ALONE IN A SILENT WORLD

The Story of the Stephensons and the Sheffield Deaf

Nick Waite

Matador
9 Priory Business Park,
Wistow Road, Kibworth Beauchamp,
Leicestershire. LE8 0RX
Tel: 0116 279 2299
Email: books@troubador.co.uk
Web: www.troubador.co.uk/matador
Twitter: @matadorbooks

ISBN 978 1785891 373

British Library Cataloguing in Publication Data.
A catalogue record for this book is available from the British Library.

Printed and bound in the UK by TJ International, Padstow, Cornwall
Typeset in 11pt Aldine401 BT by Troubador Publishing Ltd, Leicester, UK

Matador is an imprint of Troubador Publishing Ltd

In memory of Angela Waite
1940-2015

CONTENTS

List of Illustrations   ix

Acknowledgements   xi

Introduction   xiii

1. Background – before 1862   1

2. From Foundation to Institute 1862–1886   18

3. The First 25 Years in Charles Street 1886-1910   47

4. George Stephenson's final 10 years
      and retirement 1910 –1924   74

5. The Guild of St John of Beverley 1895–1951   95

6. Colin Stephenson 1920–1953   117

7. Alan and Doris Stephenson 1953-1960   141

8. The last half century 1960–2015   170

Appendix One   Profiles   197

Appendix Two   George Stephenson
                    and the Sheffield School Board   203

Appendix Three   George Stephenson
                    and Dr Symes Thompson   205

Appendix Four   George Stephenson
                    and the Guild of St John of Beverley   209

Appendix Five   George Stephenson;
                    a Weekend in London   213

Appendix Six   Obituaries of Selwyn Oxley   217

Notes on Sources   219

LIST OF ILLUSTRATIONS

Cover: Architect's drawing for Institute in Upper Charles Street, 1886

Frontispiece: George Stephenson, about 1910

Plate Section:

1   Daniel Doncaster II

2   Back to back housing in Hermitage Street Sheffield

3   First floor room at 82 Division Street Sheffield

4   The chapel/lecture hall at the Charles Street Institute

5   The reading room at the Charles Street Institute

6   Deaf ramblers in the Porter Valley Sheffield

7   George Brookes at home in Rotherham

8   Three deaf ladies signing

9   George Stephenson and Rev W H Oxley in Kensington

10 Colin Stephenson

11 Sharrow Bank, 57 Psalter Lane Sheffield

Acknowledgements and copyright

The drawing on the front cover, the photo of George Stephenson preceding the title page, and all the numbered illustrations above except 9, 10 and 11 are available on picturesheffield.co.uk (copyright Sheffield City Council) and all those except Hermitage Street were sourced from George Stephenson's 1910 Jubilee Souvenir of the Sheffield Association in Aid of the Adult Deaf and Dumb. The photo of George Stephenson and Rev W

H Oxley is amongst the papers of Selwyn Oxley in the RNID Library and the copyright would belong to the photographer or his descendants, who may have been George Brookes. The photo of Colin Stephenson is in my collection, and that of Sharrow Bank was borrowed from another local historian to whom it was given by a member of the family who owned the property before 1936.

ACKNOWLEDGEMENTS

It would not have been possible to write this book without information, ideas and support from many individuals and organisations.

Much of the documentary research was undertaken in the library of Action on Hearing Loss (formerly the RNID) in London, and in the Sheffield Archives and Local Studies Library; I also visited the Warrington library of the British Deaf History Society. Invariably the librarians were welcoming and helpful and I thank them all. My subscription to the British Newspaper Archive enabled me to transcribe items from the *Sheffield Independent* between 1862 and 1900, and other newspaper extracts were obtained from microfiches in the Local Studies Department. Most of the illustrations are taken from the Sheffield Council's picturesheffield website and I am happy to acknowledge the Council's copyright. Peter Jackson of the BDHS has kindly confirmed there is no objection to my quotations from several works published by them; I have tried without success to contact two of their authors, Anthony Boyce and Mary Hayes, but I would like to acknowledge my debt to their biography of Thomas Widd. I succeeded in tracing the immediate families of the late Kenneth Lysons and the late Rev George Firth and they were delighted that their relatives' work has been so useful.

One of the pleasures of the research has been meeting or corresponding with many Stephenson descendants. Apart from my sister, Liz Callister, and my cousin, Rosemary Gregory, I had never met any of them, and all contributed something to my knowledge of the family history. So my thanks to: Linda West, Josephine Wilson, Roger Leupold, Michael Leupold, Vicki Stevenson, Sally Anderson, Jane Hart, Leslie Bavington (Marie Stephenson's widower), Amanda McRobie, Adam Downing, and Gillian Hogg.

The Doncaster family were as important as the Stephensons in my story and I also thank their descendants or collaterals: Stephen Doncaster,

Pamela Doncaster, Suzie Doncaster, Hilary Kirkham, Jonathan Brayshaw, and Bridget Brennan. I also corresponded with Ian Dillamore, not a family member but a former CEO of Daniel Doncaster and Sons (now Doncasters Plc) whose fascinating history of the company's relationship with its bankers is listed in my Notes on Sources.

For my summary of the position since 1960 I was grateful for the chance to meet members of the Sheffield Deaf Sports and Social Club and the Sheffield Central Deaf Club. My discussions and correspondence with Martin Smith were very valuable, and I also had useful conversations with Norman Creighton, John Conway, Rev Judy Leverton, and the Directors of Communication Independence Ltd – thanks to them all. My friends Janet Howarth, John Cornwell and Kate Richards all read early sections of the manuscript and made helpful suggestions. Jude Grundy spent much time and professional expertise reading the whole second draft and making many suggestions for improvement.

I owe a particular debt to two people. Dominic Stiles of the RNID Library always answered my queries and emails, welcomed me to the library and laid out for me all the resources I requested before my visits and recommended to me others I had never considered. Julie Clarke, a former social worker with the profoundly deaf and herself the descendant of deaf members of the Sheffield Institute, was always willing to answer my queries and emails and to put me right wherever she thought I was mistaken; importantly she was my interpreter in the Sheffield Deaf Clubs with a fluency in simultaneous BSL and English which I found astounding. Without the help of Dominic and Julie I doubt I would have finished the book, but to them and everyone else mentioned above, I can only say the faults and mistakes are all mine, and you are not to blame.

Finally my greatest debt is to my dear wife Angela who supported me throughout and looked forward to publication, but died weeks after I signed the contract with the publishers. So this is a debt I can never repay.

Nick Waite,
December 2015

INTRODUCTION

'One of the Most Desperate of Human Calamities'

As a young boy in the late 1940s and early 1950s I occasionally visited a large eighteenth-century house at 57 Psalter Lane, Sheffield, originally known as Sharrow Bank. This property served two functions. The ground floor housed the Institute of the Sheffield Association in Aid of the Adult Deaf and Dumb. The first floor was home to my maternal great-uncle Colin Stephenson, the Superintendent of the Institute, with his wife Doris and their children Marie, Alan and Christine. Adjacent to the building was a chapel, and I vividly remember services for deaf people conducted by Colin in sign language. Colin himself had an artificial leg, the result of an accident in his youth followed by amputation in 1925, but the handicap scarcely inconvenienced him. I remember him as an affable, energetic and forceful character. I was dimly aware that other members of the family could converse with varying degrees of competence in sign language, but I failed to understand the nature and importance of the work which Colin undertook for the deaf community. I knew even less about his father and predecessor as Superintendent, my great-grandfather George Stephenson, who had died fourteen years before I was born.

In 1956, I left Sheffield for National Service, university and my first job, only returning to the city in 1968. Of the family members who had direct knowledge of the Institute and the family's part in its governance, my mother had already died, and her only brother a few years later. Apart from my sister and one cousin I had no contact with any of the many other Stephenson descendants. For many years I was fully absorbed in my career and raising a young family, and it was some years after retirement that I decided family history was important, partly for self-knowledge, and partly to record anything of significance for the benefit and interest of my sons and grandchildren.

Having established a basic family tree going back to the first Census, I decided that lists of names, dates and relationships were of limited interest; if I was to continue research it should have a focus. Then I remembered the Psalter Lane experience and realised that, perhaps alone in the family, great-grandfather George Stephenson had been a figure of some consequence. So I set about discovering what I could about his life and work.

I realised this would involve learning more about the Association for which he worked for almost 50 years. I could find no published account of its history and looked for original documentation in the Local Studies Department of the Sheffield City Library. It soon became apparent that it was difficult to understand the work of the Association and its Institute without some background knowledge of the problems faced by profoundly deaf people in nineteenth and early twentieth century Britain, and the development of institutions and legislation to remedy those problems. Now my enquiries became threefold – family, local and national. It was impossible to tell the Stephenson story except in the context of provision for the adult deaf in Britain, and specifically in Sheffield, during the 90 years in which three generations of the family were so closely involved.

★★★

Deafness is a diminished sensitivity to sound, crucially to sound in the speech frequencies; it is a matter of degree, varying from hard of hearing to mild, moderate and severe to profound or total deafness. This story is concerned with the extreme end of that spectrum, deafness which is so profound or severe that there is a much reduced or even non-existent capacity to hear and understand speech and great difficulty in learning to use spoken language well enough to play a full part in the society of hearing persons. In *A Journey to the Western Islands of Scotland* (1775) Dr Johnson recorded his visit to the pioneer school for deaf children founded by Thomas Braidwood and described deafness as 'one of the most desperate of human calamities'; it is a handicap which creates a degree of social isolation and less than normal socialisation. Deaf history in Britain in the last two centuries is the story of how institutions and policies were developed to remedy the situation; first by educators, philanthropists, clerics, missioners to the deaf, and deaf people themselves; and later by governments and local authorities.

★★★

Several themes run through this story, the first being the contrast between two perspectives or models of deafness. The cultural model sees deaf people as a community with a unique subculture, distinguished by shared values and experience, and above all the use of sign language. This perspective was trenchantly summarised by the American psychologist of language, Harlan Lane, in *When the Mind Hears* and elsewhere; deafness is not only a handicap or disability; society has 'medicalised' and marginalised deaf people – 'Deaf culture sees itself as a language minority instead of a disability group.' A similar British perspective is developed in *Understanding Deaf Culture* by Paddy Ladd who uses the term 'Deafhood' to describe deaf life and experience.

The alternative medical or disability model sees deafness as a physical handicap, a misfortune which requires understanding, research and treatment. The social and individual consequences can be overcome by a combination of medical intervention, hearing aids, skilled teaching, and appropriate financial and social support. Deafness is seen as a problem to be resolved for each individual; the ultimate objective is the greatest possible degree of integration into hearing society.

These two models are not just theoretical. For instance there was a debate, which continues even today, on the relative merits of teaching deaf children by 'oral' or 'manual' methods. As the names imply, the manual system relies on sign language: the use of an elaborate vocabulary of manual signs, finger spelling, gesture and visual communication with its own syntax, which is believed to enhance the pride of deaf people as a respected minority with their own history and social life.

The oralists believe that the use of sign language, in schools and families, has the fatal effect of driving the deaf community in on itself, creating an inward-looking subculture and severely limiting the capacity to play a full and equal part in society, and that many if not most severely and even profoundly deaf children could be taught to lip-read, to understand what is said and to speak clearly enough to be understood. Only by such teaching can deaf people fully comprehend the wealth and subtlety of spoken language, which sign language simply cannot encompass. For the oralists, manual teaching reinforces the social segregation of the group whereas the oral system fosters and encourages integration into society at large.

In the last decades of the nineteenth century, the debate about teaching methods drove a wedge between the schools which by government policy taught by the oral method, and the adult institutes where sign language was the everyday means of communication. At first this was not apparent in Sheffield where in 1879 the school board financed and the Association opened the first free day school for deaf children in the whole country, but by the 1890s, after poor reports from the HMI led to the closure of the school, all Sheffield's deaf children were sent away for oral teaching at residential schools, much to the distress of many parents.

George Stephenson, the central character in our story, had been appointed as teacher for the school when it opened, thereby converting a part-time post into a full-time career which endured through three generations and four members of the family for almost 90 years. How to describe that career, as exemplified by the Stephensons and many others in the deaf institutes of towns and cities throughout Britain? In all the literature the word 'missioner' (with or without a capital M) has been used more or less interchangeably with 'superintendent' to describe the occupation and functions of those men (often clerics but almost never women) who administered the voluntary societies in aid of the adult deaf. It was a unique profession, and with hindsight we have to ask whether the characteristically pious and paternalistic nature of the superintendents fostered or hindered the social development and independence of profoundly deaf people; did they create and then reinforce an isolated and inward-looking community and so reduce any hope that deaf individuals could integrate into society? An uncomfortable question for a descendant, but even in an amateur study which originated in family history, it would be wrong to ignore such doubts; they are faced in Chapters Seven and Eight.

One other theme is clearly illustrated by the Sheffield story: the relationship between the voluntary societies who first organised care for profoundly deaf adults and the belated growth of provision by central and local government. Deaf welfare is a good example of the cumulative change from the dominance of philanthropy in the Victorian era to the inclusiveness of the modern welfare state. There were, for instance, three periods where legislation profoundly affected the activities of the Sheffield Association. The first started with the Education Act 1870, supplemented by the Elementary Education (Blind and Deaf and Dumb Children) Act 1893, and led to the confrontation between the Association and the school board, described in Chapter Three. Secondly, the Local Government Act 1929 abolished the parish unions, Boards of Guardians and workhouses and created Public Assistance Committees; the placement grants they made created an uneasy but workable relationship between Sheffield Corporation and the Association which survived into the 1950s and is described in Chapter Six. Finally under Section 29 of the National Assistance Act 1948, the City Council determined to create their own inclusive deaf welfare service, and several years of mutual distrust and misapprehension culminated in the closure of the Institute in 1960, described in Chapters Six and Seven.

Within that history, the Stephensons were central to management but peripheral to policy. Ultimately, decisions were made by the Association's committee, the Sheffield School Board, and later the Education, Public Health and Social Services Committees of the City Council; yet as successive superintendents of the Institute it was the Stephensons who organised and provided practical deaf welfare throughout the city. For almost a century they were the only professionals entrusted with the work.

***

With one exception, the structure of my account is simple. The Sheffield Association was founded in 1862 and it ceased active operations in 1960, which was also the end of the Stephensons' involvement. I aimed to write the story as a straightforward chronological narrative with two strands – the development of the Association and the Stephenson family history. To top and tail the account there is a first chapter sketching the background before 1862 and a last chapter summarising the position since 1960.

With some hesitation I diverged from this plan in one respect, and set off down a curious historical path which eventually turned out to be a cul-de-sac; Chapter Five summarises the history of the Guild of St John of Beverley from its foundation in 1895/6 to its expiry in 1951. St

John, an eighth-century monk who became Bishop of Hexham and then Archbishop of York, is one of the patron saints of the deaf. I have added this chapter for two reasons: firstly because for the first nineteen years George Stephenson was President of the Guild. It remained important to him throughout his life; even in old age he relished continuing association with his successors in the Guild, and in a letter reprinted in Appendix Five he describes at length a memorable expedition to London which is the best surviving example of his style and character. Secondly, although at one stage the Guild claimed to have more than 7000 members, including 'high ranking churchmen and members of the nobility', and undoubtedly had considerable influence on the development of deaf welfare in the south and west of England, it has been almost forgotten; its history has never been written, and its very existence is largely ignored in histories of the British deaf. I think this omission should be remedied.

★★★

Finally there are a couple of issues of terminology, where I have to tread carefully. Words and phrases in common use until comparatively recently are now politically incorrect and, more importantly, offensive to deaf people. More than once in preliminary conversation and correspondence I was chided (quite rightly) for unthinking use of terms like 'deaf and dumb' and 'deaf mute'. Yet until the second half of the last century such phrases were utilised without comment, even by those involved in deaf welfare like my family. For instance, the British Deaf Association, a major pressure group of and for deaf people since its foundation in 1890, only changed its name from the British Deaf and Dumb Association in 1971; the Royal Association for Deaf People, a dominant force in deaf welfare in the London area since 1841, was called the Royal Association for the Deaf and Dumb until 1986; and the Royal National Institute for the Deaf changed its name to the Royal Institute for Deaf People in 1991 and finally to Action on Hearing Loss only four years ago. In early drafts I was therefore content to write of 'the deaf' or 'the profoundly deaf' wherever I could, but retain the old terminology when it seemed natural to do so in the historical context. Then more recently I was given specialist guidance on what is now acceptable, so that wherever possible I have tried to use the phrases 'deaf people' instead of 'the deaf' and similarly, 'profoundly deaf people'; the distinction is that 'the deaf' suggests a group apart from society as a whole, whereas 'deaf people' simply identifies a number or group of people who happen to share one particular characteristic.

Secondly, reverting to the two 'models' of deafness, some writers have distinguished between 'Deaf' and 'deaf', with the capital D used to differentiate the cultural from the disability models. In effect Deaf, whether used as a noun or an adjective, refers to the community, and deaf as an adjective to describe the handicap itself or a particular person or group; Deaf is a term of respect, deaf is purely descriptive. As far as I can see this is a modern distinction with less relevance to the main period of my account, and I therefore decided to use the capital D only where it appears in direct quotation. I realise others see the usage differently, and I can only hope they will accept the decision was made in good faith.

1

BACKROUND – BEFORE 1862

'The Forlorn Condition'

Deaf people have not been treated kindly through the centuries. For an unsparing summary of attitudes in the ancient and mediaeval worlds the reader is recommended to the early pages of *A Beginner's Introduction to Deaf History* (2004, edited by Raymond Lee; see Notes on Sources), from which much of the following material is extracted.

The Greek philosopher Plato (427–327 bc) set an unforgiving tone. Every citizen has an inbuilt or instinctive knowledge of language and understanding of ideas which develop during normal maturation, but where no speech develops there is no indication of usable intelligence, so that the totally deaf are incapable of language or ideas. In his concept of a good society there is no room for the handicapped, therefore the state should:

> *Leave the unhealthy to die and those whose constitution is incurably corrupt it will put to death*
>
> (QUOTED IN THE SOCIAL HISTORY SECTION OF
> THE *DEAFINFO* WEBSITE)

Even allowing for ambiguity in translation, Lee is clear that Plato's pupil Aristotle followed his master's analysis:

> *Aristotle (384–322 bc) in his Hist. Anim. Lib IV Ch.9 wrote that 'those who are born deaf all become speechless; they have a*

voice but are destitute of speech'. Aristotle's use of the word eveoi in this passage was rather unfortunate as it not only means 'rendered speechless' but may also mean 'senseless' and 'devoid of reason', so that if the latter meaning is adopted, the deaf were classed with idiots and those suffering from incapacity and therefore received the same treatment in the form of public disdain.

(LEE, 2004, P2)

The Romans were equally harsh. In ancient Roman law, deaf people were classified as *mentecatti furiosi,* roughly translated as 'raving maniacs' and were therefore 'uneducable'. (B L Gracer, *Disability Studies Quarterly,* Spring 2003)

For the ancients perhaps only a miracle might cure the profoundly deaf. St Mark, Chapter 8 V 32–35, tells us that Jesus cured a deaf man using the Aramaic word *ephphatha,* which we shall meet again as the title of a magazine for deaf people and as the name given to their homes by two of the main characters in our story.

32 And they bring unto him one that was deaf, and had an impediment in this speech; and they beseech him to put his hand upon him.
33 And he took him aside from the multitude, and put his fingers into his ears, and he spit and touched his tongue;
34 And looking up to heaven he sighed, and saith unto him, Ephphatha, that is, Be opened.
35 And straightaway, his ears were opened, and the string of his tongue was loosed, and he spake plain.

It seems, however, that the early Christian church took its view of deaf people from the Greeks and the Romans. St Augustine believed that they could never develop Christian faith and achieve redemption: deaf children were evidence of God's anger at the sins of their parents. According to Lee, such attitudes:

caused the deaf to be deprived of education and religious instruction for at least the next 1300 years.

(LEE, 2004. P3)

Unsurprisingly there is little positive in the history of deaf people in succeeding centuries. In Britain, the Venerable Bede recorded another miraculous healing by Archbishop John of Hexham in 685. There are isolated examples in Britain and elsewhere of profoundly deaf individuals overcoming their disadvantages, but occasional success, miraculous or otherwise, was of no use to the substantial but unknown population of the similarly handicapped.

The first important thinker to challenge the belief that deaf people were uneducable was the seventeenth-century physician, mathematician, inventor, and gambler Gerolamo Cardono, a contemporary and friend of Leonardo da Vinci. He explained that even profoundly deaf individuals could learn to read and write without either hearing or learning speech; it therefore followed they could understand concepts, form ideas, and communicate with the hearing. There was no reason why they could not be educated and lead a normal life, subject only to the limitations necessarily imposed by their handicap.

With Gerolamo's emphasis on education, it is not surprising that it was the plight of deaf children which first attracted serious practical attention. Gerolamo might argue that the capacity to read and write showed that education was possible, but for some it seemed obvious that progress would be quicker if deaf people could learn to converse with their teachers; therefore wherever possible it was crucial to develop the capacity both to understand what is said and to respond in an intelligible manner. Although there were isolated earlier cases, serious consideration of the appropriate teaching methods and the organisation of schools for deaf children were rare until the middle of the eighteenth century.

Almost simultaneously, working from the same premise that deaf children were educable, two schools of thought developed in Europe. In Germany in 1755, Samuel Heineche founded a school based on the oral method, teaching deaf children by lip-reading and reproduction of the sounds of hearing speakers; only five years later, the French Abbe Charles-Michel de l'Epee founded a school in which teaching and communication were primarily based on sign language. The relative merits of the two methods later caused much anguished debate, but this only surfaced in Britain after the momentous decisions of the Milan Conference of 1880 (formally entitled the Second International Congress on Education of the Deaf) and we shall return to this issue in Chapter Three.

In Britain there is little evidence of the education of deaf children or care for deaf adults before the late eighteenth century, only the almost universal neglect, disdain and social ostracism outlined in Lee's survey of ancient and mediaeval attitudes. Why should this be?

In the first place, deaf individuals were relatively difficult to recognise or identify in a small and predominantly rural population, so that profound deafness could seem to be rare. Exact numbers are difficult to estimate even today, but the numbers of individuals reported in the Census returns from 1851 to 1901 as 'deaf and dumb' are similar to those reported as 'deaf mutes' or 'totally deaf' by the Central Office of Information in 1947 in a survey prepared for the Ministry of Health: both these sources suggest a proportion of 0.05% or one in 2000 of the total population. We shall return to more modern estimates in Chapter Eight, but if the numbers were as small as suggested, there might be only a couple of profoundly deaf individuals in a small town and none in many villages, as easy to ignore as they were difficult to help. In 1862, the Mayor of Sheffield was astonished to be told that there were upwards of 50 deaf mutes in his town; it soon became clear this was a considerable underestimate.

Secondly, unlike blindness or physical incapacity, deafness is invisible to the naked eye or even to the perceptive stranger. It is easy to see that a blind person or someone in a wheelchair may need your help to cross the road, but much less apparent that someone who cannot hear the traffic may also require your assistance – and if he has no speech, cannot tell you so. Perhaps it is the 'invisibility' of the handicap which created the dismissive attitude to deaf people among the Greek philosophers and the early Christian thinkers and which remained prevalent for so long. Consider for instance the use of the word 'dummy' to mean someone of abnormally low intelligence, incapable of coherent thought or so stupid as to be unworthy of attention. The word 'dumb' itself is still commonly regarded as synonymous with 'stupid'. Worse than that, the inability to express oneself through intelligible speech has often been seen as humorous.

> *The deaf are at times made the butt of jokes; the blind, never. The deaf may have a place in comedies; the blind, only in tragedies.*
> (BEST, 1943, FOOTNOTE, P335)

Martin Smith recounts how in his early years in the late 1950s he had to give talks to the general public in order to obtain funds; he remembers receiving a request for a talk about Deaf and Dumb 'because we like a good laugh'. (Smith, 2011, p17) If not laughter, then impatience is a frequent social reaction to any level of deafness which is inconvenient to others; P S Taylor, a member of the commission which produced the 1960 Younghusband Report on the future of social work and training in Britain, remarked in a paper given at an NID meeting in October 1960 that 'the general public [...] pity the blind but get angry with the deaf'. (We shall return to Taylor's paper in Chapter Eight.)

If anyone thinks that the prejudicial use of the word 'dummy' is ancient history, it is worth quoting another story from Martin Smith. Only a few years ago, he was giving a talk in Leeds and remarked that deaf people were often treated disrespectfully. One of his listeners disputed this, saying that he was great friends with a profoundly deaf person with whom he had worked for many years. Thinking he probably knew the friend through his professional duties, Smith asked his name, to which the answer was: 'I don't know his name, we just call him dummy.' (Smith 2011 p viii)

In the early nineteenth century such prejudice was far more prevalent. The rapid growth of factory production and with it emigration from the countryside to the factories and slums of the industrial cities only further marginalised the disabled, whether deaf, blind or otherwise handicapped. Their plight was seen primarily in economic terms; industrial production required a more regimented working environment and maximum productivity. (Bergen, 2004, p7) The 'New Poor Law' of the Poor Law Amendment Act 1834, setting up the parish unions and the workhouses which dominated the pattern of relief for the following century, paid little attention to those formerly termed as 'impotent' as distinct from the 'able bodied', who were expected to make an economic contribution. But at least Section 56 of the 1834 Act created separate categories of the blind and the deaf and enabled the Boards of Guardians to support the schools for those two categories of disabled which were beginning to be developed as an alternative to incarceration in the workhouses; 'the growing availability of special education operated as a counterweight to economic and social exclusion'. (Bergen, 2004, p3)

So now statute had made mention of the deaf as a separate category, at least for the benefit of the children. In the public mind however, prejudice was as strong as ever; Selwyn Oxley, of whom more will be heard in Chapter Five, kept among his papers (now in the RNID library) an extract from a Victorian songbook, such as the middle class might keep on the piano and use for family sing-songs. This ditty was an arrangement of a Lancashire folk song:

> *Ther' was a bonny blade*
> *And he married a country maid*
> *An' he safely conducted her home home home*
> *She was neat and she was smart*
> *An' she pleased him to his heart*
> *But eh! Poor lassie, She was dumb dumb dumb!*

So what was life like for the profoundly deaf and speechless in the years when this song could be regarded as Sunday evening entertainment? One concerned professional was William R Wilde FRCS (better known as the father of Oscar Wilde) who gave the following bleak assessment:

> *The deaf mute claims the special attention of the philanthropist and the protection of the state owing to the forlorn condition to which he is reduced by his affliction, the difficulty he experiences in expressing his wants and his inability either to educate himself or to receive instructions through the ordinary channels; and also his constant exposure to crime from the defect of moral training and the difficulty in impressing on him a just idea of right and wrong. Degraded by his uncontrolled passions, he is, moreover, frequently the victim of cruelty and injustice; and being incapable without education of properly understanding or duly appreciating the truths of religion, he is reduced to a condition but little elevated above that of the brute creation. Alone in the world, his faculties undeveloped and shut out by his unhappy circumstances from thoroughly communicating his ideas to the rest of mankind, the deaf mute in an especial manner claims the sympathies of all.*

(WILDE, 1854, P1)

Sunk in the social abyss described by Wilde, it was difficult to imagine practical help for the adults. After the foundation of the German and

French schools, philanthropists and educators naturally looked first to the plight of the children, and the first teacher of note to make real headway in Britain was Thomas Braidwood of Edinburgh (1715–1806). Following initial success with a single fee-paying pupil, and utilising the 'combined' method involving both oral and manual teaching, Braidwood established an academy which produced a number of deaf pupils who achieved great success in life despite their handicap. Some of his pupils became teachers of deaf children themselves, and after Braidwood moved his school from Edinburgh to Hackney in 1783 there was a steady growth of public schools for deaf children during the next 70 years. Braidwood's son-in-law Joseph Watson was the first head of the London Asylum for the Education of the Deaf and Dumb in 1792, and Thomas's son John Braidwood opened a school in Edinburgh in 1810.

Following the Poor Law Amendment Act (especially Section 56) other schools followed until by 1901 there were seventeen residential schools, as well as 45 day schools provided or financed by school boards under the 1870 and 1893 Acts. Of particular significance for this study is the first residential school in Yorkshire, the Yorkshire Institution for the Deaf and Dumb at Doncaster, abbreviated hereafter as YIDD (and after several name changes still functioning as the Doncaster School for the Deaf). Founded in 1829 by Reverend William Carr Fenton, YIDD was supported by wealthy benefactors from Leeds and elsewhere headed by the Earl of Harewood. The first superintendent was the redoubtable Charles Baker, an authoritarian figure of great importance in the development of deaf education who remained in post until his death in 1873. (It was largely as a result of lobbying by Baker and his patron the Earl of Harewood that Section 56 was inserted in the 1834 Act.)

Baker and his school are significant in our story at several points; the first superintendents of all four societies for the adult deaf which originated as branches of the Leeds Society were former pupils of YIDD, as was Thomas Widd whose influence with deaf people in the city led directly to the Sheffield foundation. Charles Baker periodically surveyed the future careers of his pupils, and in 1870 reported that 'others, with missionary spirit, are engaged in promoting the welfare of their brothers and sisters in infirmity at Leeds, Bradford, Halifax, Sheffield, Hull, London and other places'. (Quoted by Bergen, 2004, p222)

Once children left the early deaf schools they naturally remained friends, recognised their common interests, and hoped to continue their association in a more organised setting, a hope achieved in the subsequent development of voluntary societies for the care, socialisation and education of deaf adults. Many such societies were referred to as missions, and their leaders or superintendents as missioners, for the very good reason that evangelical zeal was a powerful motivation amongst the founders, whether the societies were initiated on a non-sectarian basis or under the direct auspices of the Anglican or Nonconformist churches.

The first such missions were founded in Edinburgh in 1818 and Glasgow in 1822, and although the London Asylum had been founded some 50 years earlier, it was not until 1841 that a mission for the adult deaf was instituted in the capital. This deaf-led society was set up by subscription following a public meeting, under the chairmanship of Lord Calthorpe and the guidance of George Crouch, who had five deaf children himself. The first such organisation in England, it was typical of many of the non-sectarian missions, a collaboration of prominent businessmen and philanthropists with deaf individuals and their families, many of them educated in the early schools. Its aims became clear when it changed its name in 1843 to the more descriptive Institution for the Employment, Relief and Religious Instruction of the Adult Deaf and Dumb, a set of aims widely replicated in the constitutions and stated objects of many of the later foundations. In 1873, on the opening of St Saviours Oxford Street, the first church in England dedicated to deaf people, it was given the seal of royal approval and became the Royal Association in aid of the Deaf and Dumb (RADD).

From the 1840s onwards missions were established in the provinces, and especially in the rapidly developing industrial cities of the North and Midlands, including those like Sheffield which started life as branches of larger institutions and later became independent. Lysons identified two (Manchester and Liverpool) in the 1840s, four in the 1850s, five in the 1860s, five in the 1870s, ten in the 1880s, and twelve in the 1890s. The Church of England was not involved to any great extent until after 1890 and almost all the early foundations were instituted voluntarily and funded by public subscription. Supervised by voluntary committees, such organisations would typically delegate the detail of their religious, social, educational and welfare work to salaried part- or full-time superintendents/ missioners, individuals who by vocation or experience felt drawn to support, educate and in many cases to evangelise the profoundly deaf citizens of the great cities of Victorian Britain. Within this context of philanthropy, self-help and service we can place the foundation in 1862 of the Sheffield Association in Aid of the Adult Deaf and Dumb. First we must go back a few years to look at the background and families of those most closely involved.

★★★

The Doncaster family came to Sheffield from rural Nottinghamshire in the late eighteenth century. Daniel Doncaster I (1756–1819) was the son of a grocer; we have to call him Daniel Doncaster I to distinguish him from his son and grandson, Daniel Doncaster II (1807–1884) and Daniel Doncaster III (1834–1912), both of whom are of central importance in this story; for brevity we will call them Daniel I, Daniel II, and Daniel III.

Daniel I established himself as what in Sheffield is traditionally called a 'little mester', working from home or in a small workshop, alone with family or one or two employees, earning a modest income from one of many specialist trades in cutlery, iron or steel, in his case file manufacture. In 1778, at the age of only 21 or 22, he obtained his own registered trademark from the Cutlers Company of Hallamshire. The business was originally based at the family home in Allen Street, near the River Don in the town centre; the population of Sheffield was beginning to grow but was still under 40,000. The business soon became successful enough to educate all his nine children; his wife Jane was a Rowntree, and this was the first but not the last family connection with the Rowntrees of York.

It was however his youngest son Daniel II who laid the basis of the family's considerable fortune. Between the ages of 15 to 21 he was apprenticed to a draper in York, but on his return to Sheffield in 1828 he joined his brother William in the file manufacturing business. He soon realised this had been mismanaged in his absence, and after three years the partnership was dissolved and Daniel II then set up what he later described as a 'very modest steel trade' from nearby rented premises. There can be no doubt of his business abilities, as the founder of what during the following decades became a substantial and profitable business under the name Daniel Doncaster and Sons.

The 1841 Census shows that Daniel II was living with his wife Maria and the first three of their ten children in Upperthorpe, with an occupation of 'steel manufacturer'. Upperthorpe was an area of quite substantial stone-built villas, typically occupied by well-to-do businessmen and traders, on a hillside very near to but somewhat above the noxious air and crowded tenements of the factories they owned and the workers they employed. By 1861 Daniel and Maria had a total of five sons and five daughters, and the family were now living in more substantial surroundings at Broomhall Road with three resident servants; they remained at 17 Broomhall Road until their deaths. In the 1881 Census Daniel II is described as a 'retired steel manufacturer', and by then he had taken into partnership his three eldest sons, Daniel III, David Kenway and Charles.

Thus far, just one of the many success stories of the Industrial Revolution: Victorian Britain became the pre-eminent workshop and trading giant of the world, and Sheffield a world leading producer of iron, steel and engineering products, as well as its traditional pre-eminence in cutlery. But in fact the Doncaster family was untypical in two ways, both important to our story.

In the first place, they were Quakers and like so many of their co-religionists they had a deep concern for the afflictions of the poor and handicapped, a genuine philanthropy which typified the best of the Victorian middle class. Not only had Daniel I married a Rowntree, so did two of Daniel II's daughters, Helen and Anna. Another and even closer Quaker connection was with the Barbers, a family who were to play a significant role in the creation and support of the Sheffield Association. James Henry Barber was born in London but came to Sheffield as a young man to work for the Sheffield Banking Company, becoming and remaining a director to the end of his long life. The family became prominent in Sheffield philanthropic, business and professional life through several generations; of J H Barber's six sons, one was a solicitor, one a steel manufacturer on his own account, one an auctioneer, two were stockbrokers and/or chartered accountants, and the youngest, Herbert, became a partner in Daniel Doncaster and Sons. Of the five Barber daughters, Hannah Mary was married to Charles Doncaster and Emma Gertrude to Samuel.

Even more important to our story than their religion, three of Daniel II and Maria's children, Daniel III, Arthur and Phebe, were deaf from birth. For Daniel III and Phebe the severity of the affliction is uncertain, for reasons which need some explanation. All Census returns from

1851 onwards (at least to 1911) required the enumerator to identify any individual suffering from one of several conditions. In 1851 and 1861 the column giving this information is simply headed 'Whether Blind or Deaf and Dumb', but by 1871 the list had been extended to include 'Imbecile or Idiot' and 'Lunatic'. There were minor changes in the four categories in subsequent years, and by 1911 the instructions to the enumerators read as follows:

> *If any person included in the schedule is (1) 'Totally Deaf' or 'Deaf and Dumb' (2) 'Totally Blind' (3) 'Lunatic' (4) 'Imbecile' or 'Feeble Minded', state the infirmity opposite that person's name, and the age at which he or she became afflicted.*

This bald categorisation of handicap, especially coupling the deaf and blind with the lunatic and imbecile or feeble-minded could hardly be more politically incorrect and deeply offensive to those in the first two categories; not a lot seems to have changed since Aristotle equated the deaf with idiots. Perhaps this has finally been recognised with the release of the 1911 returns into the public domain, because on any attempt to identify an afflicted individual that final column is blanked out and hovering over the blank produces the message 'infirmity hidden per privacy restrictions'.

Because of this unhappy bundling of physical and mental disabilities it is sensible to be cautious about the returns. The enumerators were to some extent reliant on the veracity of informants, perhaps more so where they were of a higher social class than the enumerators themselves, and particularly where the information related to children or where diagnosis might be uncertain, sensitive or even shameful. This is another reason to be uncertain about the true extent of profound deafness in nineteenth-century Britain, and the incidence of deafness in the Doncaster family is a good example.

There was never any doubt about Arthur, the youngest. At the time of the 1861 Census he was only five and rather unusually the final column describes him as 'feared deaf and dumb from birth'. Daniel II engaged a specialist teacher of the deaf to provide for Arthur's education at home, a programme so successful that as an adult he became a successful and respected naturalist and businessman (see Appendix One). The 1871 Census describes him as 'Deaf and Dumb' and 'a student at home' but by 1881, now 25, he was living in London, described as a naturalist 'employing one man' and 'Deaf and Dumb since birth'; in 1891 the same except 'since childhood' and reverting in 1901 to 'since birth'. In fact he lived and worked in London until his death in 1931.

Phebe lived with Arthur in London from 1891 and perhaps earlier. Her case illustrates how significant information may have been withheld from the Census enumerator; perhaps in those days less care was taken when collecting information about females. It is clear from family and Quaker sources that she was born and remained deaf, yet the only time this was recorded in the Census was in 1871; she and her sister Anna were staying with a farmer in Oxfordshire, presumably on holiday, and the head of the household there and/or the enumerator had no doubt; the entry shows her simply as 'deaf'. Given that the final column is clearly intended for serious conditions it is reasonable to assume her deafness was more or less profound, whether or not any speech was possible.

In the case of Daniel III the Census evidence is equally uncertain, and perhaps his deafness was not as profound or total as Arthur's. There is no entry in the column relating to disability in any Census before 1901. He was considerably older than Arthur or Phebe and it may be that he had already acquired some speech by the time of the 1851 Census, when he was seventeen. Yet in 1901, a wealthy man of 67 and presumably perfectly capable of telling the enumerator about his own condition, the Census shows him as 'deaf from childhood'. In any event, even if his disability was not generally known outside family, friends and colleagues during his lifetime, it became clear after he died in 1912. The obituary in the *Sheffield Daily Telegraph* does not mince words. He is plainly described as 'deaf and dumb, though he learned to speak very clearly and was a remarkable lip-reader'. Perhaps his handicap explains why he never played a leading part in the development of the family business, despite being the oldest son. Though Census returns prior to 1901 describe him as a 'steel manufacturer' the obituary emphasises the extent of his philanthropic activities in Quaker and other local and national charities. Above all it is emphasised that his father had 'conceived the idea of "a place for the poor of Sheffield who were similarly afflicted"' and the very considerable part that he (Daniel III) played in this project after his father's death.

★★★

So the story of how a mission to the adult deaf was established in Sheffield originated in part with a wealthy and pious family with three deaf children, but to move from philanthropic concern to practical action required impetus from an existing institution and its local representative. This was Thomas Widd, a remarkable young man from the working class of rural East Yorkshire who only stayed in Sheffield for about six months but was as crucial in the creation of a Sheffield mission as the Doncasters. The following summary of Widd's life before he came to Sheffield is based on Boyce and Hayes' biography of Widd, *A Gift from Great Driffield* (2007), and the much shorter account by Hayes in *Deaf Lives* (ed. Lee and Jackson, 2001).

Widd was born in 1839 in Great Driffield, the second of the five children of John Hall Widd and his wife Elizabeth. John Widd was a jobbing saddler, working closely with a local blacksmith and a coach builder. The three craftsmen and their families lived in a cluster of adjoining cottages and earned a steady income as they lived on the stage coach route from Scarborough to Beverley.

With this background it is not surprising that Widd had a lifelong love of horses and it was therefore ironic that after a perfectly normal early childhood, including a year in a large class in a typical 'dame school', he suffered a life-changing accident at the age of five. He was offered a ride by a local farmer bringing his horse to be shod; the horse went to drink at a small river next to the road, dipped its head, and Widd fell into the river bottom. He was rescued, cold, wet and no doubt shocked, but worse was to follow; he contracted scarlet fever, took nearly a year to recover and it was then realised that he had totally lost his hearing.

Although not deaf and dumb from birth his speech gradually deteriorated and normal education at a local school was not a success. At the age of twelve his parents arranged for him to go as a boarder to the Yorkshire Institution for the Deaf and Dumb (YIDD) at Doncaster. This followed advice from the Driffield Board of Poor Law Guardians, who also paid the annual fees of £21, which illustrates the anxiety of his parents, their relatively low income, and the effect of Section 56 of the Poor Law Amendment Act.

As earlier explained, the YIDD school was one of the earliest residential schools for deaf children and many of its pupils and teachers became prominent in the care and education of deaf people. Widd benefitted greatly from the teaching of two of these men, Alexander Melville and Samuel Smith; the latter subsequently became the first Anglican Minister to be ordained with specific responsibilities for the care of the deaf. Clearly Widd learned enough to earn a living, because after two years his father withdrew him from YIDD and he returned to Driffield where he went to work at a local sawmill and graduated to a responsible position by the age of twenty. Notwithstanding his deafness he was a young man of considerable ability and ambition, and in 1859 he returned to YIDD, initially as an assistant gardener but soon developing an interest in printing, and became an instructor in that trade at the school.

Even this did not satisfy him for long because he came into contact with the Leeds Society for Adult Mutes (founded 1854 and subsequently or alternatively known as the Yorkshire Association in Aid of the Adult Deaf and Dumb); there he came to know the Society's Bible teacher Colin Campbell, and its Secretary James Foulston, another former teacher at YIDD. Following their discussions Widd was entrusted with the daunting task of travelling to Sheffield to set up a mission as a branch of the Leeds society; similar branches had already been established in Bradford, Huddersfield and Halifax. It seems extraordinary that a young man of 23, from a humble small town background, deaf since childhood and with work experience limited to a sawmill and a brief period teaching printing, and with no previous links with Sheffield, should have been entrusted with such a task. He must have been an impressively mature and forceful personality, as evidenced by the variety and success of his later career in Canada and America (see Appendix One). He spent a short period observing and assisting Campbell with religious teaching in the Leeds branches and was then packed off to Sheffield with no immediate resources but a promise of a salary, if and when a branch society could be established.

Widd arrived in Sheffield in September 1862. Very rapidly he managed to meet and assemble a list of some 50 deaf adults, and with a file cutter called Joseph Askew, another graduate of YIDD, he took a tenancy of a cottage in Milton Street near the town centre. There he initiated a series of meetings of local deaf people, including Askew, a tailor called William Simmonite, and 'the Stephenson couple'. It is not clear whether the couple's son George attended these meetings or whether he learned about them from his parents or from William Simmonite, a close family friend. In the Sheffield Association's *Jubilee Souvenir*, George described these early days of Widd's time in the town as follows:

> *This man was not long in the cutlery capital before he became a force among the deaf and dumb living in the town. Having obtained employment at a printing establishment, he devoted his spare time to visiting his fellow mutes, and ere long induced a number of them to meet together in the cottage home of one of them, for the purpose of mutual improvement, and on Sundays for Bible study.*
>
> (STEPHENSON, 1911, P12)

★★★

The 1841 Census shows that Benjamin Stephenson, a spring knife cutler born in Sheffield in 1817, was living in Hermitage Street with his widowed mother Martha aged 60 and two sisters, Harriet and Lydia. His late father George was also a spring knife cutler, an occupation probably carried on from the living space of their small cottage home or a workshop at the rear, performing one or more of the constituent operations in the manufacture of knives in which the blade folds back into the heft.

On the 29th August 1842 Benjamin married Sarah Mallinson aged 21, in the parish church at Rotherham. Sarah's father Joseph was a razor grinder, another outworker to the cutlery industry and one of the most dangerous of manual occupations – grinders were frequently killed or maimed by exploding grindstones or died early from 'grinder's asthma' (silicosis). In 1841 he lived with his wife, another Martha, his daughter Sarah, and a 15-year-old employee razor grinder called William Mitchell. They lived at the other end of town in Cannon Hall Cottages in Pitsmoor, originally used for the grooms or stable staff of the neighbouring Cannon Hall.

The marriage raises a couple of queries. Why would a couple who lived at home in 1841 in Sheffield get married in Rotherham in 1842? The certificate shows them both living in Westgate Rotherham, but since neither of them seems to have had any prior or later connection with the town, this remains puzzling. Secondly, in an era when travel across even short distances was difficult for working people, how or where would Benjamin and Sarah have met, living as they did at opposite ends of what was already a large town? The answer is clear: both of them were, in the unforgiving phrase of later Census returns, 'deaf and dumb from birth'.

Whatever the reason for their temporary residence and marriage in Rotherham, Benjamin and Sarah were living at 57 Hermitage Street, Sheffield, by 1845, though whether with Benjamin's mother and sisters or in a similar neighbouring cottage is not clear. Their first child George, named after his grandfather, was born there on 29th August, 1845. The couple only had two children, and George's brother Benjamin, named after their father, was born two years later. We have no direct information about any problems the two brothers encountered in learning to speak, given the total deafness of both their parents, but neither of them, nor (as far as we can tell) any of their descendants inherited the condition.

The course of Benjamin's life and career will be touched on later, where relevant to George and his family, and likewise the later life of their parents. Here we should just note what happened to their grandparents. By the 1851 Census, Martha and Joseph Mallinson were living just to the east of the town centre at Court 3, The Wicker; from that description almost certainly a back-to-back cottage and something of a comedown from Cannon Hall Cottages. Remarkably for that notoriously short-lived occupation, Joseph is still described as a razor grinder at the age of 61, but both he and his wife died in the 1850s.

We have no further information on the brothers' grandfather George, who died before they were born, but the fate of their paternal grandmother Martha illustrates the precarious nature of working-class life at the time. In the 1851 Census she is living at 58 Bath Street with a brick maker Joseph Roper and his 31-year-old wife Harriet, almost certainly her elder daughter. In the column describing her position or occupation are the words 'Receive 1/6 from Parish'. In other words, now 70 years old, without the support of either son, a widow with no occupation, she was saved from the workhouse by a subvention from the Poor Law Guardians and the wages of her son-in-law. This is a recurrent theme in accounts of nineteenth-century working-class life; the original intention of the 1834 Act had been to house the able-bodied paupers in the workhouses and rely on family support and outdoor relief for the aged, the ill and the handicapped, which was what happened to Martha, but over the decades the pattern changed, with the workhouses providing the majority of hospital wards for those poor who were unable to support themselves outside. We shall meet the workhouse again later in the Stephenson story, and with a very different outcome.

Apart from the personal details he gives in the *Jubilee Souvenir*, the only information we have on George Stephenson's childhood and youth is that by the age of twelve, having concluded whatever formal education he may have received, he was employed as a spring knife cutler like his father Benjamin, and almost certainly in his employment. What of course was different from other working-class boys who took a similar and predictable course, was the total deafness of his parents; it is clear from his 1911 account that this conditioned but in no way blighted his early life. Indeed, he seems to have had a perfectly normal and happy childhood, given the straitened circumstances of any working-class family in the 1850s. When writing about his later appointment as teacher of the deaf, he refers to the unstinting support he received from William Simmonite, the 'merry tailor' mentioned by Thomas Widd. He describes Simmonite as:

> *industrious and intelligent, and perhaps at that time the most highly respected among them (the deaf and dumb) [...] a personal friend of my own parents, a frequent visitor at our home. When I was a boy, he often took me with him when he went for a day's fishing. He was an enthusiastic angler. My first big kite was made by him, and he went with me into a field now covered by Winter Street hospital to fly it. Indeed, I was his constant companion in nearly all his leisure moments, and at these times he carefully instructed me in in the use of much of the gesture used in abbreviation by the deaf and dumb.*
>
> (STEPHENSON, 1911, P16)

So, a normal and busy youth, learning his father's trade, but also accustomed to life and language amongst deaf people, a background which stood him in good stead when he came to work on their behalf. But he was only just seventeen when Thomas Widd came to Sheffield and the Association to which he was to devote his career was founded.

2

FROM FOUNDATION TO
INSTITUTE 1862-1886

'The Beginnings of a Happy Era'

Thomas Widd arrived in Sheffield on or about 1ˢᵗ September 1862, following instructions from the Leeds Society. Apart from contemporary newspaper reports, a short memoir by Daniel Doncaster II in the Sheffield Library, and George Stephenson's historical summary written 50 years after the event, only Widd himself seems to have left a first-hand account, in the December 1897 issue *of British Deaf News*, written from his home in Los Angeles. The following account of his first weeks in Sheffield is therefore drawn in part from the Boyce and Hayes' biography, but primarily from the 1897 account on which the Sheffield section of the biography is based.

In the first few days of his Sheffield mission, even before he established a base at Milton Street with Joseph Askew, Widd realised that many of the deaf congregated in a particular public house. To interest and involve them in his work on their behalf he conducted meetings on the street outside:

> *my object was to save the poor deaf-mutes from the degradation of the saloon and to lead them to the Saviour [...] under the friendly light of a street lamp several temperance lectures were delivered; but crowds of people soon gathered around us, so as to obstruct the street, and the police ordered us to move on.*
>
> (BRITISH DEAF NEWS, 1897)

The difficulty of holding open air meetings, particularly in the vicinity of a saloon where his audience were accustomed to drink, led Widd and Askew to use part of their Milton Street cottage for their meetings. It may well have been the saloon keeper, noting the effects of Widd's meetings on his takings, who encouraged the police to move the crowd on!

It was not only an affronted publican and his allies in the police who disliked the idea of evangelising the adult deaf of Sheffield and establishing a society on their behalf. At a prior meeting in London, Widd had been warned by his former teacher Alexander Melville that Charles Baker of YIDD would object to any such development. Melville had already discovered this to his cost when leaving his post as teacher of the deaf at Swansea to set up a new institution at Llandaff, and Baker had also objected to another of his former teachers, Samuel Smith, being ordained in order to better serve deaf people. Given the proximity of Doncaster to Sheffield, Baker probably had more practical and personal issues with any development there. For one thing, some of his pupils came from the Sheffield area, and for this reason alone Widd had been advised by Leeds not to institute classes for children. And secondly, like all such institutions at the time, YIDD was partly dependent on philanthropic support, and the last thing Baker would have welcomed would be a new institution in Sheffield diverting funds which might otherwise have been to his benefit. Whatever his reasons, Baker entered into a furious correspondence with Leeds, objecting to Widd's work.

Baker had probably read a letter published in the *Sheffield and Rotherham Independent* on 13th September 1862, signed by 'one of the Adult Deaf and Dumb' (or a shorter letter published 10 days earlier by the *Sheffield Daily Telegraph*), almost certainly from Widd. Whatever the authorship of the letters – not claimed by Widd himself in 1897 – they were impassioned, evangelical, and crucial in awakening interest and concern in the town; the second and longer is worth summarising in detail.

He describes the social isolation of the deaf and dumb; after leaving school they wish to associate and converse 'in their own language' but 'at present no place is open to them but beer houses of the lowest order, where many have become slaves to passion and vice'. They do not go to church because they cannot hear the sermons or understand the services. There is a desperate need for a meeting room, as already exists in London, Manchester, Leeds and elsewhere, where the deaf can worship on Sundays and receive secular instruction on weekdays, and the writer offers to conduct a Bible class if such accommodation could be provided, which would be 'joyfully accepted by the speechless recipients'. He adds that 'associations have long been formed for the adult deaf in many large towns [...] and their value is unequivocal; and the poor deaf mutes have in many instances been stopped in their career of ruin'. His purpose is clear: 'Sheffield has upwards of 50 deaf and dumb and nothing is done for their spiritual wants, and none to point them to their Blessed Redeemer.'

★★★

Having made his public appeals, Widd's next objective was to enlist the help and support of the great and good of Sheffield, those with the wealth and influence to create an association, as others had in London, Leeds and other growing cities of industrial Britain. Not afraid of starting at the top, he secured an interview with the Mayor, John Brown. This august figure, later Sir John Brown, was the most successful of all the steel magnates of nineteenth-century Sheffield, founder of the eponymous company which by amalgamation with the firm founded by Mark Firth eventually became Firth Brown. At a time when 'conspicuous consumption' was perfectly acceptable in such circles, Sir John was the master of Endcliffe Hall, the grandest of all the Ranmoor mansions constructed by the great factory owners as homes and symbols of their success and wealth.

Widd takes up the story:

> I called on the Mayor of Sheffield, Sir J Brown, and laid the needs of the deaf before him, asking him to help with the work. He could not believe there were so many deaf mutes in the city, although I submitted to him the names and addresses of 60 persons. He said he had never met with a deaf and dumb person in Sheffield! He referred me to the Rev Dr Sale, and another gentleman sent me to a lady well known for her Christian benevolence, who, however, only asked me numerous questions to find out the extent of my scriptural knowledge, recommended me to the vicar, and promised future aid. The vicar, Dr Sale, kindly gave me a few shillings towards the expenses, and promised to do all he could to help the work – if it met with the approval of Mr Baker! It did not; and I

failed to get the venerable vicar's aid in preaching the Gospel to the poor deaf mutes.

(BRITISH DEAF NEWS, 1897)

The lady in question was a Miss Harrison of Weston Park, a well-known philanthropist who had done much for the Sheffield blind. It is not known which gentleman recommended an approach to her; it could have been Daniel Doncaster II, because it was about this time that the two men first met. Having been passed on by the Mayor, catechised by Miss Harrison, and rebuffed by the vicar of Sheffield, a lesser man might have given up, but not Widd. Following these meetings and the letters in the Sheffield press, Charles Baker started his campaign of letters to the newspaper editors and to Leeds, seeking to stop Widd in his tracks. Widd himself simply carried on preaching, organising meetings, working towards the creation of a formal association; in his own words he 'sawed wood and said nothing' (British Deaf News, 1897). It was left to Foulston at Leeds to correspond with Baker and to defend the project; after all it was he who sent Widd to Sheffield in the first place.

Baker may not have been happy with the prospect, but at this stage, sometime in the autumn of 1862, the Committee of the Leeds Society decided to set in motion their proposed creation of a Sheffield Association by holding their own annual meeting in the town at the end of the year. About the same time, having obtained details of the deaf and dumb citizens from Widd's list, Daniel II visited their homes and was of course well aware of the needs of deaf children and adults by reason of his own family situation. The next step was for James Foulston, as Secretary of the Leeds Society, and a committee member called Bent to come to Sheffield where they met several Anglican ministers and prominent businessmen including Daniel II, James Henry Barber and James Hall, another leading Quaker. Their discussions were followed by two further letters in the *Sheffield Independent*.

The first was from Foulston, published on 1st December 1862. He started by repeating Widd's estimate of the deaf and dumb in Sheffield 'whose condition is one of almost spiritual destitution [...] scarcely one degree above the darkest heathenism'. The general populace will not be aware of the existence of 'the poor mute' because (unlike the blind) 'externally he resembles the mass around him, his deep spiritual need, and not infrequently his bodily necessity, is unfortunately overlooked'. There are many Christian people, churches and chapels who would help, but the deaf never attend; 'those religious services which to the hearing person are fraught with comfort and peace, to the deaf and dumb are silent and unintelligible'. He then says that approaches have been made to Leeds from Sheffield, which his committee had not been able to satisfy until now, being fully absorbed in founding branches in Bradford, Huddersfield and Halifax, but now they 'were able to direct their most active attention to the call from Sheffield'. He then recounted the negative responses Widd had received from his approaches to the vicar of Sheffield and Miss Harrison and the more positive reaction he and Bent had encountered. Accordingly, it had been decided that the best way of involving the people of Sheffield would be a public meeting, which would take the form of the Leeds Society's annual meeting to be held in Sheffield before the end of the year; 'And they trust this will be the beginning of a happy era for those poor creatures in whose temporal and eternal wellbeing they cherish such a heartfelt interest.'

In fact there is no evidence that anyone from Sheffield had petitioned Leeds for assistance before Foulston despatched Widd there only three months earlier. There seems to have been a well-intentioned and active process of empire building at work; this may also explain the references by Foulston and in the local press to the 'Yorkshire Association'. There is no reference to any organisation of that name by Widd himself, or in Lee's list of the development of provincial associations. Boyce and Hayes refer to the Leeds Society for Adult Mutes founded in 1854 as the organisation of which Foulston was Secretary but in Boyce's earlier *The Leeds Beacon* he dates the Yorkshire Association only from 1864, and it certainly seems his research in this area is the most thorough. Lee refers to the Leeds United Institution for the Blind, the Deaf and the Dumb founded in 1850, with the associations at Bradford, Halifax and Sheffield all listed as starting out life as branches. Lysons adds to the confusion by saying that informal services for the deaf started in Leeds under the influence of James Herriott from Manchester in the 1850s and that the Leeds United Institute was originally known as the Yorkshire Association: he is probably referring to the Leeds Institute building in Albion Street which was not erected until the 1870s. The assumption must be that the original foundation was named for Leeds, but that in order to avoid any feeling in Sheffield or the other towns of being dominated by Leeds, the committee decided informally to describe itself as 'Yorkshire', a usage which was formalised in 1864 and then dropped again when each of the satellites became independent, as they all did over the next few years.

The second letter was published only four days later, on December 5th 1862, and although subscribed only 'DD' must surely be from Daniel II. He refers to Foulston's letter and describes the excellent work his society does: 'it provides rooms and a library in Leeds, and employs a deaf and dumb teacher, who devotes himself chiefly to the towns of Leeds, Bradford and Halifax, giving religious instruction on the Sabbath, and assisting in evening classes on the other days'. He then refers to the moving remarks of a Reverend E Jackson at the previous year's annual meeting in Leeds, describing the condition of the deaf prior to the formation of the society there; 'at best the deaf and dumb were so isolated as to be shut out from all those humanised and cheering associations and enjoyments which others met with, and would be improved thereby. They could neither hear the voice of affection nor the strains of music, nor the endearing prattle of their children, nor the dying words of their own parents.' He described how Widd and Askew had recently set up a centre in their own home, attended by up to 30 at a time, but those premises are 'quite insufficient to accommodate the number, and they are unable without assistance to hire another. The furniture possessed is two forms'. Having followed Widd and Foulston in describing the urgent need for action, Doncaster expresses 'the earnest hope that at the coming meeting a branch society may be formed, with a local committee, and may be so supported as may enable a room to be provided, and effectual help otherwise rendered to this afflicted class.'

★★★

The ground had been prepared and the crucial meeting took place on 29th December at the Cutlers Hall, Church Street, almost opposite the parish church. It was reported in the *Sheffield Independent* on the following day. (To add to the confusion, the headline referred to the 'Yorkshire Institution for the Deaf and Dumb', which of course is the name of Charles Baker's school at Doncaster, and not the Leeds-based association for the adult deaf.)

The report described the meeting as a 'soirée' which started with 'a tea' and 'the attendance included a considerable number of the deaf and dumb persons resident in the town, many of whom were busily engaged in their noiseless conversation with their fellows during the greater part of the proceedings'. As Secretary, Foulston then gave his annual report but emphasised the main purpose of the meeting was to establish a Sheffield branch, in part to supplement the educational work of the school at Doncaster after the children returned home as well as for those who had never attended, and also 'to provide situations and render other assistance to the distressed deaf and dumb, and above all things to care for the spiritual welfare of the deaf and dumb'. John Cole moved and John Clayton (a young deaf mute) seconded the adoption of the report, with Foulston interpreting their remarks and the rest of the meeting for the benefit of the deaf. The Mayor, John Brown, chaired the meeting and spoke next: 'He dwelt on the terrible nature of the affliction, and the cause for gratitude to Almighty God those had who were blessed with the powers of speech and hearing […] he urged that a strenuous effort should be made to obtain the funds necessary to make proper provision for their temporal welfare, and their spiritual instruction and edification.' To great applause he offered to covenant £5 per annum and to pay for the hire of the Cutlers Hall. Daniel II thanked the Mayor and 'urged the great claims of the deaf and dumb on their more fortunate fellow creatures, and expressed a hope that this gathering would be the beginning of better things for them in Sheffield'. He was seconded by the Reverend S Flood from Leeds, who stressed the dire nature of the affliction and how help was needed, and also wanted to ensure the necessary time and energy was devoted to the new branch; 'he urged the committee to be appointed for Sheffield to work earnestly in the promotion of the object and not content themselves with (only) being on the committee.' Finally resolutions were passed to establish the Sheffield branch and to appoint a committee.

Thomas Widd was certainly at the meeting and in his 1897 account in *British Deaf News* (35 years after the event), he says he worked hard to set up this 'meeting and soirée' on behalf of Foulston and even paid the booking fee of four guineas – subsequently reimbursed by the Mayor, John Brown. Widd takes up the story:

There were present over 150 deaf mutes, mostly from adjacent towns, and at which the Mayor, Sir John Brown, kindly presided. When he beheld so many afflicted ones before him, he wept and spake most feelingly on their behalf, frankly confessing that he was surprised, and that the report that I made to him of the number of deaf in the city was not exaggerated, and that they certainly needed the consolations of religion in their own language, and should have the sympathy and aid of all humane and Christian people. At this meeting a friend in need turned up. It was Mr Daniel Doncaster, who formed a committee to raise subscriptions to carry on the work. The association was established and friends of influence and wealth came forward to its aid.

(British Deaf News, 1897)

Quite why so many of the deaf should come to a Sheffield meeting, travelling 'mostly from adjacent towns' is difficult to explain until we look at George Stephenson's 1911 account. He writes that even after 49 years 'there are at present in connexion with our association four deaf and dumb who partook of that tea'. George was not there himself (he was only seventeen at the time) but it is most likely that his parents were, and that they would have told him about it. If his account is accurate, then Daniel II, the 'friend in need', did not just 'turn up': he was closely enough involved to have provided the social tea for the deaf and dumb which preceded the meeting. In view of Doncaster's later generosity to deaf people, and it being Christmas, this seems much more likely. (Stephenson, 1911, p15)

The first President of the new Sheffield Association in Aid of the Adult Deaf and Dumb was John Brown and the Honorary Secretary and Treasurer was Daniel Doncaster II, thus starting a strong if not dominant connection between the Doncasters and the Association which lasted virtually uninterrupted for almost 100 years. The other members of the initial committee were James H Barber (now related to the Doncasters by marriage) and James Wall, the Quakers who had met with Foulston on his first visit to Sheffield; the Rev J F Witty (the vicar of St Matthews Church), and John Cole, the senior founding member of the Cole Brothers department store (now part of the John Lewis Partnership), who later became President in succession to John Brown.

The Association was constituted, like those of Bradford, Halifax and Huddersfield, as a branch of the Leeds Society and did not become fully independent of that tutelage for several years. The objects of the Association remained unchanged throughout its history and are printed in each of the surviving annual reports:

> *The moral, religious, and secular education of the deaf and dumb*
> *To assist them in obtaining suitable employment; To provide an*
> *interpreter when needed; To assist in the settlement of disputes or*
> *misunderstandings between the deaf and dumb, their employers*
> *and others To visit the sick and others at their homes, and To aid*
> *them in any way that may be needful and suitable in their peculiar*
> *circumstances*

Thomas Widd's part in creating the Sheffield Association was not quite finished. Boyce and Hayes tell us that it was he, after the initial meeting, who located and fitted out the first floor premises at 82 ½ Division Street, and even paid the first quarter's rent out of his own pocket. For a period, whether months or only weeks, he carried on his work with the Sheffield deaf, though how he found the time is hard to imagine, as he was simultaneously travelling 'on some weekdays to Great Driffield or Grantham where he was employed as a journeyman printer and compositor'. (Boyce and Hayes, 2007, p24) Clearly, he was a man of quite extraordinary energy and determination, as his subsequent career in London, Montreal and Los Angeles suggests. George Stephenson, writing not only 50 years after the events but also after Widd's death in 1907, said of him 'though deaf and dumb, he had big aspirations, and also, having a high opinion of his own abilities, was fully prepared to undertake anything possible to any other man'. (Stephenson, 1911, p12)

Thomas Widd left Sheffield in March 1863 and only returned once more for personal reasons; he had become engaged to a deaf Worksop girl, Margaret Fitzakerley, who he had met when both were pupils at YIDD, and they were married at the Ecclesall Union Workhouse, Sheffield on 1st January 1864 with the Stephensons' family friend the merry tailor William Simmonite and his wife as witnesses. (Boyce and Hayes, 2007, p26)

There can be no doubt of the high regard in which Widd was held, because when he left he was presented with a writing desk with the following inscription:

Presented to Mr Thomas Widd by the adult deaf of Sheffield as a small token of their esteem and gratitude. March 10th 1863

(BOYCE AND HAYES, 2007, p24)

Widd's subsequent career demonstrates his unswerving commitment to the cause of deaf people. That career is briefly summarised in Appendix One, but for a fuller account the reader is recommended to Boyce and Hayes' biography. He was clearly able, ambitious and restless, and indubitably a fine example of Victorian progress from the most humble and disadvantaged beginnings to a respected and successful life of service to others.

★★★

The Association had now embarked on its service to deaf people which lasted uninterruptedly for the next 98 years. During that time there was almost always at least one member of the Doncaster family on the committee, in the earlier years playing a leading role, and for 89 of those years the position of salaried superintendent was held successively by four members of the Stephenson family.

Usually a basic resource to examine the history of a charitable organisation is the sequence of annual reports to its committee, supporters and the wider public, but as detailed in the Notes on Sources, apart from 1887 and two later extracts nothing has survived from the first half century. So until 1912, after which almost all the reports survive, we are largely reliant for first-hand accounts on newspaper and magazine reports, and on the Jubilee Souvenir written by George Stephenson and published on behalf of the Association in 1911. This document is not always accurate – in the first place, it was not the true jubilee, because the founding date was 1862 and not 1861 as he claimed! There is no reason to doubt the honesty of the account, only occasionally its accuracy; to be fair we should bear in mind that it was intended as a celebration as much as a history.

Following Widd's departure, the new committee's first task was to appoint his successor as teacher and spiritual guide or missioner to the deaf, subsequently entitled superintendent though probably not until the position became full time in 1879. Their choice demonstrates the leadership of the Doncasters as well as the role played in the early Yorkshire societies by deaf former pupils and teachers from YIDD. Joseph Farrar (1840–1927) was another Yorkshireman, born in Tadcaster a year after Widd. A pupil at YIDD from the age of 9 to 16 he was employed there as a pupil teacher and printer from 1856 to 1858, and then at the Swansea school for the deaf under the YIDD graduate Alexander Melville. (Apart from Census returns and the details from George Stephenson in 1911, much of the information about Farrar is drawn from a summary given by Boyce and Hayes, 2007, p 72.) In 1862 he came to Sheffield as private tutor to the Doncasters' youngest child Arthur, profoundly deaf from birth. Farrar was only 22 or 23 but he had teaching experience at YIDD and Swansea, he had presumably proved his worth in the Doncaster household, and he was already resident in Sheffield. As the Sheffield Association was established and remained for several years as a branch of Leeds, and perhaps also in view of Farrar's youth, it was arranged that James Foulston from Leeds should visit Sheffield on a monthly basis, particularly to attend the Bible studies on a Sunday, and no doubt to confirm that Farrar was performing his duties satisfactorily.

According to George's 1911 account, those duties comprised:

> *spending two nights a week teaching those who had received no schooling, holding a Bible class on Sunday, and in every way to get in touch with the deaf and dumb in the town, and bring their needs periodically before Mr Doncaster.*
>
> (STEPHENSON, 1911, p13)

Keeping in touch with Daniel Doncaster would not be difficult if his work as part-time superintendent was performed in tandem with his other duties as Arthur's private tutor. During the eight years of his employment by the Association (1863 to 1871) Farrar married a deaf girl, Elizabeth Cooper, and by the 1871 Census they were living with their first child in Gloucester Crescent, conveniently halfway between and within easy walking distance of Division Street and the Doncaster family home in Broomhall.

In the absence of any other detailed contemporary record, we can get no better feel for the activities of the Association during the first 8 or 9 years than to quote George's 1911 summary in full:

> *The teacher himself was deaf and dumb and also heavily handicapped by being very short sighted, indeed, so much so, that it was often necessary in the evenings for one of the mutes to accompany him to his home. In spite of this he was enabled to do much good among his charge, and with the aid of Mr Foulston, of Leeds, who continued his monthly visits, the classes and meetings which were held were productive of a better condition, both of mind and estate, among those who participated in them. Every year, at Christmas time, Mr Doncaster entertained the deaf and dumb to a substantial meat tea, the members of his family providing interesting and instructive entertainment afterwards. These occasions were always looked forward to by the deaf and dumb with pleasurable anticipation. Occasionally excursions into the country by bus would be arranged, and the writer can remember one such about 1866, when he, the only hearing person, accompanied them, and how earnestly and eagerly they gathered round to take in the interpretation of the guide's description of the wonders of Chatsworth House and conservatories. Thus the monotony of the lives of these people was brightened, and a feeling of hopefulness began to take the place of indifference.*
>
> (STEPHENSON, 1911, P16)

As we shall see from many later examples, the unctuous style of these remarks is typical of the mature George, though to be fair this passage could have been penned by any number of pious Victorian missioners.

George wrote that 'Joseph Farrar continued his faithful service until 1871, when he found it expedient to resign the position of teacher'. (Stephenson, 1911, p16) Quite why this was 'expedient' is not clear, but perhaps as Arthur Doncaster was now fifteen his function as the boy's private tutor was coming to an end and he needed a full-time occupation to support his wife and their intention to add to the family; they had two more children during the 1870s. It was said on his retirement that 'he performed his duties conscientiously and was very assiduous in collecting materials for the enquiry on YIDD school-leavers'. He then resumed a career as a master printer and was still occupied as such in Sheffield at the 1881 Census. Eventually, he moved to Scarborough where in 1901 he is described as a 'printer artist', clearly a considerable craftsman despite his poor sight. He went completely blind by 1911 but lived another sixteen years.

★★★

The committee of the Sheffield Association now had to find a replacement as part-time teacher and missioner to the adult deaf. George tells us that for some weeks James Foulston came over from Leeds on several occasions to fill the gap, but then:

> *the committee placed the circumstances before the writer, then a young married man of 26, and asked him to take over the work. After prayerful consideration and consultation with friends he consented, though with considerable misgivings, and entered upon the mission in September 1871.*
>
> (STEPHENSON, 1911, P16)

It is noticeable that in this account (but not elsewhere), George writes of himself in the third person, presumably because the souvenir booklet was intended for a wide readership and as a means of attracting support from the community which might not appreciate too personal a note. Quite why or how the committee came to ask him to take the post, and whether for instance other candidates were considered, is not known. As one of the sons of a deaf couple who had actively supported the work from the time Widd came to Sheffield, he would have been known to some of the committee members, and it is clear from his subsequent career and the opinions of others that he was not lacking in confidence, but it must have seemed a brave step for a young family man at the time.

George had married for the first time sometime in the early 1860s. His wife was Mary Baker, four years older than him. The daughter of an agricultural labourer from Calow near Chesterfield, and at the 1861 Census aged 21, we find her in Hanover Square, Sheffield, a stone's throw from the Stephenson family home, working as a 'house servant' for Arthur Smith, a timber merchant's cashier, and his wife Emma. George and Mary were not long in starting a family; by 1871 there was Mary E Stephenson aged seven, Albert aged five, Alice Baker just one, and George William, two months – to be followed by John in 1872 and Samuel in 1873. The family were living at 167 Milton Street, the street where Widd and Askew had started their work for the deaf community in 1862, and George was described as a spring knife cutler, the occupation he had followed since the age of twelve.

George's own account of his appointment and its early difficulties suggests that he was nervous about what he was taking on, though whether he dreamed it would occupy him for almost 50 years is unlikely. Again he coyly refers to himself in the third person:

> *Cradled among the deaf and dumb, also conversant with the manual alphabet, and being fairly proficient in communicating with them, but having had no experience in teaching or in mission work, it is not surprising that mistakes were made, and the new teacher got taken down occasionally. Nothing, however, could exceed the kindness and consideration of the committee in this respect, and affectionate regard was also shown by the deaf and dumb; all this considerably lightened his labours and relieved him of his fears, so that in a very few months the confidence of the deaf people was secured, and the future prospect became more bright.*
>
> (STEPHENSON, 1911, p16)

One other fact may explain the committee's choice: according to George himself, his name was put forward to Daniel Doncaster II by family friend and boyhood companion, the deaf tailor, William Simmonite. George goes on to say of Simmonite, now thankfully leaving behind the awkward device of writing of himself in the third person:

> *and now that his young protégé had been appointed his spiritual teacher, he was delighted, and cheerfully accompanied me to the homes of all the deaf and dumb, to whom he introduced me.*
>
> (STEPHENSON, 1911, p16)

There is a rather different account of George's appointment, also written many years after the event. This is contained in a fulsome tribute to him and his work in an 1898 article in a series entitled 'Friends of Young Sheffielders' in volume one of a monthly magazine called *Young Sheffield*. This account is certainly not accurate in every respect, as it dates the vacancy to 1869 instead of 1871, and ascribes it to 'the removal of Mr Farrar from Sheffield' whereas he was still living there at least until 1881. The article goes on to say that the deaf were then without a teacher 'for the space of a year and it became a matter of serious concern to the committee to find a suitable man for the vacancy.' There is no mention of any recommendation by William Simmonite, or of any reluctance or lack of teaching experience on George's part.

> *It was here that Mr George Stephenson volunteered to do the work, so far as his business engagements would allow. The committee very gladly recognised how the man and the work fitted each other. Mr Stephenson was then about 24 years of age, and as both his parents were deaf mutes, whilst he himself had the full advantage of hearing and speech, it was felt that the much needed 'interpreter' had come at last. From his youth he had eagerly used every opportunity of adding to his stock of learning, and had just as plainly shown himself anxious and apt to teach. His offer was therefore accepted, and Mr Stephenson threw himself into the work, and the work in turn got more and more hold of him. It grieved him much to see the sad state of neglect into which many of the deaf mutes in the town had fallen, and he felt he must do something to alter such a state of things, even though it were at the sacrifice of his growing business.*
> (YOUNG SHEFFIELD, JANUARY, 1898, PP. 56–58)

On this account it was a matter of George pushing himself forward with no reservations about his own capacity or qualifications, only perhaps a concern about the effect on his livelihood. There is no way of knowing which account is the more accurate, but all the later evidence of his strength of character suggests that he would have been capable from a young age of pushing himself forward, so perhaps there is some truth in the 1898 tribute, to which we shall return later.

★★★

To get a flavour of the first years of George's period as part-time superintendent in the early 1870s, we have to rely heavily on his own account in 1911, and in most cases, to paraphrase only detracts from his inimitable style, at once pious, optimistic and didactic. Take for instance this passage on a topic clearly central to philanthropic concern for the health and well-being of the poor and afflicted. Having bemoaned the previously limited access of the deaf to the ideas and aspirations of the hearing, he goes on to say:

> *Also, as a rule, they were easily led into intemperate habits. Knowing this weakness, Mr Doncaster had induced some of them to sign the pledge, and at the annual Christmas treat, which he provided for them, always had the blessings that accompany total abstinence from alcoholic drinks fully brought before them. In spite of all this, however, the intemperate habit was very strong with many of them, degrading them into a very low condition indeed. To combat this state of things, those of the deaf and dumb who were total abstainers and consistent in their lives were requested to form themselves into a committee of workers for the benefit of their more unfortunate brethren. It was a somewhat bold step to take with deaf and dumb people, and at once led to considerable opposition from the drinkers. The abstainers, however, held on, and organised a Temperance Society of the deaf and dumb, with a secretary chosen from among them. Fortnightly meetings were held, and presently had favourable results. One case may here be mentioned. A man called Thomas Hobbis, one of the most notorious of drunkards and wife beaters, a man whose features plainly indicated to the most unobservant the ravages of drink, was one of the first to sign the pledge. This he kept to the end of life, and it was often remarked by friends before he died that his outward appearance had changed so much that his old drinking companions would scarcely be able to recognise him.*
>
> (STEPHENSON, 1911, p17)

Fighting the demon drink was not enough, and under George's influence there were great efforts to improve the minds of the deaf. In 1873, for instance:

it was decided to invite men of science to come occasionally among
us and deliver lectures, which could be interpreted to the deaf and
dumb.

(STEPHENSON, 1911, P17)

This earnest drive for self-improvement chimed well with the enthusiasm of the Victorian middle classes for scientific knowledge and exploration of the natural world, exemplified, amongst countless others, by the Doncaster family. (Arthur Doncaster's life is summarised in Appendix One; and of his brothers, Charles was a bee keeper and enthusiastic student of bird life; Samuel created Whinfell Quarry Gardens in Whirlow, Sheffield, recently restored to its original grandeur; Samuel's son Leonard became Professor of Zoology at Liverpool University and his grandson John Priestman Doncaster was an entomologist at the Science Museum.)

Such was the success of these lectures and the welcome they received from their deaf listeners, they became an integral part of proceedings at 82 ½ Division Street:

From this time forward, every autumn and winter we had
monthly lectures, which were readily given by such men as Mr
Henry Seebohm, Mr Wm Bragge, Dr H Clifton Sorby, Mr J C
Wing, Mr G Tomlinson, Mr Byron Carr, Mr W R Marples, Mr
Charles Doncaster, Mr Samuel Doncaster, Mr Daniel Doncaster,
Miss Mawson, and many other well-known ladies and gentlemen.
Perhaps the most interesting of all the lectures given in those early
days were those by Mrs Daniel Doncaster on 'The Elements of
Food', 'Alcohol and its Work', etc. all of which were accompanied
by illustrations or chemical experiments.

(STEPHENSON, 1911, P18)

It is difficult to resist a further example of education and entertainment combined, as George recalled:

another occasion, when the late Mr Charles Doncaster unfolded the
wonderful providence of God in bird life, and then invited some
of the young men to his home and dissected a quail before them,

> *patiently explaining the various parts, and instructing them in the*
> *art of taxidermy, concluding by giving them a good supper and their*
> *railway fare from Beauchief to Sheffield.*
>
> (STEPHENSON, 1911, P18)

There is no record of how the young men felt about the instruction and largesse they received, nor what they said about the experience when they returned home from Sheffield station.

It may be that the time that elapsed between the events and the record added to their apparent importance, but George seems to have seen these early years as something of a golden age in terms of self-improvement:

> *Truly in that plain unadorned meeting room our deaf and dumb*
> *had most happy and instructive times, and upon recalling those*
> *hard-working but happy days, one cannot help feeling that, with*
> *all the advantages of our present surroundings, and the variety of*
> *organisations which now form part of our association, the deaf and*
> *dumb of those days devoted more of their time and attention to the*
> *improvement of their minds than now.*
>
> (STEPHENSON, 1911, P18)

During the eight years of George's part-time appointment, it must have become clear that the committee's choice had been justified, and likewise the committee of the parent society in Leeds. The regular visitations by Foulston ceased and the Sheffield Association became entirely self-governing; from then on there is no record of any more than a fraternal relationship between the two organisations, and for the remaining 80 plus years of its active existence, the Sheffield Association remained an independent charity.

★★★

The death of Charles Baker of YIDD in May 1874 facilitated the break from Leeds; as we have seen, Widd had been warned that Baker would object to the foundation of a society for deaf adults so near to his sphere of influence in Doncaster. His death also helped to pave the way for the next major development in Sheffield. During his frequent visits to the homes of deaf families, George Stephenson realised that many of the school-age deaf children were receiving no formal education at all; some attended YIDD as boarders but this involved fees which few could afford, and even fewer like Arthur Doncaster could benefit from home tuition. George impressed on the committee the need to cater for the 'wild and untaught' majority of deaf children. The response exemplified the influence of philanthropists, and particularly the Doncasters, because by 1879, Daniel II's third son Charles was both Secretary of the Association and an elected member of the Sheffield School Board and its School Management Committee.

No time was lost, the School Board made the necessary grant, and in January 1879 a day school for deaf and dumb children was opened in the very limited space on the first floor of 82 Division Street. George Stephenson was appointed as teacher, in addition to his duties with the adults. The school hours were from 9.00 to 12.30 six mornings a week and within a short period 20 children between nine and fifteen were enrolled. This room was also used in the evenings for meetings of the adults and on Sundays for religious instruction, a situation which could only be temporary. Pressures on space and on George's time were too great; nevertheless he wrote with justifiable personal and civic pride that the school was intended to be completely free and that 'this was the first School Board Day School for deaf and dumb opened in England, and the experiment was looked upon with considerable interest'. (Stephenson, 1911, p19) It was not compulsory for school boards to provide elementary education specifically for deaf children until after 1893, so this was indeed a pioneer foundation. Bergen referred to these new schools 'with Sheffield taking the lead in 1879, Leeds following in 1881 and Bradford making provision in 1885.' (Bergen, 2004, p239) It was just as well that Baker had died five years earlier, otherwise his objections in 1862 might have been redoubled. In his 1871 report to his committee he had commented that as he had feared, there had been a reduction in donations to YIDD because some funds had been diverted to the growing number of adult missions, but if local schools were also established they would also require funds and trained teachers, again reducing the resources available to 'his' school. (Bergen, 2004, p224/5) As we shall see in Chapter Three, this issue played a part in the eventual closure of the Sheffield school in the 1890s.

★★★

When George was first appointed as part-time superintendent in 1871, there was a potential conflict with his existing career as a cutler. The business was growing in importance; he had started as a self-employed 'little mester' like his father, and in 1871 both business and home were given as 167 Milton Street. By 1879, the local directory *Whites* still shows his business as 'cutlery manufacturer' at the Milton Street property but his home at Woodland View, a district between Malin Bridge and Stannington to the west of the city and at that time almost in the country. Clearly, he had been successful enough to separate work from home. Now, however, he had a full timetable of responsibilities for the Association as the children's teacher and as missioner and superintendent for the adults, and he could scarcely have managed even if he had a settled personal life. Unhappily, that had not been the case for several years.

Mary and he had six children by 1874 (as explained below there may also have been a seventh). Plenty for a family with an expanding business and charitable work, but then tragedy struck; two days after Christmas 1874, in his presence and at their home, his wife Mary died of phthisis, defined in the *Concise Oxford Dictionary* as 'any progressive wasting disease, especially pulmonary tuberculosis'. TB was a common cause of death among the Victorian working class, but we can only imagine how long George and his young children watched their wife and mother decline to her death at the age of 34. Suddenly the conflict between business and work with deaf adults was magnified with single parental responsibilities for six or seven young children.

We do not know how he coped in the four years following Mary's death, but we can make a reasonable guess from what then happened. On 5th August 1878 at Stannington Parish Church, George Stephenson, widower, 'missionary and agent', was married to Lena Spencer, aged 25, widow, and the address for both of them is given as Woodland View, Stannington.

Lena (otherwise Selina, her given name at birth) was born in Sheffield in early 1853 and in 1861, aged eight, was living with her parents John Parker (like George and his father Benjamin, a spring knife cutler) and Emma in a back-to-back cottage in Taylor's Yard, Park, until its demolition one of the most crowded, insanitary and deprived of Sheffield slums. In late 1869, aged only 16, she married Job Spencer, a 20-year-old silversmith, originally from Middleton in Derbyshire, where his father was a farmer and publican. In 1871 Job and Lena were living in Bigod Street, Park. At this point the genealogical picture gets fuzzy, because my research has failed to find any record of Job Spencer's death, despite the facts that Lena is clearly described on her marriage to George as a widow, and that the two witnesses to the marriage are Thomas and Alice Spencer, presumably relatives of her late husband. (There is a further mystery. Looking ahead, to the 1881 and 1891 Census returns, George and Lena's household includes a Laura Stephenson, a 'daughter' aged seven and seventeen at those two dates, the same age, but possibly as much as a year apart, as George and Mary's last child Samuel. In the column giving the place of birth, which for the rest of the growing family is Sheffield, the entry for Laura is Birmingham, a city with which none of the Stephenson, Parker or Spencer families had any known connection. Research has so far failed to elucidate Laura's parentage, origins or indeed her life after 1891.)

We can guess what may have happened in those difficult years between Mary's death and the marriage to Lena. George was trying to care part-time for many deaf citizens, run a business, and raise at least six children; Lena was widowed, presumably with no means of support, and perhaps caring for a young daughter. By the date of their marriage, they were living together, and it seems likely that at some stage both their immediate problems had been resolved by George employing Lena as housekeeper and carer for his young family. In January 1879, he assumed the even more onerous task of teaching deaf children six mornings every week; perhaps if he had not formalised the relationship with Lena by marriage his appointment as a teacher of children might have been unacceptable to his employers. A marriage of convenience, perhaps, but it gave both parties the security and stability they needed and produced seven more children, of whom six survived to adulthood, and lasted 32 years until Lena's death.

What of the description of George on the marriage certificate as 'Missionary and Agent'? Almost certainly Missionary should read Missioner. The word Agent suggests how George may have already reduced his business activity, by withdrawing completely from manufacturing but continuing to act as an agent or merchant, using his knowledge and contacts to market the products of others. *Whites Directory* gives us a fuller picture for 1879. In the commercial section George Stevenson [*sic*] is given as a cutlery manufacturer at 167 Milton Street (his home with

Mary, certainly until her death) but under the residents section George Stephenson is described as Superintendent of the Deaf and Dumb Institute with 'H' (for home) as Woodland View, Stannington. However, we know from an announcement in the local press (see later) that by early 1880 the family were living at 57 Countess Road. This was one of a street of new working-class terraced houses, a few hundred yards from Hermitage Street where George was born and Milton Street where he had lived and worked in cutlery and Widd had started his mission in Sheffield, and not much further from the Association's premises in Division Street. This is confirmed firstly in the 1881 Census and then in *Whites* for 1883, where there is no longer any mention of George as a cutlery manufacturer or of Milton Street, and he is described as 'Schoolmaster at the Deaf and Dumb Institute', resident at Countess Road.

In the same year as the appointment as teacher and the marriage to Lena there was another family death which probably made it easier to abandon the cutlery business completely. George had been a spring knife cutler from the age of 12, following his father, and as he became independent and successful he acted as agent for other producers, who could well have included his father; if so he would be reluctant to retire completely for as long as his father was dependent on him for an outlet. But on 29th May 1879 Benjamin Stephenson, spring knife cutler aged 62, died from paralysis at his home in Court 16, Portobello Street and the informant was his son George of Wood Lane, Stannington. The marriage to Lena and the death of his father enabled him to see his future more clearly; with the opening of the school earlier that year he had accepted a full-time post with the Association and the family were back in the city centre at Countess Road. The life of a working cutler or agent for others was over; at the age of 34 he was now a full-time salaried superintendent of the Sheffield Deaf and Dumb Institute where he remained in post for another 41 years.

To get a flavour of the next few years we return to the fulsome tribute by the *Young Sheffield* magazine in 1898 which gave a clear impression of the volume and variety of his functions, even if some of them such as the natural history lectures were given by others like the Doncasters:

> *On Mr Stephenson giving his whole time to the work, a fresh impetus was given to every branch of operation in aid of the deaf and*

dumb of the town. To a growing number of adults he gave lectures on natural history, along with such general instruction as they seemed to need. Rambles were taken on Saturday afternoons; and every opportunity was seized of awakening an interest in natural objects, and of turning the attention to healthy innocent pursuits; whilst abreast of this religious, moral and secular instruction were kept the equally necessary work of the interpreter, the assisting of the deaf mutes in the finding of employment and the settlement of disputes or misunderstandings between them and their employers and others, the visiting of the sick in their homes, and generally the aiding of the deaf and dumb in any way that was needful or suitable to their peculiar circumstances.

(*YOUNG SHEFFIELD*, JANUARY 1898 PP. 56–58)

In 1884, five years into this frenetic activity, supported by an active committee of wealthy philanthropists but with George Stephenson as the only full-time employee, the Association suffered a double bereavement. The first was Daniel Doncaster II, in George's phrase 'our beloved founder'. In poor health for some time, he had relinquished leadership of the family business and the honorary posts of Secretary and Treasurer to the Association, in both cases to his son Charles, but retained his concern for the deaf almost until his death. The obituary in the *Sheffield Independent* (18th August 1884) said his was:

a name long associated in the minds of Sheffield people with words of sympathy and acts of kindness and benevolence towards every movement which had for its object the alleviation of human suffering and the promotion of temperance, morality and religion.

In a lengthy obituary, the reporter nevertheless had insufficient space to mention every example of Daniel's good works, but after summarising his activities with the Quakers, the greatest prominence is given to the deaf community:

To Mr Doncaster and his family more than anyone we owe the formation and the continuance of the Sheffield Association in Aid of the Adult Deaf and Dumb, a class of poor unfortunate creatures for whom he felt the deepest sympathy and concern.

After detailing his leadership of the Association's committee as well as its foundation, a more personal note is struck:

> *Once a year at Christmas he invited the whole body of the deaf and dumb to dinner, and that custom was continued from the formation of the society down to last Christmas... a memorable event in the lives of the poor afflicted.*

The obituary then details his concern and work for temperance, the Sheffield Infirmary and the Peace Society, with a substantial section on his political stance ('a sound Liberal'). The account of the funeral, in the *Sheffield Independent* two days later, again makes clear the primary significance of his work for deaf people. It was noted that (in line with traditional Quaker simplicity) the funeral procession for the half mile from his home to the General Cemetery was:

> *devoid of most of the trappings of woe, [nevertheless] a carriage was provided for the servants at the deceased's house and at the rear of this came several vehicles containing members of the Sheffield Deaf and Dumb Institute [...] and in Mr John Cole's carriage were that gentleman, Mr Robert Renton Eadon, and Mr George Stephenson as representing the trustees and committee.*

We shall meet Mr Eadon again later. He was a committee member from 1879 until 1900, variously described as a saw, file and steel manufacturer; he was the only committee member apart from Daniel Doncaster III who was deaf himself, 'from childhood fever' according to the Census. Other mourners included the Quakers James H Barber and his sons Jonathan, a solicitor, and Jarvis William, a chartered accountant.

Worse was to follow, for both the family business and the Association, with the death at Christmas 1884 of Daniel III's son Charles, only 45, successor as head of the family firm as well as Chairman of the Sheffield School Board. In 1911 George described him as:

> *a man of sterling character, with high ideals, practical and full of energy, he had put into his short life great work. Revered by all who*

knew him, and beloved by the young men, his death was a great
loss not only to our association but to Sheffield.

(STEPHENSON, 1911, P20)

The obituary in the *Sheffield Independent* (December 26th 1884) was shorter than that of his father, but no less laudatory:

All movements which had as their object the benefiting of his
fellow men, whether morally, socially or religiously, found in him
a warm and cordial supporter [...] and without the slightest show
or ostentation.

This included support of temperance and Quaker activities, especially teaching both at the Friends Sunday School and adult classes, as well as the assumption of his father's duties as Secretary and Treasurer of the Association, work in which 'he ever evinced the deepest interest'. His main contribution to Sheffield life however was in education. Like his father he was an active supporter and participated in the management of the boys' and girls' Lancastrian schools, providing free education on the monitorial system developed by Joseph Lancaster. Following the Education Act 1870, he was elected to the first Sheffield School Board, and by 1882, when he succeeded John Cole as Chairman, he was the sole survivor of the original board. A businessman, nature lover and a staunch though not prominent Liberal; like father, like son, the very paradigm of the Victorian philanthropist.

Charles was succeeded as head of the family company by the fourth son Samuel (the second son David Kenway having died in 1881) and as Secretary and Treasurer of the Association by Daniel II's oldest son Daniel III. Perhaps passed over for the leadership of the family business because of his congenital deafness, Daniel III now assumed the role for which he is best remembered.

★★★

The excessive pressure on George Stephenson's time and energy had been relieved by his second marriage and by relinquishing all his business interests, but the pressure on the Association's premises became acute after the foundation of its school. There was a desperate need for additional space; there are no surviving plans or measurements of the single room on the upper floor at 82 Division Street but its growing inadequacy was realised as early as 1878, before the school classes had even started, and the Association already held £200 as the nucleus of a building fund. It was decided to hold a bazaar to raise more and it is a tribute to the philanthropic fervour of the Association's wealthy supporters and their wives that in order to push this project forward:

> *Mrs Daniel Doncaster junior and the Misses Doncaster (followed by Mrs Edward Tozer and the Misses Tozer) kindly consented to take over the control of weekly sewing meetings of the deaf and dumb women.*
>
> (STEPHENSON, 1911, P19)

It is not recorded what the deaf women thought about being taken over in this way, but the efforts of all were rewarded. On 22nd, 23rd and 24th May 1878, the bazaar was held at the Cutlers Hall, opened by the Mayor, and produced a profit of £450 which was invested and added to the building fund.

Efforts continued to maximise the fund during the next few years, and Charles Doncaster in particular searched for a suitable building. Failing to achieve this, he included the following appeal in his last annual report as Honorary Secretary before his death:

> *SITE WANTED. Can any of our friends help us to a small plot of land, say 300 yards, centrally situated, but not necessarily on a main thoroughfare?*

In the early 1880s Sheffield Corporation was redeveloping a large area in the town centre around Pinstone Street, Cambridge Street and Charles Street, demolishing old tenements and extending Charles Street towards Cambridge Street, naming the extension Upper Charles Street. In the course of these operations, vacant land became available. Robert Renton Eadon had joined the committee in 1879, and his father Alderman R T Eadon was a member of the Town Council. Edward Tozer, another prominent steel manufacturer whose wife and daughters had joined the

Doncasters in supervising the deaf women's sewing class, had joined the committee at the same time as Daniel Doncaster III; he was a Town Councillor and had been Mayor in 1879 when the association took on the education of deaf children and Charles Doncaster had been Chairman of the School Board. No doubt George was right to say that it was the collective influence of these prominent citizens which in 1885 enabled the Association to purchase from the corporation for the very reasonable sum of £750 a triangular piece of land of about 250 square yards at the junction of Upper Charles Street, Cambridge Street and Cross Burgess Street.

Edward Tozer's efforts and influence were not exhausted. According to George he was instrumental in persuading many other prominent citizens to add substantial donations to the building fund. Writing some 25 years later, George must have had access to complete lists of donations, because he gives details of three donations of £100, seven of £50, eleven of £25, eight of £20, twenty-five of £10 or guineas, and 'a large number subscribed smaller sums [...] the deaf and dumb collected £36 6s 6d.' The Town Trust, a long-established civic charity, donated £500. The fund was now large enough for the committee to instruct the prominent Sheffield architects Flockton and Gibbs to prepare plans for the new building. The requirement comprised a schoolroom for 50 children, a large meeting room, a reading room, ancillary accommodation and a superintendent's house.

That left only the legal formalities. Looking ahead for precise evidence, in June 1894, the Charity Commissioners conducted an enquiry into the Endowed Charities of Sheffield. Their report shows that the Association was represented at the enquiry by James Henry Barber's son Jonathan of Watson Esam and Barber, solicitors of Sheffield. (This long-established firm, always led by Quakers, was still in existence into the 21st century and acted for the Association throughout its history.) Jonathan Barber produced to the enquiry a trust document and a conveyance, both dated 10th September 1885, which between them formed the legal basis for the remainder of the Association's active life.

The trust document provided that R R Eadon, Daniel Doncaster III and E H Marples (all members of the committee) should hold the land purchased from the corporation as trustees on behalf of the committee who had funded the purchase. The land and any buildings were to be under the control and management of the Association acting by its elected committee. They were empowered to erect buildings 'to be used for religious, educational, recreative and other purposes for the benefit of deaf and dumb persons of either sex residing in and around Sheffield and their relations and friends', but with an absolute prohibition of the sale or consumption of alcohol, dancing or gambling. The committee were further empowered to frame, enforce and amend such rules, regulations and bye-laws as they deemed necessary for the proper conduct of the premises within the bounds set by the conveyance and the trust deed.

So the Association had the funds to build an Institute commensurate with its needs and ambitions, a site on which to build, a legal framework for its continuing management, and architects had been appointed. Contractors and sub-contractors were selected and the building work commenced in the summer of 1885 and was completed at the end of September 1886 at a total cost including furnishings of £2700 plus the £750 to purchase the land. Everything was ready for the grand opening, the next and perhaps the most auspicious chapter in the history of the Association.

★★★

There is one postscript to the construction of the Institute which had an entirely unexpected echo in 2012, which illustrates how the wealthy Victorian philanthropists who devoted energy and resources to help the poor and disadvantaged were not themselves immune to personal sorrow. It concerns James Willis Dixon, a very successful silver plate manufacturer with works at Cornish Place. With his wife Fanny, he became one of the most active supporters of the Association and its deaf members. During the course of research for this account, I visited the modern City Council building which houses the Sheffield Deaf Sports and Social Club and facilities for various other handicapped citizens. Behind a closed set of shutters, I was told, were the remaining items salvaged from the chapel at the Institute's last home in Psalter Lane, now no longer used for religious services because there is so little demand. After some delay, the shutters were unlocked and my companion and I were able to see the altar, font and various other items heaped together in no particular order. I noticed a rather battered but elaborately carved oak chair and thought I had seen an image of it somewhere before and therefore took a photograph. Reaching home, I looked back at George's 1911 Jubilee souvenir and realised where I had seen it. Let George take up the story:

About this time (January 1886) the precious little daughter of Mr and Mrs James Dixon died. Mr Dixon, being interested in the building scheme, sent to the Hon Treasurer, Mr Daniel Doncaster, the amount of his child's savings, with a request that it might be expended in some special article of furniture for the new institute, as a memorial of the little one. This was done, and one of the deaf and dumb members, a cabinet maker named Hugh Gough, was instructed to make an oak chair, upholstered in morocco leather, with the result here shown. On the back of the chair is a silver plate, bearing the inscription:

In Memoriam
Margaret Dora Dixon
Born Jan 29th 1883
Died Jan 30th 1886

After this expression of the interest shown in the association by Mr and Mrs Dixon, it is small wonder that at the Annual Meeting held in March, Mr Dixon was unanimously elected a member of the committee.

(STEPHENSON, 1911, p23)

The silver plate has gone, but it seemed rather poignant that 126 years after the Institute was built and over 50 years since the Association closed its doors, the last remaining physical memento should be this reminder of a purely personal tragedy.

3

THE FIRST 25 YEARS IN CHARLES STREET 1886-1910

'Well Ordered and Self-respecting Townsfolk'

On 8th October 1886 the Institute was opened by Sir Frederick Thorpe Mappin Bart, MP for the Hallamshire division of Sheffield, in the presence of the Mayor J W Pye-Smith, the Master Cutler G F Lockwood, the Vicar of Sheffield, and the Association's Chairman, Edward Tozer. The building is described in the Sheffield Independent on 9th October as constructed with:

> *brick and red terracotta in the Flemish style of architecture, this quaint style being especially suitable for these materials.*

On the lower ground floor was a schoolroom for 30 children with a covered playground. From there, a stone staircase with glazed brick walls led up to a hall 41 feet long, 35 feet wide at one end, narrowing to an octagonal platform at the narrow end (this being a triangular site). So that the audience or congregation could see the speaker clearly, there were no windows behind this platform, which was illuminated by windows in the roof and side walls of the hall. On the same floor there was a reading room, 23 x 16 feet, and toilets for men and women. The superintendent's private quarters shared the main entrance on Charles Street but had a private rear entrance at a higher level on Cross Burgess Street, and included a small hallway, office, storeroom, living room, scullery, pantry and four bedrooms; this substantial accommodation remained the

Stephenson family home for the next 50 years, until the move to Psalter Lane.

Although the new Institute was in use until 1936 and the building was only demolished in 1964, no photograph of the exterior has been found, probably because it was always surrounded on all sides by equally high buildings which would make photography difficult. However the illustration we have appears in many articles as well as in the annual reports of the Association, and there are photographs from George's 1911 Jubilee Souvenir of the Lecture Hall/Chapel, the Reading Room and the Billiard Room which replaced the school room in the 1890s when the school closed.

In his speech on behalf of the Association, Edward Tozer said that the new Institute would provide its services to a deaf and dumb population in Sheffield of 160 adults, of whom 140 were already involved; these numbers increased considerably over the following years. He itemised the total expenditure to date of £3500 including the £750 cost of the land; there was a funding shortfall of £200, though half of this had been promised in letters from supporters who were unable to attend the opening ceremony. Sir Frederick Mappin also spoke, first to praise George Stephenson as teacher and superintendent. As a total abstainer himself, he drew particular attention to the fact that George had increased the number of abstainers from 10 to 39 since his full-time appointment seven years earlier. George also addressed the audience, which he said included 'many prominent ladies and gentlemen of Sheffield'. He took the opportunity to join the debate about marriage between deaf couples and its consequences for their children. As so often in such remarks, there is an apparent discontinuity between figures and conclusions: on one hand he says that of the 31 children at the school 27 had hearing parents, and yet also suggests that three out of four children born deaf in England were the result of 'infringement of the laws of consanguinity'. He also said that the children were taught by a combination of 'finger spelling' and lip-reading, another issue which caused much discussion and distress in the next decade.

Despite any such controversy, the opening of the Institute was a most significant step for the Association and the Sheffield deaf. As George remembered:

*there was much jubilation among the deaf and dumb, who were,
on the same day, entertained to a good tea by the members of the
committee.*

(STEPHENSON, 1911, P23)

★★★

It is not easy to picture the early years of life in the Institute when only
one of the annual reports from the period has survived. One other
source is *Chosen Vessels* by the late Rev George C Firth, himself a long
time missioner/superintendent to the deaf in Stoke on Trent, Reading,
and elsewhere. Firth's chief source for material on Sheffield and the
Stephensons was George E Robinson (1911–1982), born in Sheffield of
deaf parents, superintendent of the Deaf Institute in Swansea for fifteen
years and then superintendent of the Liverpool Adult Deaf and Dumb
Benevolent Society. As a boy, Robinson's parents regularly took him to
the Institute in Charles Street. Some, if not most, of what he told Firth
must have been derived from his parents, as Robinson himself was only
born in 1911. On the other hand, he spent at least an informal part of
his training period under George's son and successor Colin during the
late 1920s or early 1930s, and for instance his remark about the hearing
children being a nuisance within the Institute may have referred to Colin's
children. In any event, whether the information is second- or third-hand,
the various extracts quoted here and later give a clear impression of life at
the Institute. Of the building itself, Robinson said:

> *The Charles Street Institute was built on a slope; and inside there
> was literally a mountain of steps. The first room on the left was the
> billiard room from which children were barred – by a prominent
> notice and by the policing of the deaf themselves. In the billiard
> room there were sawdust-filled brass spittoons. Halfway up the
> stairs to the right was a door leading to the superintendent's living
> quarters; and at the top of the stairs, on the right again, was the
> Chapel-cum-Hall; and in front at the top of the stairs was a small
> reading room [...] The hearing children ran around playing up
> and down the stairs with nothing else to do, making themselves a
> thorough nuisance!*

(FIRTH, 1985, P98–99)

So what of the activities of the Association and its committee and superintendent in their grand new Institute – in what ways was it serving the deaf people of Sheffield and how many of them were involved? How far was it fulfilling the objectives set out at the foundation of the Association? Although no other annual report from before 1900 has survived, we are fortunate that a fragile copy of the report for 1888 is held by the Sheffield City Library. Despite the formal language, it tells us much about the Institute's activities, finances and its central place in the deaf community.

The most important event of the year had been the visit by members of the Royal Commission on the Education of the Deaf and Dumb, who had inspected not only the children in their schoolroom but also 'the weekly sewing meeting of the deaf and dumb mothers conducted by Mrs James Dixon'. The Chairman, John Cole, said they were looking forward to the report and hoped that further financial support for the children's education would be forthcoming. In fact, before the Institute was completed Cole and James Barber had already written to the school board, requesting further financial support so that when the new schoolroom was available the school hours could be extended from the mornings to the whole day. In order to provide the necessary teaching skills, a second teacher should be employed as assistant to George, in view of all his other duties with the adults. As they said, most of the parents were very poor, and could not afford the fees payable for residential education at YIDD or elsewhere out of Sheffield. The outcome of this appeal is dealt with below when we look at the fate of the school in the 1890s.

The financial section of the report contains several features which are repeated with minor variations right through to the 1950s. The revenue account shows three heads of income; a grant of £18 from the school board, bank interest of £1 8s 3d and subscriptions and donations of £124 0s 6d; in other words a heavy reliance on the generosity of private individuals. The subscription list is given in full; around 150 individuals and institutions, including £10 from the Town Trustees, £5 from John Brown and Co, and donations from local dignitaries like John Cole and members of the Doncaster family, but the great majority were subscriptions of 10 shillings or a guinea or half guinea.

The main item of expenditure was the superintendent's salary of £80, not an excessive stipend for a post of considerable responsibility and many and various functions, but accommodation was provided for him and his family. The remaining expenses are detailed, including repairs and maintenance, coal, coke, gas, stationery, cleaning, insurance, etc. to a total of £46 19s 1d. There is one further item, simply summarised as 'Relief Cases', amounting to £3 10s 7d, a reminder that in those days of the workhouse and a total absence of state relief for poverty, the Institute was dealing overwhelmingly with working-class families. At this early stage in its existence, the Institute was comfortably able to fund any modest shortfall of income over expenditure, as the balance sheet shows an opening figure of £244 11s 3d at the bank, bolstered during the year by two legacies of £100 each plus bank interest and dividends; there were investments in Sheffield Corporation Consolidated Stock, a Midland Southern and London Railway debenture and a healthy closing balance.

George's annual report shows that the Institute had on its register a total of 125 adults and 46 children. Of the adults there were 30 married couples, seven widows and the rest were young single men and women; of the children, about 30 were taught in the schoolroom, the remainder being in residential schools elsewhere, mainly at YIDD. The Reading Room was now 'self –supporting', i.e. the nominal subscription from readers paid for new magazines and books, and gymnasium equipment had been provided for the young men through the 'liberality of several committee members'. Social life continued as before, and it is reported for instance that on Whit Wednesday the adults and children were 'conveyed by wagonette to Ashopton' (a Derbyshire village subsequently drowned by the Ladybower Reservoir) and there 'entertained to a substantial tea by James Dixon, the Master Cutler that year, and Mrs Dixon'.

Apart from the daily lessons for the children, the report also gives the average daily attendance at meetings, Sunday services and classes: 26 on Sunday mornings and 46 in the evenings, 23 on Mondays, 17 on Tuesdays, 20 on Wednesdays, 10 in the gymnasium on Thursdays, 9 in the Reading Room on Fridays and 25 on Saturdays. Teaching the children, however, and supervising these activities, did not exhaust the range of George's duties. During the year, he made no less than 520 home visits (then and subsequently a central part of the superintendent's duties), 127 visits to hospitals, workhouses and other institutions 'with or on behalf of deaf individuals', and a further 152 visits to factories and other workplaces 'to solicit employment', resulting in twelve jobs being obtained.

Several later tributes demonstrate the high reputation which George earned through this ceaseless activity, but the dry details in an annual report give little impression of the man himself or what the deaf members felt about his work. Some sense of his personal authority and style can be gleaned from what George Robinson's parents told him, and he related to Rev Firth:

> *Like a lot of the early pioneers he (George Stephenson) did a lot of home visiting; and George Robinson said to me that he remembered Stephenson calling on his mother in the daytime, wearing a top hat and frock coat, having a chat, and then going off to visit other deaf people in the vicinity – all on foot, of course. [...] He had a bald head and a goatee beard, so the deaf had one of two 'signs' for him: either the sign for a goat (the fingers dangling down under the chin) or a sign denoting the bald head (the palm stroking the top of the head).*

> (FIRTH, 1985, P98)

Perhaps nothing better reminds us of the traditional relationship between deaf people and their missioners than this tiny vignette: the former working cutler, now salaried and secure both socially and financially, professionally attired in accordance with his status, striding from home to humble home, having a chat and being seen by his charges as rather grand. Firth also describes George as a disciplinarian who ruled the deaf 'with a rod of iron' but despite his authoritarian ways was 'greatly beloved by the Sheffield deaf people'.

In truth, the position as superintendent or missioner in an Institute like Sheffield, replicated in a similar form in many towns and cities of late Victorian Britain, was demanding, all embracing and largely isolated from others with the same responsibilities. That George could have felt something of this isolation may help to explain his involvement from 1896 in the Guild of St John of Beverley, as detailed in Chapter Five. For now it is worth noting a personal communication from Rev Firth to Lysons in 1963:

> *The traditional missioner did not look after himself any better than he did the deaf. He spent his whole life in a deaf atmosphere. His*

friends and playmates were deaf. Very often his parents and perhaps his wife were deaf. He kept no office hours and regarded himself as available 24 hours a day. He went for his holidays as part of a deaf outing. His salary was small and he often lived on the premises of the deaf club. Very often he spent a great deal of time begging money to raise his own salary. He was often employed by a committee of delegates from diocesan or other bodies who knew nothing about the deaf and only saw them once a year at the Christmas party. He had no other supervision and was miles away from his nearest colleague.

(LYSONS, 1963, P269)

The value of this isolated role for the social and individual development of deaf people was later questioned, not least by Lysons and Firth, but no such doubts were raised in the early years or during George Stephenson's long career; there is a full discussion of the issue in Chapter Seven.

★★★

However independent the local missions, and however isolated the individual superintendents, they could hardly fail to make some contribution to national debates. Chief amongst the issues which came to a head in the last quarter of the nineteenth century was whether deaf children should be taught on the manual or oral system. The debate came to a head, with long-term consequences believed to be extremely damaging by proponents of sign language, at the 1880 Second Conference of Educators of Deaf Mutes, usually known as the Milan Conference, an international gathering of teachers of the deaf and government representatives, dominated by proponents of oralism.

The conclusions and recommendations of the Milan Conference could not have been clearer; all deaf children should be taught by the oral method and every effort should be made to ban sign language from the schools. This meant that the many teachers who were themselves profoundly deaf and taught by signing could not continue in the careers for which they were suited by experience and vocation. The acceptance of these recommendations by the British government transformed the teaching of deaf children and signalled the victory of the oral method with profound consequences for the children, their families and their teachers, not least in Sheffield.

The strength of feeling engendered by the Milan decisions can be gauged even to this day, for instance in the remarks in Lee (2004, p42–3) that the consequences of Milan were 'truly appalling [...] one of the greatest injustices ever done to deaf people'. According to Lee, 'many thousands of deaf teachers' lost their jobs because of their inability to teach the oral method, and many deaf children lost the opportunity to learn to read and write. Being unable to speak English does not necessarily inhibit literacy, provided both teachers and pupils can converse in sign language. The website www.deafinfo.org.uk succinctly summarises the consequences of the Board of Education's acceptance of Milan as:

> The biggest influence on the education of deaf children for the next 100 years. Within a generation there were almost no deaf teachers in deaf schools and sign language was banished from the classroom and usually from the playground as well, and Harlan Lane (see Introduction) called Milan 'the single most important cause – more important than hearing loss – of the limited educational achievement of the modern deaf man and woman'.

Martin Smith, who struggled mightily to make the case for sign language in the Leeds education system from 1966 to his retirement in 1992, described the Milan conference as 'the Deaf Dunkirk':

> A most violent act of repression was enacted at a conference in Milan in 1880. The conference voted to ban the use of all manual forms used in the education of deaf people. It marked the return to illiteracy for many deaf people.
>
> (SMITH, 2011, P53)

Oralism was adopted by nearly all the residential schools for deaf in England, with consequences for the Sheffield deaf community which we can now examine in some detail. The closure of the Sheffield school for deaf children, which had been operating under George Stephenson as sole and then as one of two teachers since 1879, and the removal of the children to residential schools away from Sheffield, would necessarily take them firmly into the oralist camp, with considerable social and familial consequences. As will be seen, the members of the Sheffield School Board were aware of this, so how did it happen? The following account is based primarily on detailed examination of school board minutes in the Sheffield Archives, contemporary newspaper reports of the board's meetings and letters to the local press, supplemented by Bingham's *The Sheffield School Board 1870–1903.*

One reason why Charles Baker of YIDD had objected to the foundation of the Sheffield Association in 1862 was the potential loss of pupils and income from the town, but at that time there was no local provision for the education of deaf children. Joseph Farrar resigned as superintendent and was replaced by George Stephenson in 1871, the year after the creation of local school boards under the Education Act 1870. Farrar himself had been trained at YIDD and had come to Sheffield as tutor to the deaf Arthur Doncaster, but George had no formal teacher training, only his knowledge of sign language as the son of profoundly deaf parents. Although the Act itself made no mention of deaf children, at one of the first meetings of the Sheffield School Board in 1871 (*Sheffield Independent*, 4th February) it was reported that Joseph Farrar had proposed deaf children should attend 'his school' at Gloucester Crescent; the decision was deferred, and this seems to have been the first and last reference to any school operated by Farrar.

By 1879, with the school board now chaired by Charles Doncaster, consideration was given to providing a school for deaf children within the complex of education offices and central school then being built in Leopold Street in the town centre. Instead, perhaps because it would be cheaper, the board's School Management Committee decided to finance a school in the cramped accommodation at Division Street. George Stephenson was appointed as teacher at a salary of £50 per annum and the Association was given a grant of £12 per annum 'for cleaning and warming'. (Bingham, 1949, p219)

At the time the school was created, the debate about teaching methods for deaf children was already raging. An extract from the *Daily News* was reprinted in the *Sheffield Independent* (20th May 1879) contrasting the merits of 'lip conversation', leading to a greater involvement in hearing society, with 'finger conversation', which at least gave deaf people a sense of identity within their community. Sensibly the article concluded that as not all pupils could benefit by purely oral teaching, both systems should be used as and when appropriate. This was certainly the approach in the new Sheffield school: the first report by the school board's inspector in 1880 was positive; despite the obvious limitations of the accommodation, some of the older pupils were said to have good lip-reading skills, and the younger ones were taught by 'signs and finger language'. (Bingham, 1949, p219)

Coincidentally the 1879 meeting of the British Association was held in Sheffield, and its Economic Science section discussed the education of deaf children at length, as reported in the *Sheffield Independent* (26th August 1879). There were reckoned to be 20,000 deaf mutes in Britain, historically regarded as uneducable: an unnamed delegate is said to have remarked that 'to instruct the deaf, no art could reach, no care improve them, and no wisdom teach'. (This is surely a quotation but I have been unable to trace the source.) The advantages of the oral and manual methods were discussed, and the combined method seems to have been favoured; nonetheless a resolution was passed that more teachers of the oral method should be trained as a matter of urgency. This was the view which came to dominate the Milan Conference in the following year and which in due course played a part in what happened in Sheffield.

The government had set up the Royal Commission on the Education of the Blind and the Deaf and Dumb following Milan and before the Sheffield Institute was built, and in early 1886 the Sheffield School Board wrote to the commissioners, pointing out they had set up a school for deaf and dumb children some seven years earlier without any central government funding. As most of the parents were very poor and could not afford the fees for residential schooling, they requested that such support should be recommended in the commissioners' final report. At this stage it is clear the school board were still in favour of maintaining the Sheffield school; as we have seen, John Cole and James Barber had written to suggest that teaching hours should be extended and an additional teacher should be appointed. The board had agreed, and authorised the appointment of an additional teacher at a salary of £13 per annum. Moreover they also agreed to increase 'the Master's salary' to £100; this was of course George Stephenson and the increase was presumably intended to reflect his greater responsibilities as the head teacher in what was now a full-time school. From early in 1887 the school was transferred from Division Street to the ground-floor schoolroom and play area at the Charles Street Institute, and now operated for five full days a week instead of the previous six mornings.

The Royal Commission, which had visited the Sheffield Institute in 1888, reported in the following year. Although the commission was thought by many to lack authority, with only two of the members having any experience of teaching deaf children, the report suggested that the deaf and dumb should be taught in ordinary schools 'to prevent deaf children leading to subsequent marriages and the population of a deaf race' and specifically that the teaching should be on the oral system and that manual teaching should only be permitted where it was already well established in existing schools. (Bergen, 2004, p242)

There was much anger and pressure brought to bear on these issues, not least by the British Deaf and Dumb Association, founded in 1890 specifically to combat the oralist conclusions of Milan and to defend sign language. Such was the strength of the protests that the Elementary Education (Blind and Deaf and Dumb Children) Act of 1893 specifically provided government aid for the education of blind and deaf, to be channelled through the local school boards. Such grants were only forthcoming to those institutions which met the approval of HM Inspectors. The Act permitted school boards to decide the form of education for deaf children and then satisfy the HMIs of the quality and nature of their proposed provision; inevitably the outcome in each case would depend in part on the attitude of individual HMIs but the commission expressed a preference for residential schools 'except under favourable conditions in the large towns'. (Bergen, 2004, p239) As a residential school with Charles Baker's successor James Howard as a convinced oralist, YIDD would be safe, but not necessarily Sheffield, which in both Institute and school was accustomed to work in sign language.

These were not the only potential problems for Sheffield. First there was the admitted inadequacy of the ground-floor schoolroom at the Institute, given the importance now given to deaf education by the Act and the growing number of children. Secondly, George Stephenson had realised that with the expansion of his duties with the adults following the opening of the Institute he no longer had enough time for teaching the children, so that the second teacher was now carrying most of the burden alone.

Given these problems, the Sheffield School Board would have to decide how best to discharge its duty under the 1893 Act to provide efficient education for deaf children; whatever the decision there would be profound implications for the children and their family lives. I make no apology for the detail in the following account of how and what was decided; it is the first of several examples of how legislative requirements could create disputes between the voluntary and statutory approaches to deaf welfare, without suggesting that either side had any but the best interests of the children and their families at heart. Nevertheless it should be noted that the detailed minutes give a somewhat different impression from the public discourse, and reveal that the school board had effectively made its decision well before the debate reached the deaf community and the wider public through the press.

The first HMI inspection of the Sheffield school at Charles Street was followed by a certificate issued in 1894 but in heavily qualified terms; there would be no renewal unless plans were urgently submitted for a new school building, and moreover a second teacher should be appointed without delay. The inspector had written a damning report; this was 'a purely sign school'; there was only one teacher for 38 pupils, she only gave basic instruction in reading, writing and arithmetic; there was no 'articulation' (oral teaching); and very little equipment or teaching aids. (Bingham, 1949, p220)

The inspector stipulated that any new building should have three classrooms to allow for either oral or combined teaching methods. Late in 1894, to relieve the immediate pressure, the school board agreed to rent from the Association the upper-floor lecture room/chapel as an additional schoolroom during the day. Clearly the school board had a great deal to think about, and this arm's-length transaction is the first evidence of a difference of approach between the board and the Association. It has to be remembered that when the school was first created and funded by the board in 1879, Charles Doncaster was both Chairman of the Board and Honorary Secretary of the Association; but he had died in 1884 and the personnel of the two organisations was now quite distinct.

In early 1895 the Association was clearly worried what the school board might decide, because there was a meeting between the buildings sub-committee of the board and representatives of the Association's committee. This was followed by a formal letter to the board, signed by Daniel Doncaster III's son Edwin, now a committee member. The letter proposed the construction of a new school on land adjoining the Institute which the Association had already purchased; coupled with this was an offer to either lease or sell that land to the school board and also, if required, to lease the 'caretaker's house' and the existing schoolroom and playground. Architects advised that this was a feasible proposition, if tight on the site, and the board's buildings sub-committee recommended the proposal should be pursued, provided further adjoining land still in the corporation's ownership could also be incorporated. In April 1895, the scheme was approved in principle by the government's Board of Education, as it seemed to meet the inspector's requirements for a renewed certificate and thus qualify for funding approval under the 1893 Act.

Very soon, however, the Sheffield School Board had second thoughts, following receipt of a carefully worded memorandum from the board's clerk, comparing the likely cost of three alternatives. First, sending every deaf child to residential institutions outside Sheffield, costing at least £480 per annum; second, building a new school for all the deaf children, estimated at £440 per annum to include the interest on the capital required to fund the construction; and third, a combination of both proposals to allow for the fact that some parents actually preferred their children to go away to school, whilst still allowing the majority to stay at home and attend the new school in Sheffield.

It seemed the last alternative was a financial non-starter because the full cost of the new school would still be incurred, plus the fees of £16 per annum at YIDD for each child who went away. Faced with this conflict between the different wishes of the parents, the school board asked the Board of Education whether they could refuse to pay the fees for the residential schools on the grounds that they were providing an efficient local alternative; the answer was equivocal. Two cases gave rise to particular concern; one boy was being housed and educated at the Jews Deaf and Dumb Home in London, and another at the Roman Catholic school at Boston Spa near Wetherby. (Bingham, 1949, pp. 223–4) Given these intractable problems of divergent parental wishes and the need for financial certainty, the sub-committee baldly recommended that the proposal to build a new school on the suggested site should be abandoned. In the middle of all this, there was a further inspector's report on the Charles Street School. He said that the teacher had worked very well but the accommodation could only be regarded as temporary. There were now both oral and manual classes, so that two teachers would now be required, and 'the children taught on the oral system mix too freely on Sundays and at playtime on workdays with the children taught by sign'.

It would be difficult to imagine a clearer example of the prejudice against sign language as a means of education and communication; children who were taught by the alternative oral system should not be contaminated by contact with signers, even out of school hours.

There were discussions between representatives of the school board and the management committee of YIDD in Doncaster, who doubted whether they could absorb 40 or more pupils from Sheffield, and stipulated that if necessary a building would have to be found in Doncaster for their living accommodation, the additional expense of which would fall on the Sheffield School Board. Nevertheless, it seems from the board minutes that by October 1895 the decision had been made in principle. Despite the potential difficulties of overcrowding at YIDD and the likely additional costs, the advantages of the 'excellent' oral training at the long established YIDD were too great to ignore, and those advantages 'should outweigh the objections which some parents may have to sending their children to a boarding school.'

So the need to separate orally from manually educated children, the apparently manifest advantages of the oral training at YIDD, and perhaps the feeling of the school board that it was better for others to deal with a difficult small minority of children, were together sufficient to ignore the possible objections of the parents and any additional costs. The shadow of Milan was apparent if unspoken.

Then, this decision not yet communicated to the Association, the deaf children or their parents, another problem appeared. The school board much preferred to send all the children to YIDD; Doncaster was the nearest alternative and the fees were lower than elsewhere. But within a month the YIDD Committee's reservations had hardened, and in November 1895 they told the school board that they could not house or teach 40 new pupils so the proposal could not proceed. The board requested a further discussion; the chairman of YIDD said there was no point in meeting again. At this point the issue became public with a report of the first school board meeting of the New Year in the *Sheffield Independent* (January 17th 1896), including YIDD's rejection of the proposal to educate the deaf children from Sheffield and that the board had therefore 'felt themselves unable to proceed in the matter'.

In fact the board were not prepared to accept this setback. The minutes of the February meeting show their determination to send as many children to Doncaster as YIDD could accommodate and meanwhile to invite Charles Baker's successor James Howard to the next meeting to give a talk to the parents. At this 'special' board meeting (reported in the *Sheffield Independent*, 25th March 1896) the Chairman Newton Coombe pointed out that the 1893 Act permitted the board to provide for deaf children's education in either day schools or residential institutions, and the board had decided in principle to support YIDD and the Catholic school at Boston Spa. The meeting was then addressed by Howard, unlike his predecessor Charles Baker a noted and convinced exponent of the exclusively oral system. It was reported that several of his pupils gave impressive demonstrations of their abilities, and that George Stephenson interpreted the proceedings for the benefit of the deaf and dumb in attendance – in sign language of course, an irony which might not have been lost on his audience.

Now that the problems were public knowledge through the press reports of the school board meetings, the discussion became very heated indeed. Prominent in the debate was another of those larger than life characters who appear regularly in the history of deaf people. Robert Renton Eadon (1854–1917), already mentioned as one of the committee members who negotiated the purchase of the Charles Street site and one of the trustees, derived his wealth like most of the committee from the steel and engineering industries and he lived near the Doncaster family in Broomhall. But his prominence in the debate, despite he and his wife being childless, was surely explained in the 1891 Census; he was 'deaf from fever in childhood' and as far as I can ascertain, with Daniel Doncaster III, one of only two deaf members of the committee throughout its history.

On 14th April, the *Sheffield Independent* published Eadon's letter to Coombe, complaining that the report on 25th March was the first deaf people had heard of this momentous decision. The parents were most anxious and required clarification; in particular, what were the relative costs and merits of the day school and residential alternatives? The answer appeared only three days later in the report (17th April) of the next school board meeting. Coombe confirmed the board's intention to ask the parents to choose a school of their preference as soon as places were available, and that when all the children were gone, the Association's Sheffield school, established 17 years earlier with the financial support and approval of the school board, would be closed. Even if the board was to finance a new school building, there would be no guarantee the children would choose to go there, and in any event it would not be possible to provide any choice of denominational teaching as at YIDD and Boston Spa. As to cost, the fees would undoubtedly be less than providing a complete new school.

Eadon's riposte was printed on 21st April. He accepted the present school was inadequate, but the board had failed in its duty under the 1893 Act to rectify the deficiencies. In any event, he said, the residential institutions were incapable of absorbing the 50+ children being educated in Sheffield. The problem of religious differences had never arisen in practice, and all the evidence suggested that deaf children of average ability would make better progress at home with loving parents than isolated in distant institutions. As to cost, the institutions would charge £16 per head per annum, which he calculated was double the cost of providing adequate premises in Sheffield. There is no sign of a detailed rebuttal of these arguments. The school board's next report (17th July) admitted that a letter had been received from the Board of Education clearly indicating the state of deaf children's education in Sheffield was unsatisfactory, which the chairman put down to the 'transition stage' of the day school (i.e. it was being slowly run down towards final closure); he said the board saw no reason to change its now settled policy.

The anger of Eadon and the parents he represented was very clear from his response, published 18th July. He believed their position was being misrepresented. In fact the school had been unsatisfactory for several years, understaffed and under-resourced as the board tried to implement its policy of removing the children from the school, the town, and their family homes. On June 14th the parents had sent a deputation to the school board, without result, and now there was a petition, following a meeting at the Institute, signed by 27 parents. It had been unanimously resolved that the board be requested:

to provide an efficient school for the education of deaf children in Sheffield, as we, the said parents, are unanimous in opposition to your proposed plan of sending the children to boarding institutions away from Sheffield.

Reading the minutes of the June meeting attended by Eadon and five representative parents, it is seems they were already spitting in the wind; the minutes rather tartly referred to receiving demands from 'a number of gentlemen, being a deputation, from whom is not stated'. (Bingham, p234) The board had given very serious consideration to the decision, and despite any additional costs, they were convinced it was in the best interests of the children. It is also fair to infer from other evidence in the minutes that Eadon did not represent all the parents; there were 27 who signed his petition but at least 40 children involved, and several parents had actually petitioned the board to send their children away. That was why the board had asked the government for confirmation they could refuse such applications if they provided adequate facilities in Sheffield. The board had also assured the deputation that the Sheffield school would remain open until it proved possible to send all the children away, though they could hardly have said otherwise given their statutory duty under the 1893 Act.

The petition was the last throw, and it had no effect. At the tenth anniversary celebration of the Institute (reported in the *Sheffield Independent* for 7th October 1896), the chairman remarked that the school board was about to remove the children from the schoolroom at the Institute to temporary accommodation in the newly constructed central school buildings. There were still insufficient residential places available, at YIDD or elsewhere. He tried to look on the bright side; now there would be more room for adult activities in the Institute, and the schoolroom henceforth housed a billiard table. Mr Stephenson would have to sever his connections with the school and there would be a consequential financial loss to the Association.

Eadon had at least been right in one thing; the residential institutions simply could not cope with so many new pupils at short notice. In July 1896, the same month as the last meeting between the parents and the school board, YIDD managed to find just three places for deaf Sheffield boys and none at all for girls, though an unexpected vacancy occurred for a single girl a few weeks later. The government reluctantly agreed to reissue certificates to the school for as long as it took to find residential places for all the children, provided that the premises were only to be used on a temporary basis. (Bingham, p226) In fact it was not until 16th June 1900 that the school board reported without comment that:

> the school for deaf and dumb children is about to be closed, the children being sent to institutions in which they will have a complete and continuous training.

Eadon was right too, about the cost and the numbers; on 1st July 1900 a further report stated that one girl was being sent to the school at Leeds at a cost of £28.16s per annum, and that the board were sending about 40 more to the same school. YIDD, the nearest and most closely connected with Sheffield, still could not cope with the numbers.

Sheffield Education Committee (which replaced the school board in 1903) did not open a school for deaf children until 1921, when after much pressure from one of the committee members, Miss Maud Maxfield, a specialist school named after her was opened in East Bank Road; an entry in the log book of the Leeds Deaf School reads that 'deaf children from Sheffield were withdrawn to the new Maud Maxfield school for the deaf, Sheffield'. (Boyce 1996, Appendix Two)

As late as 1911, George Stephenson reported that there were 30 deaf and dumb boys and 20 girls of school age in Sheffield who were being taught at YIDD, the Leeds School, or the Old Trafford Institute for the Deaf and Blind in Manchester, and a further seven who were to be assigned to such residential schools 'as soon as practicable'.

This was a sorry chapter in the history of the deaf community in Sheffield and their treatment by the local authority, which over a period of more than twenty years exiled numerous deaf children from their homes and families. George Stephenson played no part in this acrimonious dispute until it was too late, perhaps because he had relinquished his teaching duties soon after the 1893 Act, and perhaps he also felt it would be inappropriate for a salaried missioner to argue openly with the school board. Finally he made his real feelings known, scarcely hiding his contempt for the school board in a letter to *British Deaf Monthly* in June 1899. To get the full flavour, the whole letter is reproduced in Appendix

Two, but as the teacher who ran the pioneering Sheffield school handedly in the early years, his anger is abundantly clear:

> To think that the very first provincial town to open a day school for deaf children, after the Act of 1870, should now cowardly wish to shirk their responsibility and cry out, 'This little bantling of ours has become unmanageable, and so we have decided to put it out to nurse,' is enough to raise the shade of the Right Hon A. J. Mundella, who so ably represented the town in Parliament for 26 years, and who, when Vice President of the Council, took a lively interest in the promotion of this very day school.

★★★

Although George kept out of the Sheffield education debate when was still an issue, it was clearly part of the debate with another of his opponents, Dr Symes Thomson MD FRCP, revealed in correspondence in the *British Deaf Monthly* earlier in 1899. The dispute concerned the wisdom of marriage between profoundly deaf couples. The 1889 report of the Royal Commission on the Education of the Blind and Deaf and Dumb had recommended the education of deaf children in ordinary schools, specifically to avoid their intermarriage and 'the perpetuation of a deaf race'.

Now it was Dr Thomson who returned to the fray, perhaps bravely if not wisely in the columns of a journal devoted to the interests of deaf people. He summarised the arguments of the report: marriages between deaf couples should be discouraged because they might have deaf children and thereby increase the ranks of the handicapped. This was not a new idea, but it was the introduction of a specifically clerical element into the argument, favourably contrasting the influence of local Anglican vicars with that of the deaf institutes, which really angered George, a lifelong Wesleyan. In a circular which George had received, Thomson wrote:

> With the possible exception of consanguineous marriages, the most fruitful source of congenitally deaf children are the societies for the adult deaf which bring both sexes together and too frequently lead

quite out of court, and not qualified to offer any opinion on the rival systems of instruction of the deaf.

But suppose we take him seriously, which I confess is somewhat difficult...

He was careful to say that in general he had great respect for the clergy, many of them very helpful to the deaf, *but* his institute was within 150 yards of the gates of his parish church (the church of St Peter, demolished as surplus to Church of England requirements in the 1930s and now the site of the Peace Gardens), and he could:

confidently affirm that the vicar of the parish knew absolutely nothing about the deaf; and he did not believe that he had ever evinced any interest in their condition, whether spiritually or morally.

It will be recalled that Thomas Widd met with similar lack of comprehension and interest from the vicar of Sheffield nearly 40 years earlier; the response of the Anglican Church to the problems of deaf parishioners was still patchy at this stage, especially in the industrial North (see Chapter Five).

George then quoted figures from his own records to dispute the idea that marriage between deaf parents produced deaf children. In Sheffield, he said, there were 168 deaf adults plus 35 school-age children and four infants. There were 34 marriages where both parents were deaf, producing in total 79 children; seven of those couples had no children, and the other 27 had between them 76 hearing and only three deaf children. Of the seven couples where only one of the parents was deaf, two of them were childless, and the others had produced five hearing and six deaf children. Modern genetic research renders such disputes unnecessary; figures from Action on Hearing Loss suggest that at least half of the profoundly or severely deaf children currently receiving special educational support have been deaf since birth and their handicap is therefore genetic. However, this does not mean their parents are deaf; 90 per cent of profoundly deaf children are born to hearing parents.

The facts on either side may have been doubtful or confusing but the dispute revealed two aspects of George Stephenson's character. First, he was always prepared to stand up in public to defend the work of the institutes against allegations he felt were untrue or unfair. Secondly, and this is a little surprising and recurs in several different contexts, he chose to keep his own family's experience quiet; he could have added that both his parents were profoundly deaf but neither he nor his brother, nor any of his twelve or his brother's eleven children were affected in any way.

★★★

It is not easy to sketch a rounded picture of George Stephenson during this central and perhaps most satisfying period of his career. Now in his fifties, ensconced in the spacious quarters above the Institute with his large family, we have few personal comments or insights beyond the public record, the contemporary tributes and the final obituaries. Occasionally we can read between the lines and get a flavour of the attitudes and values of both George and his deaf members. Here for instance is an extract from an account of Sunday at the Institute in an 1893 issue of *Young Sheffield*:

> *In conduct and in bearing the members of the Sheffield Institute for the Deaf and Dumb – and they form 90 per cent of the deaf mutes of the town – now simply stand with the rest of Sheffield's well-ordered self-respecting townsfolk. To see that Mr Stephenson has succeeded in a high degree in bringing moral and spiritual influences to bear upon his charges, one has only to attend a Sunday evening service in the lecture hall, the one difficulty then being to determine which to admire the more, the tireless zeal of the teacher in rendering in manual signs, with marvellous skill and grace, the hymns, prayers, lessons and sermon for the day, during a whole hour and a half without cessation and without assistance, or the fixed, earnest and reverent attention of the deaf mute congregation from beginning to end of the service. This is the third meeting today – one being held in Rotherham in the afternoon – and tomorrow and all through the week the now spiritual guide will be speaking on behalf of one or more or all of his mute charges as occasion arises whether with enemy or friend at the gate, and seeking in every way to secure and promote their interests. And this he has done unfailingly for 26 years.*

And what did his 'mute charges' make of all this? There is little evidence but perhaps the gentle comment of George Robinson to Rev Firth does a little to lighten such an austere and humourless account.

> *Robinson's parents regularly took him to the deaf Sunday services – which he found excruciatingly boring – but as a wee boy he would watch fascinatedly as Stephenson, standing on the platform, would now and then magically produce a handkerchief from behind his bottom, use it, and put it away again. It was many years before Robinson found out that there was indeed a secret pocket beneath the jacket's long coat tails.*
>
> (FIRTH, 1985, P98)

Long sermons and little magic tricks – a curious combination.

★★★

Whatever light moments George introduced to his unending activity, there can be no doubt of the seriousness and high moral purpose which informed all he did. As one of innumerable examples, his superintendent's report in 1907, twenty years after the opening of the Institute, gives the full flavour:

> *Probably never before have our members taken such an intelligent interest in local and imperial subjects, following with keen interest the doings of both City Council and Parliament. And our married members are decidedly improving in their manner of living. A decided distaste for debt is growing very strongly amongst them, and it is not too strong to affirm that in the management of their household affairs, and in the numerous matters in which as householders they have to come into contact with people outside, they conduct their business with equally as much intelligence and integrity as the best of the labouring classes in the community.*
>
> *Year after year we have young people brought within the influence of this Association, and there is no question that these young people who come back to their homes after passing through school life just*

need the same patient labour and wise and tactful treatment as those
adults who are now so promising; thus it will be seen that our work
will be necessary as long as there are any Deaf and Dumb.

How paternalistic all this can sound to modern ears! 'Improving their manner of living', acquiring 'a decided distaste for debt', coming into contact with 'people outside' and showing 'as much intelligence and integrity as the best of the labouring classes'. But we have to remember the context of late Victorian working-class life, particularly for those with a profound disability; self-improvement was seen as the only practicable solution, supported for the more fortunate by the wealth of philanthropists and the energies of the managers and missioners they employed. We should also remember that George Stephenson himself rose from a similarly disadvantaged background to a position from which he was able to give that support as unstintingly as he did for almost 50 years.

A busy life indeed. The eulogies, the authoritarian figure in the frock coat and tails, striding from home to home with his message of self-help and sobriety, preaching in sign language three times on Sundays, not afraid to enter into public debate, hugely respected by his fellow citizens, even if regarded with a little amusement by his 'charges'; all this we can get from published sources and not least from his own account in 1911, a clear picture of the man in relation to his life's work during 25 years of unceasing activity. What those sources do not reveal is anything about the personal life and family history which we left with marriage to the widow Lena in 1878.

★★★

There are no diaries or correspondence and precious few photographs from this period, and little personal information in the 1911 Souvenir or the annual reports of the Association. To reconstruct that part of the story we have to rely on Census returns and the registers of births, marriages and deaths.

George's father Benjamin had died in 1878, the year in which George had finally devoted himself full-time to work for the deaf community. Benjamin had remained a spring knife cutler all his life, moving several times between terraced or back-to-back cottages near the town centre, playing his part in the development of community amongst the deaf. He would surely have been proud of the success of George and his brother, the silver engraver, Benjamin junior. Their mother Sarah survived another twenty years and her story tells us a little more about the harsh nature of Victorian life for a poor widow, with its uncomfortable echoes of her mother-in-law Martha's reliance on a weekly subvention from the parish.

Unlike Martha, Sarah had no married daughter to provide a home, and seemingly neither of her sons, with growing families and busy working lives, was able or willing to take her in. In 1881, Sarah is a lodger with a deaf and dumb couple, the 'merry tailor' William Simmonite, George's boyhood friend and fishing partner, and his wife Mary. Sarah is described as a dressmaker, perhaps connected with Simmonite's business. The house was in Clarence Street, not more than 300 yards from Hermitage Street where she had started married life and her sons were born. For some reason this arrangement did not last, because although the Simmonites continued to live in the same house for many years, by 1891 Sarah was living as a lodger at 28 Gell Street (even nearer the town centre) with a brother and sister, Thomas and Annie Powell. Neither is shown as deaf in the Census. Annie was an elementary school teacher but like Sarah's husband and father-in-law, Thomas was a spring knife cutler.

We can infer from her death certificate that at some time during the 1890s Sarah developed what we now call dementia. Added to her handicap as a deaf mute, this would seriously limit the alternatives; there were few facilities to shelter the old, frail and incapable; hospital provision for these categories was largely confined to the workhouses. The records held in Sheffield Archives show her admission to the Ecclesall Union Workhouse on 18th March 1898, a fate which her mother-in-law Martha had avoided. The Ecclesall Workhouse, erected in 1843 in a more or less rural setting in Nether Edge but soon to be surrounded by the substantial villas of mid-nineteenth century business people, was transmuted in the twentieth century into Nether Edge Hospital and has now been converted into an upmarket housing estate, an irony which might have been lost on its original founders and inmates.

According to reports in the local press by Dr R J Pye-Smith, surgeon at what became the Royal Hospital, who visited the Ecclesall Workhouse in 1896, there was provision for persons of Sarah's age, sex and condition. Dr Pye-Smith inspected:

*the accommodation for aged and infirm inmates, the hospital, and
the lunatic wards in which there were beds for 27 of each sex, but
such was the excessive number that 30 lunatics had to sleep in the
main building.*

(FLETT, 1985, P9)

Whether categorised as aged, infirm or a lunatic, Sarah died there on
20th June 1899, aged 79. The death certificate gives the causes of death as
'senile decay and heart failure' and the informant, present at the death,
was her daughter-in-law Adele, the wife of George's brother Benjamin.
The certificate describes Sarah as 'widow of Benjamin Stephenson of
23 Ratcliffe Road'. In fact Benjamin senior never lived there; it was the
family home of her son Benjamin junior, only a ten-minute walk from
the workhouse. So it is not surprising that Adele should be summonsed
to her mother-in-law's death bed. It is also possible Sarah had been living
at Ratcliffe Road after leaving her last lodging, though it would have been
very crowded since by 1898 Adele had given birth to eight of her final
total of eleven daughters, all raised in a modest terraced house.

★★★

George and Lena had soon added to the five surviving children of his
first marriage to Mary. The newly-weds quickly left the Malin Bridge
area; by 1881 they were living at 57 Countess Road, the only one of
George's homes which still survives. This was a move back to his origins,
as Countess Road was a new street of terraced housing no more than a
quarter of a mile from his birthplace in Hermitage Street and within easy
walking distance of his then workplace in Division Street.

At Countess Road, the couple first suffered a tragedy common enough
at the time, but unknown by their descendants until I stumbled across a
brief announcement in the *Sheffield Daily Telegraph* of 5th April 1880 of 'the
death on April 3rd at Countess Road of Cyril the beloved son of George
and Lena Stephenson aged 10 months'. They were more fortunate on six
further occasions; the next child was born in May 1881, the rather grandly
named Oswald Kenway, my maternal grandfather. Oswald was followed
by Margaret in 1883, Hilda in 1885, and then (at their new home in the
Institute) Norman in 1888, Douglas in 1890 and finally in 1893, Colin,

who would eventually succeed his father as superintendent.

Unsurprisingly, this brood of twelve moved (or were moved) out as soon as practicable. By 1891, Albert, Alice, George, William and John of Mary's children had left, and by 1901, only Norman, Douglas and Colin were still at home; within a few years there was only Colin. Other than George Robinson's parents' remark that they had nowhere to play and could be a thorough nuisance round the Institute, there is no surviving record of George and Lena's domestic life; indeed Lena is scarcely mentioned anywhere, despite the considerable social activities of the deaf women within the Institute. We can only imagine that George was so completely involved in work for the deaf members of the Institute that in many ways their daily lives and routines would be quite different. It is not as if George came home to relax with his family after a hard day's work; the family lived, quite literally, on top of a job which had for many years occupied him day and night, seven days a week.

***

By 1910, George Stephenson was 65. Of his twelve children, all except sixteen-year-old Colin had left home; three of his eighteen grandchildren had been born, with another three in the next twelve months – but by then George had been widowed again. After 32 years of marriage, Lena Stephenson died on 3rd January, 1910, aged 56. The death certificate gives the causes of death as cirrhosis of the liver and 'dropsy' (the old-fashioned term for oedema, an excess of liquid under the skin). To speculate on the cause of cirrhosis and dropsy in a household and Institute so devoted to temperance may be unkind, but if Lena did have a drink problem it might explain why she played no part in the many activities of the Institute and is never mentioned in any surviving document of the Association. In the circumstances nobody could have begrudged George retirement after nearly 40 years of unremitting service to others. In fact it seems he had no such intention; where would he go, what would he do, and perhaps uppermost in his mind, who would succeed him?

4

GEORGE STEPHENSON'S FINAL 10
YEARS AND RETIREMENT 1910-1924

'A Real Foster Parent'

Lena Stephenson's death left George and Colin rattling around in
the domestic quarters on the top floor of the Institute, probably not
well versed in the domestic arts. There is no sign that the family had
ever employed domestic staff, but the 1911 Census shows that George
had decided it was necessary. The Census enumerator may have been
confused, because his original entry shows a third resident of the Institute,
Fanny Emma Stephenson aged 42, described as a 'Housekeeper', but
then this was neatly crossed out and replaced by 'Daughter'. In fact the
deleted description is more accurate, and the explanation takes us back
into family history.

George's only brother Benjamin, a successful silver engraver, had
travelled twice to work in America but returned with enough savings to
buy his own and then two more terraced houses in the developing suburb
of Hunters Bar; it was his wife Adele who had registered the death of
George and Benjamin's mother Sarah in the workhouse.

Between 1869 and 1903 Adele gave birth to no less than eleven
daughters. Fanny Emma was the eldest and went into domestic service.
In 1891 she was a cook in the home of the vicar of St Matthias and
his family, but by 1901, she was resident cook at Brincliffe Towers, a
substantial suburban estate created by a wealthy Sheffield solicitor in the
mid-nineteenth century, just up the hill from the workhouse where her
grandmother Sarah had recently died. How George persuaded her to

move from comfortable surroundings at the Towers to the city centre and service in the Institute is unknown, but she joined his household, and stayed for the remaining fourteen years of his life.

★★★

From 1912 it becomes easier to follow the history of the Institute, as there is an almost unbroken sequence of annual reports from then up to 1957; moreover the layout of the reports is virtually unchanged throughout, which helps with analysis. In contrast a more informal note is apparent from the few surviving examples of *Dacty*, a penny magazine specifically for the Sheffield deaf which George utilised to entertain, instruct and lecture his readers.

1912 was a sad year for the Association and the deaf community, as the chairman and George as superintendent made clear in their reports – Daniel Doncaster III died on 12th October. Although never mentioned in Census returns before 1901, George confirmed in his appreciation that Daniel was 'deaf himself', as did the obituary in the *Sheffield Telegraph*. However, the Doncaster family connection continued without a break. Daniel's son Edwin had been a committee member for a number of years, and his cousin Charles Mallinson Doncaster (the son of Samuel, now head of the family business) had been Hon. Secretary since Daniel III withdrew from active participation because of ill health; he now replaced Daniel as Trustee and Hon. Treasurer and the new Hon. Secretary was George Bates, a senior employee of the Doncaster company who became George Stephenson's friend and the executor of his will.

Bates' first report as Secretary emphasises the importance of the Association's work in obtaining jobs for the deaf:

> *The employment of the Deaf and Dumb continues to be satisfactory except in a few cases, where great perseverance on the part of the superintendent has been necessary to obtain work. In nearly every case where employers have been persuaded to employ our members, the result has justified the Committee's contention that the Deaf and Dumb man as a workman is equal to the standard of his hearing brother.*

George confirms his success in work placement; in his own report he says that 'at present there is only one able-bodied deaf and dumb man out of work'.

Apart from this vital function in persuading firms to employ his members, George's account of his other activities gives a clear picture of the Institute's work and its importance to the 212 adults now registered with the Institute as 'members'. In addition, there were now 60 deaf children being educated out of Sheffield.

Spiritual guidance had always been a high priority. George reported that attendance at the Sunday evening services was 'exceptionally good' but less so in the mornings, when there were 'rarely more than twenty'. In addition to two Sunday services (and often one in Rotherham as well) he conducted or supervised a Wednesday evening Bible class at which the average attendance during the year was 26. Temperance was always closely allied with spiritual concerns, and George had instituted an 'Ephphatha Lodge' of the Order of Good Templars, which met every Monday, when there were 'many interesting and instructive programmes, with occasional lantern lectures and lecturers from outside, and visits from other Lodges'. (The Good Templars, now an international order, was founded in America in the mid-nineteenth century; it was based on the Masonic model but with membership of both sexes and all races, devoted to abstinence or at least moderation in alcohol consumption.)

Not all the social activities were as serious and pious. There was an Angling Club with 40 members, of whom 28 travelled all the way to Ely for the annual match competition. More anglers than attendees at Bible class or services or improving Lodge lectures? Well, yes, but it should be remembered that apart from the pub, the two main leisure activities for Sheffield's working class males in the first half of the last century were said to be football and coarse fishing; it was reputed that each weekend anything up to 50,000 fishermen would leave the city by charabanc and train for the rivers and dykes of Lincolnshire and the Fens. Rambles into Derbyshire were a regular feature, and although the summer of 1912 was very wet, walking groups went out on fifteen Saturday afternoons. No doubt in winter, many of the same men would be at Bramall Lane or Hillsborough, to support the successful and hugely popular football clubs; only a few years later, under Colin's guidance, the Institute had its own football team, an early example of organised sport among the deaf community.

The deaf women were far from neglected. They had worked hard to mount a Sale of Work to help fund the building of the Institute 30 years earlier, and this tradition had continued. There were regular meetings, preparing for the sales, sewing classes, making finished garments, all under the indefatigable guidance of Mrs Matthews and the Misses Matthews, wife and daughters of the committee member Henry Matthews. There was also a Mothers Circle Christmas Club, preparing to dole out welcome largesse on Christmas Eve, much of it no doubt supplied by supporters like the Matthews, the Doncasters, and the Dixons. In 1912, we are told, 40 couples and eight widows were given 'reasonable parcels of provisions and clothing', each of the Good Templars was given 'a packet of cocoa' and regular attendees at the Bible Class each got a parcel of clothing. This cloying mixture of philanthropy, self-help, and rewards for piety, sobriety and good behaviour may grate on modern ears, but is typical of George and the age. There must have been backsliders, but there is no mention of them anywhere in the annual reports, or of any court appearances, criminal offences, or other deviant behaviour.

Given the multiplicity of these activities, the number of 'visits' which George carefully recorded each year is astonishing. He was now 66, and the total for 1912 was 1036, an average of almost three a day throughout the entire year. They comprised 639 calls at the homes of the deaf, many of which would be within walking distance of the Institute, but also 174 visits to employers seeking jobs for the deaf, 42 hospital visits, eleven to the two Sheffield workhouses and the lunatic asylum at Wadsley, and a further 120 he described as 'miscellaneous'.

At the end of each annual report were the year's accounts, always in three sections comprising much the same categories of information we saw in the surviving annual report for 1887. In 1912, these were a Cash Summary (income and expenses), Investments and Properties, and a detailed list of Subscriptions and Donations with the names of all the donor institutions or individuals – this third item is repeated in exactly the same form each year.

In 1912 the financial situation seemed very healthy. Rounding the figures up or down to the nearest pound, the Cash Account shows an opening balance of £903 plus income of £429 (subscriptions, donations and a legacy to a total of £247, interest and dividends of £155 and £27 miscellaneous); expenditure was only £275 including George's salary of

£180. The surplus of income over expenditure meant that the Association was able to add to its investments by purchasing £500 Preference Stock in the Great Northern Railway.

Investments and Properties (which we would now call the Balance Sheet) is similarly healthy; the assets comprised investments at cost of £5200 and the Institute land, building and fixtures at cost of £3773. The list of subscribers and donations contains about 140 names, including no less than five members of the Doncaster family, but with the exceptions of ten guineas from the Ecclesall Bierlow Board of Guardians, £20 from the Town Trustees, £10 from Edwin Doncaster, and £5 from John Brown & Co Ltd, almost all were a guinea or less.

The overall picture might seem healthy but with hindsight we can see how difficulties could arise over an extended period. Any charitable organisation depends on the width and depth of its support, even if the balance sheet and cash flow seem satisfactory. For a city approaching half a million people and a comfortable and sizeable middle class, a list of 140 looks quite short and the size of almost all the donations and subscriptions is small. If or when overheads and costs began to rise, it would soon become clear that charitable donations would have to increase substantially or be supplemented by alternative sources of income. As we shall see, that is exactly what transpired over the coming decades; the philanthropic model had a limited life.

It is worth summarising the activities and finances of the Association in such detail for the single year of 1912, and not only because it is the first of an unbroken series of reports; in some ways it marked the high water mark of the Association's history and George Stephenson's life. The Great War was only a couple of years away, with profound social and economic effects; Daniel Doncaster III had died; and George himself, for all his energy, piety and self-belief, was already of an age when the strongest of constitutions might begin to weaken.

★★★

At a purely personal level, however, perhaps George's vigour remained unimpaired, as could be seen from his superintendent's report for the following year, 1913:

The Institute having been licensed for the solemnisation of marriages, the first marriage took place on 14th March, 1913, the Reverend John Thornley conducting the ceremony. The meeting room was filled with the friends of bride and bridegroom.

The extraordinary feature of this item is not what it contains but what it omits, namely the identity of the happy couple. This was another example of how the personal was resolutely separated from the professional; in fact the bridegroom was George Stephenson, and the bride his third wife, Mary Hannah Nicholson, a widow of 67. The daughter of Thomas Cossey Varley, a bed and mattress manufacturer, Mary was born in or about 1845, and successive Census returns show clearly why she remained unmarried and at home until her late thirties, and how she probably met George: she was 'deaf and dumb from birth'. Moreover, so was her first husband John Herbert Nicholson, originally a general labourer from Halifax but later a self-employed lithographic printer, working from the marital home in Attercliffe Road; he had died in 1903. John and Mary had two sons, Thomas and Arthur, respectively six and four at the time of the 1891 Census and therefore born when Mary was about 40 and 42. Thomas was a witness to George and Mary's wedding, but neither of the brothers lived at the Institute. We know very little about Mary; her wedding photograph in the local paper rather reinforces George Robinson's childhood recollection of her as a grand figure 'in a poke bonnet and cape'. (Firth, 1986, p99) There is no evidence that Mary played any part at all in the conduct of the Institute except as one of the deaf members. Quite what it says about the characters of either George or his three wives is difficult to say, but it does seem odd to modern eyes that nowhere in any of his annual reports as superintendent, or in his more informal messages to his deaf members in the surviving issues of *Dacty*, is there a single mention of any of his wives, and precious little about his twelve children and eighteen grandchildren, except of course his youngest son and eventual successor, Colin.

★★★

1913 was similar in scope and activities to the previous year; the gathering war clouds could still be ignored in the day-to-day business of caring for the deaf community and financing the Institute. The number of deaf citizens registered with the Association had risen to 242, employment was almost full amongst the able-bodied, and only five members were wholly or partly dependent on out-relief from the Poor Law Guardians. At this stage, the inception of Old Age Pensions was beginning to supplant the Guardians, and George reported that two 'aged men' and two widows were receiving OAPs. A football club had been added to the range of leisure activities, and the financial situation further bolstered by legacies of £100 from Daniel Doncaster III and £946 from a Joseph Rowland.

By the end of 1914, George could summarise the effects of the outbreak of war in August. Perhaps surprisingly in a city dominated by heavy iron and steel industry – therefore armaments and munitions – the deaf suffered initially from short time working. However, heavy industry was a difficult option for deaf workers and their usual trades such as cutlery, printing, boot making and tailoring were temporarily less in demand. George said his members were coping well, by greater household economy, assistance from the Association and by some deaf women obtaining jobs in areas vacated by hearing men volunteering for the army. Being profoundly deaf and almost or completely bereft of normal speech meant that deaf men were ineligible for military service, which may have irked the more patriotic and adventurous but ensured that the deaf community in Sheffield lost not a single life in the slaughter of 1914–18.

One change of importance to the ageing George was the committee's agreement to the part-time employment of his youngest son Colin, then aged 21, 'to assist Mr Stephenson in the evenings'. The move may have been grudging because there is no evidence from the accounts that Colin was paid for this employment. This situation was only marginally remedied in 1915, notwithstanding the secretary's report that 'the engagement of Mr Colin Stephenson to assist his father has been efficacious, especially in regard to recreation'.

George himself remarked that:

> The assistance of my youngest son has been a relief to me in the prosecution of some of the duties which have been incumbent on me in the past at the Institute, notably those in connection with the recreation of the young men. At the age of 70 one is not expected to be very enthusiastic in the pastimes of the young.

The work was only part-time, as for some years before he took over as superintendent, Colin was employed by Thomas Firth and Sons; the accounts show a figure for the salaries of the superintendent *and* assistant of £179, an increase of only £9 over George's own previous salary.

One minor item in George's report for 1915 illustrates the contrast between the Association's reliance on donations and the tiny income generated internally; it is also the first mention of a curious feature of his career. The Institute made a profit of about £2 on its Shrovetide Festival, of which half was donated to 'Mr Selwyn Oxley's Van Mission'. There is scarcely any other mention of Mr Oxley or his mission in the annual reports and yet this is an indirect reference to an organisation devoted to the advancement of deaf people which during two periods had a national profile; George had been one of the four founders and its president for almost twenty years (see Chapter Five). This is another example of the complete separation of his function as superintendent of the Sheffield Institute and his personal life and activities.

The 1916 annual report was much shorter due to wartime restrictions and the 1917 report is missing, alone in the sequence 1912–1957. In fact the abridged 1916 report contains little new, apart from one section in George's report as superintendent, which is characteristic of his style and approach. Writing of the employment situation, he says:

> *There has been trouble with deaf and dumb from other places, who have come to Sheffield hoping to get better wages. As a rule these are the least desirable class and do not appreciate what is done for them. However I am glad to be able to state that our own deaf have not been influenced by them, but are, on the whole, contented, and have confidence in the missioner.*

Note the phrase 'on the whole'; perhaps we should leave to the imagination what might have been the relationship between the missioner (George himself, of course) and those of 'our' deaf who actually *were* discontented and had less confidence in him.

There is additional evidence for 1917 in three surviving issues of *Dacty*, the monthly magazine 'for the Deaf and Dumb', founded by George in 1901 and always edited by him; it was provided for purchase by the deaf and their friends and was intended to pay its way, though rarely did so. George Robinson recalled:

> *the reading room being crammed on a Saturday night with people sitting round, Stephenson at the far end keeping them enthralled with tales of one kind and another; while in front of the table there were copies of the monthly magazine Dacty – which everyone was expected to buy!*
>
> (FIRTH, 1985, P99)

The surviving copies of *Dacty*, including one from 1901, and quite a few but far from a complete set from February 1917 to October 1921, are held in the RNID Library as part of the huge collection assembled by the same Selwyn Oxley who visited Sheffield with his van in 1916. They are valuable because they were produced primarily for a deaf readership, in contrast to the factual approach of the annual reports, and also because they tell us more about George's character. The magazine did not survive as a monthly after George became ill in the last years of his retirement; it was revived as a quarterly for about three years in the late 1920s but no copies exist from that period.

The first surviving issue of the middle period, for February 1917, shows the importance of *Dacty* to George and his paternalistic approach to his deaf readers. Signing himself as 'The Editor', George first apologised for the late publication of the previous issue and continued:

> *For some time I have been somewhat anxious about our decreased circulation. This ought not to be; I am sure that if our deaf members would each one make up their minds to help they might easily more than double our present circulation. The continuance of the magazine depends upon this, for if we do not have a large circulation, business people will not advertise in our pages, and without advertisements we could not continue. There has been a loss of over £2 on last year's issues; this ought not to be. It has been kind of those who have continued their advertisements, in spite of a small circulation, and I sincerely hope that all our readers will patronise them in business. I do myself and I know that we get good value for our outlay. I suggest that every deaf member get*

four other people to take Dacty, and so bring our circulation to
1500 per month, then people would gladly give us advertisements.
Remember that Dacty is printed for you and it rests with you to
press your friends to buy it every month. Now I have had my say,
please do your part.

Whatever the result of this sales pitch, the real interest lies in what Dacty says about George. In the remaining surviving issues for 1917, for March, May and August, his Editor's Notes give some idea of life at the Institute and the hopes he had for self-improvement of the members. In February for instance, he gave details of the Christmas treats provided for adults and children, with fulsome thanks to those members of the committee and their wives who had contributed to the cost and the organisation of the events. He then reverted to the main thrust of his work as missioner; there is no certainty about the outcome of the war, but:

there can be no uncertainty about our duty. There is a plain path
before you and me. It is quite simple. Be true to yourself, seek only
that which is good. Remember the times for meeting at the Institute;
I do not mean the Billiard Room, I mean those meetings where
you will get good (presumably not 'good' at billiards). *I do not*
wish to discourage recreation, I do wish to see all of you anxious to
improve your minds. The Bible class will be resumed on Wednesday
Feb 7th when I hope to meet with an increased attendance. We
shall continue with the Sunday afternoon services until the end
of February. The evening service at 6.30 will resume on Sunday
March 4th. There is still a goodly number of our young men and
women outside, who would be much better inside the circle of our
Good Templar Lodge on Monday nights (i.e. in the Institute listening to lectures, rather than enjoying themselves in the pubs or downstairs in the billiard room). *Hoping to see*
improvements all round during the year of grace 1917.

The tone of the March editorial was even more astringent. He reminded his readers of a contemporary wartime poster exhorting all men and women to enrol in some form of National Service which ended 'there must be no shirking'. Then the rhetorical question 'What does shirking mean?' It means firstly those who fail to give a full day's work for a full day's wage, 'any man who indulges himself and thinks only of his selfish desires with no regard for his wife and children', secondly, the wife who takes drink or is lazy and untidy or who 'never darns her husband's or her children's stockings'; all these and many more are shirkers. He then finishes: 'If the cap fits any of you take it off as quickly as possible; do not on any account remain one of the shirkers.'

However moralistic this seems today, his righteous anger was not directed only to self-indulgent men and slatternly women, but also to the government of the day. In his May editorial he railed impressively against the slaughter of millions in the Great War.

> *I believe God is love and I cannot for the life of me see what love has to do with the dreadful carnage which is now taking place [...] He has nothing to do with this war, it is altogether the outcome of man's lust for power [...] What is our country doing to follow the example of Christ – to save man?*

And then, though he suggests no alternative by way of strategic or military policy, he embarks on an entirely characteristic diatribe on one of his favourite hobby horses, and this in the year in which the government introduced strict licensing hours for public houses:

> *There is an enemy in our midst, a destroying enemy, a liar and a cheat; hundreds and thousands of poor innocent and ignorant men and women are being destroyed body and soul, and yet the government allows this destruction to go on, not daring to take away the enemy. We have just entered upon a campaign of trying to persuade the people to sign the total abstinence pledge. Pray God that it may be successful. I do earnestly pray that all of you, my deaf and dumb friends who have not signed the pledge, will do so.*

So, in February, buy *Dacty* and come to services, Bible class, and the Good Templars Lodge meetings; in March do not be a 'shirker'; and in May an attack on the immorality and horror of the war and a fervent appeal for abstinence. No more of *Dacty* survives until August 1918. George, now 73, was nearing retirement; his main article is not signed as 'Editor' but from 'your sincere friend George Stephenson', probably because Colin had now taken on the editorship. George's first contribution summarises his views on love and marriage, in essence asking 'my dear deaf friends' not to expect the dreams of everlasting happiness in marriage but to accept that the only real and lasting love is that we have for God and he for us, so that only with that in mind can we make a worthy and successful marriage.

The second piece is quite different and informative about George's life and future. The heading is 'Deaf and Dumb Anglers at Sutton on Trent' and the article is signed 'One of the Bagmen' but the style is so similar to George's own that we can assume it was written by him or perhaps by Colin who was certainly in the 28-strong party, because one of the three anglers who caught nothing all day was 'the youthful superintendent'. The day was beautiful, the competition was enjoyable, and the highlight was the substantial tea including English beef which almost banished the thoughts of war and rationing. The day's pleasure closed with one and a half hours spent in 'the large garden of the superintendent'. This is the first mention of the cottage and garden in Sutton on Trent to which George retired.

Returning to the annual reports, there is nothing of significance in 1918 except an extraordinary omission: the end of the Great War. 1919, however, is very different, with significant developments for both the family and the Association. The first of these is not mentioned in the reports of either the secretary or George as superintendent – it was the death at the age of 73 of his third wife, Mary Hannah, from 'dilatation and atrophy of the heart.' The marriage had lasted six years but there is no evidence whether it was successful or not, only that neither marriage nor death was thought worthy of mention in the Association's report, and also that like Lena, Mary played no part in the work of the Institute, in marked contrast, as we shall see, to Colin's wife Doris. However, it is likely that his wife's death precipitated the last decision of his long career:

> The superintendent has notified the Committee that, owing to increasing years and failing health, he wishes to resign on 25th March next. During 49 years Mr Stephenson has faithfully and energetically carried out his arduous duties, always to the entire satisfaction of the Committee. His work has been marked with a high degree of success, and the deaf and dumb themselves will

*always owe a debt of gratitude to him for his untiring efforts made
on their behalf.*

George gave his own summary. He surveyed his work for the Association
and described himself as:

*a foster parent to the whole of the deaf and dumb in this district
[…] The deaf need help. There is scarcely any relation in life in
which the deaf are independent of outside help. In every large centre
of population the deaf and dumb need a real foster parent […] His
duties are manifold. Practically they cover the whole of the relations
of life.*

It would be hard to better this as a definition of paternalism. How far
deaf individuals accepted him as a 'foster father' cannot be known. More
significantly, the job description he was passing to his youngest son must
have seemed daunting.

★★★

Retirement for George meant Sutton on Trent, a rural backwater between
the Great North Road and the River Trent some 40 miles from Sheffield.
Now only an easy eight miles on the A1 from Newark, it must then have
seemed a haven of peace after the bustle, noise and smoke of Sheffield.
We do not know when or how George took possession of his cottage,
which true to form he named Ephphatha, but certainly not later than
1917 when it is first mentioned as a base for the Institute's annual angling
match. Probably it was rented because his salary was too small for him to
purchase. His third wife Mary Hannah came from a business family and
although in a codicil to his will George describes her as 'well provided
for', it seems unlikely she would have funded the purchase. In any event
the cottage was not mentioned in his will or inherited by the family.

My mother and other relatives had good memories of summer
holidays in Sutton with the august but ageing patriarch and his faithful
niece Fanny Emma, who was already 51 when they left the Institute, but
there are no surviving letters and only one photograph. Otherwise, the
only evidence is derived from the surviving issues of *Dacty*. Retirement was

one thing, but neglecting his flock was another; in every surviving issue, from December 1920 to October 1921, there is a long monthly letter to 'My Deaf and Dumb Friends'. The first letter, dated 15th December,1920, starts in elysian mood, describing the pleasures of a snowy winter in the country, watching the birds in his orchard, shrubbery and garden, his niece throwing them bread crumbs, and identifying a bullfinch 'with its markings of blue, red and white, helping itself to the corn scattered for the fowls in the fowl run'. Idyllic, for him and for the village children, who were building a snowman. Characteristically this is an occasion for moral reflection:

> *I dare say the children who made this snow image said the Lord's prayer before retiring to bed at night, but I venture to think that as they laid their young heads on the pillow their thoughts went out to the image and the anticipation of the fun they would get out of it the next day, so that it is quite plain that they thought more for the image than of the child Jesus and his mission.*

This thought led him to the story of the King of Babylon, the golden image he constructed and his threat to throw any of his subjects who refused to worship it into the fiery furnace. And from there he reminded his readers of the annual Christmas service at the Institute, how much pleasure they all had from the floral decorations, yet how these too were mere images to which we should not bow down. Quite a lesson to draw from his picture of country children enjoying themselves in the snow!

In fact George was capable of detailed accounts of rural life of genuine interest to social historians as well as his deaf readers. His letter in March 1921 was all about his adopted home, so closely bound up with the river Trent. As he said, the interest of the masses who came from Sheffield and Doncaster on summer weekends was limited to the fishing, and for them the village was 'only a convenience'. Apart from agriculture, the major occupation of the inhabitants derived from the willows which grew in great abundance on the river banks. Originally the 'rods' or young flexible shoots were cut by enterprising villagers and sold to basket makers far and wide, but then they realised they had a more lucrative trade to hand. First a flourishing economy of basket makers developed, and then extended to many related products; cradles for babies, fish baskets for Grimsby, Hull and Yarmouth, clothes baskets, coal baskets and others. George described the trade and manufacture in considerable detail, and as we shall see his knowledge and interest were fuelled by a final change in his domestic life.

One reason for his approval of this honest and sober trade was its moral superiority to the previous occupation of many of the male population, which gave him scope for another of his homilies. He proudly describes Sutton as being 'almost, but not quite, a model village [...] there are three places of worship, and only four public houses'. Clearly much better than the old, pre-basket making days about 50 years previously, when he was told there were no less than eleven ale houses. The majority of the patrons had been bargemen from the Trent, though from the middle of the nineteenth century their numbers were much reduced by the advent of the railway. They were, according to his local informant, 'very rough and uncultured' and spent much of their time in the alehouses:

> *it was no uncommon pastime for them to sit (in pairs) on each side of an oblong table and order their drinks from the landlord, and as they drank they commenced kicking each other's shins with their heavy clogs, and continued in this brutal manner until one of their number could not bear the pain and loss of blood any longer, and so cried out that he had had enough; in consequence of giving in first, he had to pay for all the drink both he and his opponent had consumed.*

The reader may suspect that George's friendly informant was gently pulling his august neighbour's leg, but the story allowed for another lesson in sobriety and good living:

> *I am sure that you my deaf friends will agree with me that those ways did not conduce to the respectability of the village, and happily those times have passed away, never to be resumed.*

The following month he told his readers that he was 'not yet weary of my adopted home'. He regularly attended the Wesleyan Chapel which 'stands only a few feet away from my cottage' and much enjoyed the excellent music provided by the choir. George taught Sunday School at the chapel and the musical elements were accompanied by a twelve-year-old girl on the harmonium, taught like many of her schoolmates by the same lady whose aged father had preceded her in this work for 40 years. One throwaway remark in this story is the first and only evidence of George's own hearing loss; 'as most of you know, my hearing is not strong'.

The next month he described another most important Wesleyan resident of Sutton, the village blacksmith, with copious quotations from Longfellow; 'the smith a mighty man is he, with large and sinewy hands', etc. To gain George's approval, of course, there had to be a strong moral aspect to his personality and the blacksmith, always ready to give advice or help whether to householders or farmers, was like his father before him, 'Secretary of the Brotherly Love Lodge of the Order of Foresters, of which there were at one time over 100 members in the village.'

A rural idyll indeed; busy, prosperous, populated by pious and hard-working citizens, and with far fewer ale houses than in the rough past, yet conscious of the troubles of the outside world. In the same letter of May 1921 George assures his readers that he and the other villagers are aware of the poor economic conditions and industrial unrest plaguing the rest of the country, including the employment and living standards of the Sheffield deaf. By July it seems even Sutton had reason to complain; though the village is near the Nottinghamshire coalfield, 'the great coal shortage has created a positive famine' and even firewood was now in short supply.

And so the pattern continues; a mixture of detailed reportage of the minutiae of village and country life, pious homilies, awareness of the outside world, a holiday visit from his daughter Hilda and her three children, a trip in a motorcycle side car (he was 76!) to Newark, passing a brand new sugar beet factory with appropriate comments on its significance for the rural economy. His greatest excitement and most detailed report are reserved for Chapter Five and Appendix Five, but after October 1921, there is nothing. There are no more surviving copies of *Dacty*; he is said to have suffered several strokes before his death in 1924 so perhaps there were no further letters to his 'deaf and dumb friends' at the Institute.

Neither is there any direct mention in surviving records of the final change in his domestic life. In 1923, his 'loyal and devoted niece' Fanny, now 54, married Albert Edward Woods who carried on his father's trade as osier or basket maker. Given George's authoritarian personality, it might seem surprising that he consented to the marriage of his middle-aged niece, with the possible loss of the housekeeper he had employed since 1911, but it seems that Albert played a full part in caring for George at the end of his life. On the Grant of Probate of his will George's address is given as 'The Willows', either Albert's house or a basket maker's renaming of Ephphatha, and Albert was present at and then registered the death.

George Stephenson died on 17th April 1924, and the cause of death was 'cerebral haemorrhage' (apoplexy). There were several obituaries, in the *Sheffield Daily Independent* and in two of the deaf journals, *British Deaf Times* and *Ephphatha*, but all three are so similar it seems likely they were based on the Sheffield example.

Friend of the Deaf and Dumb – Death of Former Superintendent

The deaf and dumb of Sheffield have lost a good friend by the death of Mr George Stephenson, which occurred on Thursday afternoon at his home in Sutton on Trent. For 49 years Mr Stephenson was superintendent and missioner of the Sheffield Association in aid of the Adult Deaf and Dumb. During this time he devoted himself wholly to the teaching and guiding of the deaf and dumb in a manner which earned him the commendation of all who came into contact with his work. Both Mr Stephenson's parents were deaf and dumb, and it was this early experience which led him to take up the work of helping those so afflicted. He first started the work by conducting a Bible class for the deaf and dumb at the request of the late Mr Daniel Doncaster. At first the work was voluntary but eventually Mr Stephenson started a school for the deaf and dumb children, a post which he held for 15 years. However he found the work exceedingly heavy, and decided to devote the whole of his time to the adult sufferers. In October 1886 the Sheffield Institute for the Deaf and Dumb was opened with Mr Stephenson as superintendent missioner, a position which he held until March 1920, when, at the age of 75, he retired owing to failing health. He was succeeded by his youngest son Mr Colin Stephenson. The deaf and dumb, at various times, showed their appreciation of Mr Stephenson's work on their behalf, by making presentations to him, among these being a mahogany secretaire and illuminated address; also his portrait in oils, which now hangs in the Institute.

The piece in *Ephphatha* adds an example of his devotion to the deaf community not recorded elsewhere, relating to the death of his third wife Mary in 1919.

> *A splendid Christian act must not be forgotten. Mr Stephenson had just buried his wife – he left the graveside, travelled to York, and interpreted for his grace the Archbishop of York, when seven of the York deaf were confirmed.*

The body was brought back to Sheffield. The Ephphatha report tells us that at St Paul's Church, a stone's throw from the Institute, a special service was conducted by the Rev Canon Elliott MA, who gave a short address on the words 'inasmuch as ye have done it to one of these the least of my brethren, ye have done it unto me'. All George's surviving sons were there, and 'the church was crowded with the deaf and representatives of the Association, and many other institutions in the city, and they followed in procession to the cemetery.' This was the General Cemetery, about a mile from the church, privately funded for the benefit of those who could afford to be buried in their own plot or vault. Opened in 1836 it provided sites for 87,000 Anglican and Nonconformist burials before it closed in 1978; it is now recognised by English Heritage in its list of historic parks and gardens, a conservation area cared for and renovated by a charitable trust. George was interred in the family grave of his third wife Mary Hannah.

The obituaries were unstinting in praise, yet there is one gap in the written accounts which I find extraordinary. We have seen that in the annual reports of the Association there is no mention of the deaths of either of George's second and third wives, nor is his third marriage identified, even though he proudly reports the ceremony as the first to take place in the Institute. The reports faithfully record the deaths of various benefactors and committee members, yet *nowhere* in the 1924 or any other report is George's death even mentioned; not at the AGM, not in the reports of the secretary, his friend and executor George Bates, or of the superintendent, his own son Colin. He may have been retired for four years but until his series of strokes he regularly visited Sheffield and the Institute, he wrote to 'My Deaf and Dumb Friends' on a monthly basis, and he had been the dominant figure in the life and management of the Association and its

Institute for almost 50 years. So why is there no mention of his death in the annual report?

There was the carefully worded appreciation from the committee when George retired, and a measured approval of his work in some of the annual reports, but all of it rather strained and distant by modern standards. There seems to have been a substantial gap, social and personal, between the Doncasters, their colleagues and successors on the one hand, and George on the other. It may have been that as his grandeur of style and piety grew with the years, and as he became more experienced and knowledgeable than successive committee members, they, like George Robinson and his parents, came to see him as a little distant, hugely impressive but also an occasional figure of gentle fun. We should also gauge the relationship through the prism of late Victorian and Edwardian society, rigidly class based; a milieu in which anything personal between employer and employed – well-to-do businessmen and charity worker from a working-class background – might be regarded as inappropriate.

★★★

It is difficult to summarise George Stephenson's life and career. There are no contemporaneous personal records, letters or diaries of relatives or friends; he died 90 years ago, so there is no one alive who knew him personally. I remember stories from family members who visited him in Sutton, but none who recalled his time in the Institute; they loved his cottage and garden, but their recollections of the man himself were less detailed. The old-fashioned word 'august' seems appropriate; the family were rather in awe of him. Others of the many descendants have been asked for any recollections from their own parents or grandparents, and the search yielded only one item. This is a short letter about family history written in 1979 for the benefit of his brother Benjamin's descendants by Winifred ('Auntie Win'), one of Benjamin's eleven daughters and a sister of George's faithful niece and housekeeper, Fanny. The sisters remained close throughout their long lives; the family have a photo which shows eight of them in Sutton to celebrate 'Auntie Fan's' 80th birthday in 1949.

Interestingly, Auntie Win describes her uncle George in almost the same terms as George Robinson. She writes that George was 'quite a character in Sheffield, as he wore a beard, a tall hat and a frock coat – much respected'. August, respected, a little distant, a civic dignitary rather than a family member – is it fanciful to suggest that he had become the role that he played? Although it is not a direct recollection, this thought is echoed in an interview given in 1956 to the *Sheffield Star* by Alan Stephenson, his grandson and eventual successor as superintendent. The interview formed part of a descriptive piece about the life of the deaf community by a staff columnist, and Alan told her something of the history of the Institute and the family connection. Of his grandfather George, who died two years before he was born, Alan says:

> *He was an incredible old man. He is still remembered by our older members with a mixture of admiration and fear. He would stand no nonsense from anyone.*

The photographs that survive show a confident, mature figure, serious and self-possessed. Two from near the end of his life are of particular interest, both in the Selwyn Oxley papers in the RNID Library. The first, posed outside the cottage in Sutton, is the nearest we have to anything remotely informal. The second relates to his participation in the Guild of St John; it shows him standing with Rev W H Oxley outside the Oxley family home in Kensington. He looks rather grand, and exactly matches the description given by Robinson to Rev Firth and by his niece Winifred nearly 60 years later. There was also a portrait in oils presented to him and hung in the Institute and given to him on his retirement. In his will this was gifted to my grandfather Oswald, the eldest son of his second marriage, and eventually it passed to me. We tried hanging it in one of our homes, but our three young children found it unnerving, so it was taken down and lost or destroyed on a subsequent move, which I now much regret. The reaction of all those family members who saw it was similar; respect for a significant ancestor, rather than affection. As far as I know, there is only one remaining item from George's life in the Institute; the secretaire given to him to mark his first 25 years of service to the deaf is in the home of my sister Elizabeth Callister.

The published records have been quoted and tell much the same story. His own written style, in the letters to the *British Deaf News* and the address to the Guild of St John reproduced in the appendices, was always serious and impassioned. Only in the letters from Sutton to the

Sheffield deaf and the Robinson stories is there any lightness of touch, not quite humorous but capable of simple enjoyment. Otherwise, he always seems to have been well respected, held somewhat in awe, and only 'loved' in some sense by the deaf for many of whom he was their only and lifelong guide, helpmate and teacher; as he said himself, a 'foster father'. As with many of the superintendents of the voluntary societies whose lives were summarised by Rev Firth, his vision of the role was paternalistic, pious and evangelical, epitomised in the Victorian title of 'missioner': a missionary, not to darkest Africa but to one of the darkest and most neglected corners of British society. As I say in the Introduction it was only long after George's death that this role began to be scrutinised more critically, and we shall return to the issue at the end of Chapter Seven. For now we need only say that in many ways George Stephenson was the very paradigm of Victorian piety, service and endeavour, the ideal character to give practical shape and continuity to the philanthropic vision of the wealthy and equally pious families who dominated business and social life in nineteenth-century industrial Britain.

The life's work speaks for itself. For half a century he devoted his life for only modest rewards to the service of his fellow men, with courage in public debate and unexampled and single-minded vigour in his daily tasks. He may have seemed an awkward customer to some, a little distant and imperious to his deaf 'charges', but he fulfilled a vital function for a deeply disadvantaged section of society. It originated from family experience, but became a career, a commitment and a lifestyle which took precedence over everything. He was a man of consequence; his story needed to be told.

5

THE GUILD OF ST JOHN OF
BEVERLEY 1895-1951

'A Scheme to Unite the Whole of the Deaf and Dumb
Attached to the Various Societies into One Great Federation'

At the end of his first *Dacty* letter of 1921 from Sutton to the Sheffield deaf, George added an afterthought:

> *I was closing my letter without telling you that yesterday Mr Selwyn Oxley of London was here and delivered a very interesting lantern lecture (200 slides) upon the educational and mission work among the deaf and dumb. I have not space to give even a very abridged description of the lecture, suffice to say that he traced by pictures and speech the whole history of work among the deaf, from the time of St John of Beverley; also in India and Japan. A large portion of his lecture was devoted to Denmark, where the lecturer spent considerable time in visiting and obtaining photographs and information concerning the deaf and dumb.*

Quite what the basket makers and farm workers of Sutton made of this lecture is hard to imagine, though George did say that 'I have been much gratified by the encomiums I have heard from some of our village folk'. Who was Selwyn Oxley, and what brought him to give such a specialist address in a small Nottinghamshire village? Part of the answer can be found in an 'appreciation' of George by Oxley which was added to the obituary in *The British Deaf Times*. The first line reads: 'The home call has come to one of the very few existing founders of the Guild of St John of Beverley.'

The Guild is scarcely mentioned in the Association's annual reports, and there are few and fleeting references elsewhere in deaf history, yet it meant a great deal to George Stephenson and this chapter summarises its curious story and the careers of two eccentric characters, Ernest J D Abraham and Selwyn Amor Nathaniel Oxley.

★★★

In his Editor's Notes in *Dacty* for December, 1916, George had reported that:

> *I have just received a long and very interesting letter from Mr Ernest J D Abraham, the superintendent of the Victoria Deaf and Dumb Association, Melbourne, Australia. Many of you older members of the Institute will remember Mr Abraham, who for some years had the care of the deaf and dumb in Bolton, Lancashire. And was also the editor of the Deaf Times and other periodicals published in the interests of the deaf. A restless, enthusiastic personality, always on the lookout for ways and means to uplift the deaf and dumb, for whom he had great affection, and to whom he has devoted the whole of his talents. He was the first in the country to draw up a scheme to unite the whole of the deaf and dumb attached to the various societies into one great federation, the object of which was to unite the members into a grand and true Christian Fellowship, under the name and title of the Guild of St John of Beverley.*

'A restless, enthusiastic personality' was an understatement. Born in London in 1868, orphaned at nine, he was adopted by a deaf mute minister, Rev John Jennings, and given an education; he assisted Jennings in the South London Gospel Mission to the Deaf and Dumb and an associated school for deaf children. Aged only sixteen, Abraham took over the school on Jennings' death, and the following year was elected minister to the mission. Restless indeed, his next move, still only nineteen, was to what became the Bolton Mission to the Deaf, from which he also contributed, edited, managed and part owned a series of magazines for the deaf – *Deaf and Dumb Times* which became *The Deaf Chronicle* in 1891, then *The British Deaf Mute* in 1892/3, *The British Deaf News* in 1896 and finally, *The British Deaf Times* in 1904 under which name it remained a leading journal for deaf people until 1954. In this journalism he worked closely with Joseph Hepworth; Abraham, Hepworth, Walter McCandlish (Missioner to the Hull Deaf Institute) and George Stephenson were the 'four founders' of the Guild referred to by Oxley. Of the four, only Hepworth was deaf; the son of a Wakefield businessman, he was Assistant Missioner at Leeds until he moved to the Cardiff Institute in 1896.

Missioner, campaigner, and journalist, Abraham is characterised with some asperity by Rev F W G Gilby (1865–1949), at the time Superintendent Missioner at the Royal Association for the Deaf and Dumb (RADD) in London. Based at St Saviours Church for the deaf in Oxford Street, Gilby was also a journalist, editing *Church Messenger*, which later became *Ephphatha*. The following assessment was written in old age in Gilby's unpublished autobiography (see Notes on Sources):

> *Mr Ernest J D Abraham, son [sic] of the late Rev John Jennings, in South London, was a popular young preacher among the deaf in those days. He was a freelance (not under our association), and we felt it a grievance that there should be a rival mission in S London. He wore clericals and lemon kid gloves with fur collar and cuffs; he was only about 20! I now see that he had really great gifts. His power of signing with his hands was in no way inferior to my own, and his journalistic powers were way in advance of any that I possessed. He was a born advertiser, eaten up with the modern spirit. And so his magazine beat mine to a frazzle. When he had to leave London and become missionary to the deaf of Bolton, Lancs, the war went on between his British Deaf Times and my Church Messenger and I or 'we' lost quite £200 in the struggle... I had a certain pull over the British Deaf Times in that it promoted beauty competitions for deaf girls, which all the missioners to the deaf were pretty well agreed in condemning.*
>
> (GILBY, 1947, P121)

So – a restless personality, a born advertiser, a successful journalist, a flamboyantly dressed and popular young preacher and signer, and a promoter of beauty contests; not your typical social worker in late Victorian London, and certainly not in industrial Lancashire, where he must have seemed an exotic figure.

In the November 1895 edition of *The British Deaf News*, under the florid Latin headline '*Societas Sancti Johannis Benerfaci*', accompanied by a four-page history of St John written by Walter McCandlish, Abraham introduced his great vision in grandiloquent style. The deaf of France, Germany and America had already honoured their pioneer saints, but what about the British?

> *Are we to understand then that the British Deaf do not appreciate the efforts that have been made on their behalf, that they are wanting in gratitude, patriotism and enthusiasm? No! Ten thousand times NO!*

He sketched his vision of a Guild which would 'bind the deaf, and those interested in their welfare, into a bond of good fellowship'. On each anniversary of St John's death (7th May) there should be a service at Beverley Minster, with an oral sermon interpreted by one of the Nonconformist missioners, followed by a 'congress, dinner, picnic, etc.' There would be no bar to entry, certified by a beautifully designed 'card', bronze and silver badges, an executive committee, and local branches; as soon as 200 names of prospective members were received, they would all be printed together with voting forms for choice of local officials.

There is no evidence (and Abraham never claimed) that this grandiose vision originated from anywhere but his fertile journalistic imagination, but it certainly struck a chord. Within three months there were two branches established at Hull and Sheffield, the membership had reached 500 including some from as far away as Bristol and Cardiff, and George Stephenson had addressed preliminary meetings in Leeds and Manchester – though no branches appear to have been founded there or anywhere else.

In March 1896 an editorial gave the date of May 9th for the first 'annual Pilgrimage' to Beverley, with a proposed programme of events and a hope that 'hundreds' of the deaf would attend. Abraham 'cordially invited' members of the National Association of Teachers of the Deaf, the Union of Teachers of the Pure Oral System, the Institute of Missionaries, the British Deaf and Dumb Association, and the National Deaf and Dumb Teetotal Society 'to join our Guild of St John' and to attend the pilgrimage, though there is no sign in Abraham and Hepworth's journals that any of these organisations participated. Abraham commissioned a special prayer for the pilgrims from the Bishop of Beverley and expressed his hopes for the future:

> *In addition to the deaf mute members of congregations, associations and institutes, I most earnestly hope to see a large number of the missionaries, masters, and teachers of the deaf – especially those who are themselves deaf – present at Beverley.*

In the June issue, Abraham's report of the pilgrimage described it as 'a glorious success'. The delegate conference created an elaborate structure with George Stephenson elected as President, McCandlish and Hepworth as Joint Secretaries and an Executive Committee including McCandlish doubling up as Hon. Treasurer. Later these posts were supplemented by an 'Aldermanic Bench' and the appointment of a Warden. It is however noticeable that all these posts were created and seem to have been filled by the four founders who also proposed, seconded and passed the Resolutions. The sense of a small cabal of zealots taking full charge of the nascent Guild is unmistakeable. Abraham also had to admit, in his fulsome praise for his colleagues, that the attendance was not what he had hoped:

> *Then there is Mr Stephenson, who took nearly 100 of his congregation to Beverley. What a gigantic gathering we would have had if other missionaries had worked with the same zeal! Mr Stephenson has set us all a grand example, and it is to be hoped one that will be followed next year. Fifty deaf friends from fifty different institutions – 2500 persons. What a glorious gathering that would be! And why not? Indeed such an assembly could be brought about by quite a moderate effort on the part of the missionaries.*

Abraham complained of a last-minute refusal of the railway companies to arrange special low excursion fares for the occasion, otherwise 'we should have had thousands of deaf friends rather than hundreds'. Quite how the small town of Beverley or the railway network would have coped with such an influx is difficult to imagine. The head of the Manchester school for the deaf expressed his support for the Guild but also complained about the cost and the venue, having had to leave Lancashire before 6.00 am and not expecting to get home until after midnight.

George Stephenson addressed the pilgrims; what might now be called a keynote speech was reproduced in full in *British Deaf News* and is printed here in Appendix Four. Like the letters of dispute with Dr Thompson and the Sheffield School Board in Appendices Two and Three, it shows George as pious and opinionated to the point of aggression. He clearly feels there is already an undercurrent of opposition to the Guild, perhaps to the dominance of the founders, and certainly connected to the mutual suspicion of Anglican and Nonconformist missions, but struggles to clearly define the Guild's objectives. He bemoans the absence of delegates from the South, perhaps realising that Beverley was an unsuitable centre for a hopefully national membership. In *British Deaf Mute* Abraham again tried to set out the purpose of his brainchild, but what he wrote scarcely clarified the issue:

> *This annual gathering will thus aptly symbolise the prime object of the Guild, which is the UNION of the deaf in religion, in business and in pleasure. The Guild does not exist for the Annual Festival alone. It is an organisation for everyday religious, social and recreative work among the deaf. Above all it seeks to unite them – to heal up petty divisions – to bring mutually antagonistic bodies into harmony, so that in the end all the deaf may pull all together all the time, and so immeasurably strengthen their hands.*

George Stephenson shared the fervour and the grandiose vision; he accepted the presidency, enrolled a large number of his deaf members and gave them a day's outing to Beverley. From the outset, however, the scheme had several weaknesses. It lacked coherent purpose or specific policies; it failed to attract a national membership or the adherence of other organisations; it was based on an annual festival in a remote town in East Yorkshire; it appeared from the outset and continued in fact to be dominated by the three missioners who shared Abraham's enthusiasm. But above all it was basically the product of Abraham's personal ambition, and there was a problem with his leadership. Even before he left London he had suffered from nervous exhaustion, and on two occasions in the first few years of 'his' Guild he had to withdraw from active participation in both the Guild and journalism.

Daniel Doncaster II, philanthropist, steel master, and founder of the Sheffield Association in Aid of the Adult Deaf and Dum, photographed about 1861

Back to back housing in Hermitage Street, Sheffield, where George Stephenson was born, raised and started work as a cutler, photographed before slum clearance in the 1930s

The first floor room at 82 Division Street, Sheffield, which was the Association's only home from 1863 to 1886 and also its school premises from 1879, date unknown

A group of deaf ramblers from the Institute photographed at Porter Falls on the outskirts of Sheffield on New Year's Day 1902.

George Brookes, deaf bee keeper, cabinet maker, and professional photographer, seen at home in Rotherham in 1904

"I am thine, O Lord" signed by three ladies of the Institute about 1910

MR G. STEPHENSON, THE FOUNDER AND WARDEN OF GUILD

1219

George Stephenson and Rev W H Oxley outside the Oxley family home in Victoria Road Kensington in 1921, and perhaps photographed by George Brookes – see Appendix 5

Colin Stephenson, robed as Diocesan Lay Reader, about 1938.

Sharrow Bank, 57 Psalter Lane, Sheffield,
home of the Institute and the Stephensons from 1936 to 1960,
photographed before purchase by the Association.

Without Abraham's energy and self-belief the Guild would be difficult to sustain, and this became apparent within a few years. In April 1901 his resignation as missioner at Bolton was announced in *British Deaf News* because his health had been unsatisfactory 'for some years', and he wished to 'further some of his old schemes for the benefit of the deaf.' 'Furthering old schemes' was more evidence of his restless nature; after an earlier unsuccessful application, he was given a three-year contract as the first full-time missioner to the deaf in Melbourne, Australia, and in June 1901 it was admitted that he had never recovered from 'the nervous collapse of a few years ago.'

Like Thomas Widd, Abraham's departure from Britain marked only the beginning of a life of service to deaf people, summarised briefly in Appendix One. *The British Deaf Monthly* amalgamated with Rev Gilby's *Ephphatha* and when it changed its name to *The British Deaf Times,* the editorship passed again to Joseph Hepworth, now missioner in Cardiff. This did not mean the end of the Guild, only that it operated on a much reduced and more parochial level and was less frequently reported in *The British Deaf Times*.

George Stephenson and Walter McCandlish continued to be involved, retained their official titles and attended more or less annual services and meetings at Beverley. Attendance was much reduced, for instance in 1902 all the names were listed, most of them women (unusually the meeting was fixed for a working day) and all from East Yorkshire. For some years there is no report at all, but in April 1912 *The British Deaf Times* presages the May service at Beverley with a generously worded piece by a Miss Mason:

> *Once a year the streets of the old world town are filled with pilgrims who have flocked from all parts of the country to celebrate the patron saint of the deaf within a Guild whose function was to bind the deaf and dumb and all those interested in their welfare with a bond of good fellowship.*

This reads as if Miss Mason did not expect many subscribers to have heard or know much about the pilgrimage and reflects a much lower level of activity. The report of the actual occasion, printed two months later, is more realistic; rather than 'flocking from all parts of the country' the attendees included George as President, McCandlish as Secretary, several clergymen from Beverley and Hull, and 'deaf persons present from Hull, Driffield, North Frodingham, Cottingham and Beswick'. There is only one conclusion: the Guild was now confined to the deaf of a limited area of East Yorkshire and would not have survived at all but for the enthusiasm of George Stephenson and Walter McCandlish.

There is no mention of a pilgrimage in 1913 and only a formal report in June 1914, *except* for one change in the attendance list; 'the Rev W H Oxley, who came down from Kensington for the purpose, and also his son, Mr Selwyn Oxley, honorary worker among the deaf'. On the same page there is a column and a half devoted to the younger Oxley.

> *We have much pleasure in informing our readers that Mr Selwyn Oxley (hon. worker for the deaf) will be prepared to address drawing room and other meetings on behalf of the deaf, with or without lantern slides.*

The report outlined the terms and subject matters of his lectures, and offered to lend Oxley's 'irreplaceable' lantern slides to other lecturers provided that they pay carriage, 'railway glass rate', both ways, and a small fee of 3/-. He says that he will embark on a two-month driving tour in July and August, to visit 'those parts of England which have no Deaf Missions' and asked to be informed by readers of the addresses of any deaf persons they know on his proposed route. Nearly all the first three pages of *The British Deaf Times* for December 1914 were devoted to:

The First Annual Report of Honorary Work done by Mr Selwyn Oxley (late Pembroke Coll Oxon), honorary worker for the Deaf, April 1913 to April 1914

A summary of this report would only list the many places Oxley had visited and the impressive number of people who had given him introductions and hospitality, but it is curiously short on what he actually achieved. He was able to visit and presumably support in some unspecified way a number of isolated deaf individuals in rural areas; he also spent much time collecting and preparing up to 300 lantern slides for his lectures. What is abundantly clear is the enormous energy which he devoted to these endless journeys, including spending his 'holiday' visiting deaf institutions in Milan, Florence and Rome.

★★★

After Abraham emigrated the Guild had ill-defined aims, a limited geographical area, and lacked a leader able and willing to devote himself to the cause. Perhaps only a character as eccentric and single-minded as Abraham would fit the bill; someone with the energy, time and financial security to reinvigorate the Guild on a different but equally grandiose basis. Such a man was Selwyn Oxley, whose story has scarcely been told except in the posthumous biography by his wife Kate. For my purpose it is significant in its early stages because of the largely honorary role played by George Stephenson for which Oxley was clearly grateful. The support of established missioners like George and McCandlish was vital for him to be taken seriously.

Rev Firth described Selwyn Amor Nathaniel Oxley as 'undisputedly the unique figure in the Annals of the Deaf'. (Firth, 1985, p112) Born in Penarth in 1891, Oxley came from a wealthy Yorkshire landowning family. His father Rev William Henry Oxley (1849–1924) was a younger son and after Cambridge he took Holy Orders. After a few years as a vicar in Grewelthorpe near Ripon, he held posts as chaplain to expatriate communities in Sorrento and Sicily before returning to a living in Penarth and finally as Vicar of Petersham in Surrey. In 1913 he retired to a suitably large and comfortable house in Victoria Road, Kensington, which remained Selwyn's home until his marriage in 1929. (Apart from his initial role in the Guild, Rev Oxley's only claim to fame was *The Fisher Folk of Filey,* a set of poems in Yorkshire dialect now held in the National Archives. His wife, Rosamund (aka Nelly) was not physically strong; she had congenital curvature of the spine, a weakness inherited by Selwyn in the form of a pronounced stoop, and was described by her daughter-in-law Kate as 'the smallest woman I ever knew.') (Oxley, 1953, p193)

The Oxleys enjoyed the benefits of inherited wealth, and Selwyn was expected to go to Oxford but failed the entrance exams ('Smalls') in 1911. The following year he got as far as entrance to Pembroke College but after a term in lodgings suffered what Kate described as 'a nasty nervous breakdown' and on medical advice withdrew and planned a cruise to recover. On the train to Liverpool docks he chanced to meet Rev Payne, a distant relative, the son of a deaf headmaster and later chaplain to the Liverpool deaf, and this chance encounter seems to have enthused Selwyn with a purpose in life which became an obsession.

Rev Payne could not have guessed what he had unleashed, and certainly not the incessant, almost manic programme of travel, lectures and meetings which occupied Selwyn and all those closest to him for the next 25 years. It was an extraordinary life, now almost completely forgotten. It is hard to find any detailed and unbiased account of Selwyn's character or motivation; he seems to have been regarded by some as a secular saint and by others as a 'nosey parker, or as an amateur diletttanti [sic] or as an outsider of doubtful motives'. (Firth, 1985, p113) Fortunately, two years after his death in 1951, as instructed in his will and at the expense of his estate, his widow Kate published her biography of *A Man with a Mission*, modestly said to be derived from his papers and diaries. Well, yes and no: in fact Kate Oxley (née Whitehead) was not only profoundly deaf herself but as unusual and strong-minded as her husband. Notwithstanding the almost complete devotion with which she served him and his purposes, she was perfectly capable of clear and sometimes acerbic judgements.

Kate Oxley's life and career are summarised in Appendix One. She first corresponded with Selwyn in 1922, moved to London about 1925 and married him in 1929. So her summary of his first year of touring in 1913 and 1914 is based on his diaries, the recollections of others and her own experience of travelling with him a decade later, but it encapsulates the mixed reactions he always attracted:

> One feels he was happy and contented throughout this period as he was to a great degree pioneering new ground, a novelty to himself and to those others he came across. It says something for his singleness of purpose that despite rebuffs, setbacks, disappointments, jealousies and all the rest, he let nothing divert him from his chosen path [...] (He) was greatly misunderstood by many who should have known better; they doubted his motives, his singleness of purpose.
>
> (OXLEY, 1953, p144)

It was a 'singleness' which brooked little opposition. Kate said in her Introduction that he 'liked a chat' but much preferred an argument, and woe betide the other party whose facts and logic failed to match his own:

*If you could not, you were back at the start, arguing all over again.
I know to my cost: I have endured them by the thousand, all the
years I have known him.*

(OXLEY, 1953, P. XIII)

She says she formed her assessment early in their relationship, as she
became more closely involved with him and his work:

*I think it was then I suddenly realised the real truth of his
psychology. It was that he would never really care for anyone as
a single individual: things would for him more or less be on the
collective system. And he would value a thing far more if it was
unobtainable: once he had possession it was just one more on a long
string of what he already had. I knew then he was good at starting
things but got tired of them ere he finished. This latter part others
had to do! I was to understand this point a good deal more in the
years to come.*

(OXLEY, 1953, p194)

Rev Firth gives an entertaining picture of the endless tours:

*Many deaf people remembered that first visit of Selwyn Oxley, in
a motor van decorated with posters about the Deaf, standing in the
town square or on the village green, while Oxley went the rounds
of the local vicar, the squire, the doctor, the postman and the village
gossip, to discover where deaf people were to be found [...] (but) he
was not always given a welcome by established organisations and
their professional workers, either in schools or established societies
for the adult deaf.*

(FIRTH, 1985, p112-3)

So much for Selwyn's character and impact; what he actually achieved
will be examined later. When he first embarked on his endless journeys,
looking for deaf individuals in areas where no organised help existed
and proselytising on their behalf, he was only 22; he had failed to fulfil
expectations of an Oxford education, was prone to nervous debility, and
had decided almost accidentally on a life dedicated to deaf people; his

only support was his recently retired father. What he needed was an established, respectable and pious organisation to give credence to his personal mission and a title and a history to satisfy his own romantic, obsessive nature. What could be more appropriate than the Guild of St John, dedicated to a patron saint of the deaf and led by august missioners of impeccable reputation?

Although the early journeys concentrated mostly on the south and west, where the Guild had never been strong, he also visited most of the schools and missions in the north; he may well have met George Stephenson before he first appeared at a Guild conference and he certainly knew Walter McCandlish of Hull who was chiefly responsible for keeping the Guild in existence between Abraham's emigration and Oxley's arrival.

Both George and McCandlish were impressed by the enthusiasm (and probably the resources) of the dedicated young Londoner, and the sequence of events is clear from the detailed minute book of the Guild held in the RNID Library, starting with the first committee meeting after Selwyn Oxley completed his 1913–14 tour. Apart from 'Brother' Stephenson (all the members were called Brother) the committee were all from Hull and the meeting was attended by both the Oxleys. As Chairman, George welcomed Selwyn Oxley and his proposal to establish a branch in the south, whereupon he is there and then elected a Vice President of the Guild.

Within a year, George Stephenson had resigned as President, and it had been agreed that Rev Vernon Jones should be President of the new southern branch, which thereafter always met at the Oxleys' Kensington home. Rev W H Oxley threw himself with gusto into his son's venture, and he was elected as Warden of the Guild, a function with a supervisory role over all the branches (there never seems to be more than three: Sheffield, Hull and now 'the South'); he had a second home in Filey on the East Yorkshire coast. He was also commissioned to draw up a shortened version of Anglican service appropriate to a deaf congregation; according to the minutes, this was then approved for use in the Church of England by (or perhaps on behalf of) the Archbishops of Canterbury and York.

Very rapidly, and particularly from 1917 onwards, whilst always respectful of the surviving founders, the Oxleys came to dominate the Guild. There are no further committee meetings attended by anyone from the North and little mention of any activities by the Sheffield or

Hull branches, although there are brief pieces in *The British Deaf Times* to which Selwyn Oxley made frequent contributions under his own name, his initials, or other noms de plume. Selwyn had found the organisation which enshrined his energy and enthusiasm in a pious cloak of venerable origin which he could and did use for the rest of his career.

★★★

Of the three references to the Guild in *Dacty*, the first was George's report in 1916 of the letter from Ernest Abraham and the second his report from Sutton of Selwyn Oxley's lecture to the village. The third is his account of an occasion which affected him deeply; it is the last and most personal example we have of his own writing, recounted in his letter to 'My Deaf and Dumb Friends' in *Dacty* of June 1921. I make no apology for printing this account in full in Appendix Five; as the last record of George's long life and work, it says much about his energy, character, and continued devotion to the deaf community. It also shows his faith in the motives and importance of the Oxleys' 'take-over' of the Guild of which he had been President for almost 20 years.

George was now 76, suffering various 'disablements' and nearing the end of his life. Reading this heartfelt description of what must have been his last expedition, it is impossible not to admire his strength of will and undimmed enjoyment of life, work and friendship. Thrice widowed, retired to a rural life of which he had little previous experience but clearly loving it, travelling to and around the 'great metropolis', preaching to another flock with his hands, shopping in Selfridges, royally entertained by his wealthy friends the Oxleys, and taking tea at a Corner House with the profoundly deaf naturalist Arthur Doncaster who he may not have seen for 40 years: this was quite a coda to an extraordinarily full and satisfying life, captured in a photograph with Rev Oxley in front of 75 Victoria Road in all their finery as Warden and Founder of the Guild.

The photograph may well have been taken by George H Brooks, one of several professionals who helped Selwyn Oxley assemble the huge cache of images now stored in the RNID Library. Brooks himself was profoundly deaf, a native of Rotherham and like his father a member of the Sheffield Institute; he was not only a photographer but a cabinet maker and a bee keeper, another example of how native ability, ambition and determination could overcome disability. Another surviving photograph shows Brooks himself and George outside the Finsbury Park Centre with the description 'teacher and pupil', and there is an earlier photograph of him as a bee keeper in George's 1911 Souvenir. It is not difficult to imagine George's pride if in fact this last great occasion in his life had been recorded by someone whose family he had encouraged and supported in the Sheffield Institute.

★★★

The London visit was more than a personal coda, it was nearly the end of an era. Between this happy if exhausting adventure, and his death almost three years later, George had several strokes and was cared for by the devoted Fanny. There is no evidence of any more visits to the Institute after the first couple of years of his retirement. As for the Guild, it was now based entirely at the Kensington home of the Oxleys; the minute book, which was kept in great detail up to the mid-1930s, shows Selwyn Oxley's obsessive round of ceaseless activity. At a meeting of the committee on 10th July 1924 it was reported that:

> a note of deep sympathy was passed to the relatives and friends of the Rev (sic) G Stephenson, one of the four original founders of the Guild, and the Secretary (Selwyn of course) stated that he had absented himself from the Royal Association stone laying at Shepherd's Bush on April 22nd on account of the funeral which was taking place that day.

George was the second of the founders to go; Joseph Hepworth had died in 1921. Walter McCandlish spoke warmly of his old colleague at the Sheffield Institute, but within months he had also died. So three of the four founders had died within three years, and Abraham had been in Australia for 20 years. This left only one senior figure as a link between the Guild's original base in the industrial North and its revival in the South. Selwyn's father Rev W H Oxley had been in poor health for some time and had retired to Exeter, where he died on 2nd August 1924. It was a great personal loss to Selwyn; it is clear from Kate Oxley's account that his father had supported him loyally and energetically in his chosen mission and from now on Selwyn was the sole and undisputed leader of the Guild.

He did have loyal and continuing support from other individuals, including several influential clerics, but none of them based in or connected with Sheffield, Hull or the northern missions. There is no indication that George Stephenson and Walter McCandlish objected to the centre of Guild operations moving to Kensington, and after their deaths no evidence that either Colin Stephenson or anyone else in Sheffield or Hull played any substantial part in the conduct of the Guild. In Colin's time there is no mention of the organisation or of Selwyn Oxley in any annual report. Nor is the Northern branch of the Guild mentioned in any detail in *British Deaf Times* after the deaths of the founders. There is a record of the annual Guild pilgrimage to Beverley as late as 1932, with about 100 attendees 'mostly from Hull', but the Guild officers are named as the Vicar of Beverley and the superintendent of the Hull Mission, with no mention of Oxley or any of 'his' committee. The formal link between North and South seems to have been broken and apart from Hull I have found no evidence of activity in the North after 1924. For this reason, the remaining years of the Guild and the life of Selwyn and Kate Oxley can be told more briefly.

★★★

There are few references to the Guild or the Oxleys in published deaf histories, and even Lysons has only one paragraph in his summary of national and local organisations for deaf people:

> *Nor did deaf work lack a hagiology. The Guild of St John of Beverley which included among its objects the adequate national commemoration of the death of St John was inaugurated in November 1895. The society which had fallen into desuetude was later revived by Selwyn Oxley Esq., and was disbanded after the latter's death in 1951.*
>
> (LYSONS, 1963, p183)

If it were not for another product of Selwyn's ferocious energy it would be impossible to tell the Guild story at all. In addition to incessant travel, journalism, propaganda, founding at least one new voluntary mission and encouraging others, and administration of the Guild, he also set about assembling a Guild library of books, pamphlets, magazines and cuttings, together with his ever expanding collection of photographs and slides, intended for the use of anyone who wished to learn about or foster work for deaf people. The library was housed first in his parents' house in Kensington, then his own married home in Ealing and finally in the Oxleys' last home in Cheltenham; it now forms a substantial part of the RNID Library. Rev Firth summarised both the eccentric origin of the library and its importance:

> *His method was to save any book, pamphlet or press cutting where deafness was mentioned, quite indifferently as to what else the document might contain. Thus the NID received copies of Arthur Mee's Children's Encyclopaedia because it contained a diagram of the finger spelling alphabet [...] (but)a great deal of this material has genuine historical importance.*
>
> (FIRTH, 1985, p113)

The library includes all the books and magazines which remained after Oxley had given some away in the last years of his life, together with his personal papers and the bound volumes of Guild records and the collection of photographs and slides, but the source of most of the published material is unclear. Probably Selwyn bought anything he could find from any available source, it is likely for instance that he purchased part of the library assembled by Abraham Farrar (no relation to Joseph Farrar of the Sheffield Association's early years), a well-to-do deaf polymath and bibliophile.

The Guild's most active period lasted only until 1935 but the minute book and other documents reveal the frenetic level of Selwyn's activities. He was not alone. Apart from Kate Oxley, his greatest support after she moved to London in 1925 and became his wife from 1929, there were a number of active committee members, most of them Anglican ministers already involved in deaf welfare, including Vernon Jones, F W G Gilby, and William Raper who had welcomed George Stephenson to South London in 1921 and later officiated at the Oxleys' wedding.

There were also the 'members' of the Guild, claimed to number thousands. The ledger containing their full details is another example of Selwyn's idiosyncratic character. One section lists animal members including several of the Oxleys' pedigree cats; the main human entries, arranged alphabetically and by date of entry, also specify the 'benefaction' which entitled the individual to membership. The benefactions included 'hospitality', 'gave books', 'wrote poem', 'reduced hotel bill', 'helped deaf woman' and many other items both trivial and important; it seemed almost any connection with deaf people or the Guild was sufficient. The entries started in 1917 and finish in 1927.

Notwithstanding the support of his committee and the large 'membership' there is no evidence that the Guild sought or attracted substantial funds. Selwyn was supported by his committee colleagues but was much the most active and provided most if not all of the funds. It was essentially a one-man-band, which was recognised by the National Institute for the Deaf; it was reluctantly reported to the Guild Committee in 1932 that Selwyn was no longer a member of the NID Executive Committee because of the Guild's 'peculiar constitution'. There is no sign of a formal constitution in the surviving Guild papers but we can guess the NID had realised that it was basically a pious cover for Selwyn's personal crusades.

The time and energy he expended is evidenced by three long reports which he made to his committee. 'A Short Resume of the Guild's Work 1920–1922' details efforts to expand operations to Southern Africa, India, Ceylon and Denmark as well as the south west of England.

> *Grants have been made for deaf work in Paris, Scandinavia, India and Ceylon and [...] grants to missions at Bath, Bristol, Salisbury, Swindon and Gloucester amongst others have been made [...] it may justly be said that it was through the direct pressure exerted by the Guild that it was found possible to establish the new Gloucester Mission for the Deaf in 1920.*

Six closely typewritten pages headed 'Epitome of Car Work Done in the years 1924–1928' would do credit to a successful commercial traveller. The caravan had been replaced by a succession of chauffeured motor cars. A total of 50,000 miles, three cars, one chauffeur, every English county except four visited at least once, three accidents ('very slight'), seven punctures, and only one police interview, for speeding in Radlett, Hertfordshire. There are fifteen major tours listed, 25 deaf missions and the same number of deaf schools visited, eighteen 'Special Visits' to conferences, congresses, 'various deaf teas', at least two international or league football matches and the Henley Royal Regatta – though the relevance of these last three items to deaf welfare is not immediately apparent. Again, the impression is irresistible: the scattergun approach of the true obsessive.

The third document summarises the period as 'Twenty-One Years of Honorary Work for the Deaf', now travelling with and, he says proudly, 'married to a very gifted and totally deaf Yorkshire novelist'. He pays tribute to other organisations including the NID, RADD, BDDA, the Church Benefit Society and the newly established Deaf Welfare Education Board but it is difficult to pinpoint exactly what he and the Guild actually achieved by all this ceaseless activity. The annual pilgrimage to Beverley, though it continued at least fitfully until the early 1930s, is scarcely mentioned by him after the deaths of the founders in 1924.

There is ample evidence in *The British Deaf Times* and elsewhere of Selwyn's continuing journalism and correspondence on behalf of deaf people, and there is little doubt that he and his father were instrumental in the foundation of the mission at Gloucester. Kate Oxley claimed that with another committee member, his distant cousin W E Bolton, he was responsible for the foundation of several other societies in the South and West, and Rev Firth says much the same, but it is more likely that he did no more than suggest, cajole, and press the Church for such foundations, and quite possibly part finance them as well, as he certainly did in Gloucester. His family background, the occupations of the majority of his committee and his own faith meant that he sought to work largely through the Church and, perhaps thinking of him as an 'interfering busy body' they seem to have been reluctant to acknowledge his support or encouragement. As Kate said, he was a 'starter rather than a finisher'.

As Lysons makes clear, the Church had instituted few if any missions for deaf people after the foundations of the 1890s, until discussions starting in 1916 between the Convocations of York and Canterbury finally led to the foundation in 1922 of the Central Advisory Council for the Spiritual Care of the Deaf and Dumb. Lysons gives considerable detail of the impetus this gave to the development of specifically Anglican missions in some dioceses and the support the Church gave to existing societies elsewhere, but significantly does not mention Oxley or the Guild in this context.

In 1956, Rev T H Sutcliffe, a Canon of St Pauls and Organising Secretary of the Central Advisory Council, wrote a two-part account of 'The Origin and Development of Missions to the Deaf and Dumb' in the September/October and November/December issues of *British Deaf News*, the successor to *British Deaf Times*. It is not as detailed or as academically rigorous as Lysons' thesis, but given his official position Rev Sutcliffe would have been well informed about the creation of missions during the 30 years of his council's involvement, and yet he also makes no reference at all to Selwyn Oxley or the Guild.

None of this devalues completely what Selwyn and his Guild achieved, but it is difficult to quantify. The uncertainty is amplified by the nature of his personality and his enormous restless energy; he was the facilitator par excellence, pushing here, encouraging there, persuading others to set up and then operate institutions in which he then played no part, but supplying seed finance if necessary out of his own ample resources. In some ways he was a typical Victorian philanthropist, operating in an era when that style could already be seen as anachronistic.

***

25 years of frenetic activity took its toll on a constitution which was never robust. In *Man with a Mission* Kate Oxley is perfectly frank about Selwyn's faults as well as his virtues, but curiously non-specific about the nature and extent of his physical and mental frailties. However, by the mid-1930s it was clear that his energy and capacity were declining. The Guild's written records become less complete and precise after about 1935; by then, Kate was beginning to worry about her husband and feeling that he ought to take things easy for a time.

First she persuaded him to take a three-year lease on a house in Harrogate, but he spent only occasional weeks there. Both of them were increasingly worried about the growing threat of European war, especially its likely effects on the Guild Library and the menagerie of pedigree cats which shared their Ealing home and increasingly seemed as important to them as the Guild and the library. Eventually, they settled on a large Regency house called Southlands at 53 Queens Road, Cheltenham. They moved there shortly before the outbreak of war; the move of the library was delayed which could have been tragic, because the Ealing house was badly damaged by a land mine in 1940 and an uncertain number of books and documents were destroyed; the remainder were hastily moved by lorry to Cheltenham. As Kate wrote:

> *Selwyn seemed to get much older overnight; it meant the wreck of all he had built up [...] At this time (his) nervous system began to suffer more than we knew.*
>
> (OXLEY, 1953, P232)

Before the move to Cheltenham there was a final acknowledgement of Selwyn's significance as a self-appointed spokesman and literary warrior for the deaf. Kate tells the story:

> *the reconstruction and world extension [sic] of the Guild of St John of Beverley had progressed a good deal in the years it had been under Selwyn's control. Perhaps 1938 was in a sense its peak year, though we were not to know it. It was marked by one outstanding event: the Gallaudet College for Deaf Students in America endowed Selwyn with their M.A. degree. He was very proud of it, though I recall that when the letter first came, he did not at once take it in and threw it in the waste paper basket.*
>
> (OXLEY, 1953, P128)

He soon got over this, and had his MA robes made for use if a suitable occasion should arise.

The move to Cheltenham meant the end of the Oxleys' national role. They lived out their life together in social comfort, surrounded by their cats and cat memorabilia (see the piece on Kate in Appendix One), the Guild Library and all the papers and ledgers relating to Guild administration. The visitors' book for the library, once full of daily entries, shows only four visitors in 1940, three of them from Cheltenham, and then no more. Selwyn became involved as honorary assistant missioner in the Gloucester mission which he and his father had founded; its missioner acted as their chauffeur whilst their own was on war service. They offered their home as a local branch, and Selwyn gave 100 guineas to pay off the mortgage on the Gloucester Institute.

This gave him some satisfaction, but it is clear from *Man with a Mission* that his physical and mental health was deteriorating. He found it difficult to come to terms with deaf welfare practice and administration after 1945 and with the successive deaths of all his colleagues on the Guild Committee:

> *it did not take much to make him really happy. I think he sometimes felt a bit left out of things, as both deaf mission and school work was on a new basis, more advanced, and many of the workers he had known and loved had 'passed over', often causing him to feel lonely.*
> (Oxley, 1953, p229)

Later, Kate added:

> *Personally I think he was tiring of deaf work, since it was (now) amply provided for compared with the times when he had to pioneer isolated places before the era of the motor bus.*
> (Oxley, 1953, p268)

In the last few years he felt the need to deal with the mass of books and materials. Several lots were parcelled up and sent to other deaf institutions in Britain and abroad. Near the end he even started to destroy books and Kate had to hide them from him.

Finally, in the last week of January 1951, both Selwyn and their favourite Siamese cat Soko got much worse. It is difficult from Kate's account to decide which concerned her most, but within days Soko had to be put down and on 29th January Selwyn died of influenza, pneumonia, bronchitis and heart failure. Or so said the doctors and his wife; it is difficult not to surmise that he simply gave up because he had nothing left to live for.

It was a low-key end to a remarkable life. I have only traced two obituaries, in *British Deaf Times* and the *Cheltenham Echo*. Both are printed in full in Appendix Six. It is notable that in *British Deaf Times* no mention is made of the Guild or the formation of any new missions, whereas the *Cheltenham Echo* refers to the Guild and the foundation of the Gloucester mission, presumably based on information from Kate Oxley. This supports the overall impression which Kate identified in her biography

– a starter, not a finisher. It also reinforces the belief that the Guild was a usefully respectable cloak for the enthusiasm of the Oxleys – father and son – and that it declined in importance as Selwyn matured and then withered completely as his health deteriorated.

For historians of the deaf community, Selwyn's will contained one invaluable clause; it provided for the costs of composition and publication of his biography, which Kate wrote as *A Man with a Mission*. Although not mentioned as such in the will, the bulk of the Guild Library, comprising all the books not gifted elsewhere and all the documents, slides and photographs, was lodged with the NID. When Kate Oxley died in 1978 she divided the residue of her estate (about £30,000) equally between YIDD (where she had been educated) and what was now the RNID 'in the case of the latter to be used for maintaining the Selwyn Oxley Deaf Library'. I am not the only one to be grateful for this last act of a wife's loyalty.

6

COLIN STEPHENSON 1920-1953

'Their Anxieties are Ours'

To succeed George Stephenson would be a challenge, but there never seems to have been any doubt that his son Colin would be appointed. In 1920 there was no established career structure or salary scale for welfare workers for the adult deaf at local, regional or national level, and there is no evidence that the committee looked any further or saw any need to do so. Perhaps Colin himself felt he had no real choice; the authoritarian side of George's personality is clear and Colin was the only son still at home after Norman and Douglas left to get married some dozen years earlier.

The 1911 Census describes Colin, aged 18, as a 'Student in art – Decorative' and as an employee, but whatever this involved, it did not last. Aged 21 at the outbreak of the Great War and unmarried, he might have been expected to volunteer (or later to be conscripted) for the slaughter which followed, despite George's strong views on the conduct of the war and the pacifism of the Quakers who dominated the Association's committee. However, he would have been rejected on medical grounds: an accident in his youth left him with one leg shorter than the other and he wore a built-up shoe, a disability of greater significance in his later life. Perhaps as a replacement for the many able-bodied young men who did volunteer, he took a clerical job in a steelworks which lasted almost until George's retirement. He had continued to live with George and Fanny and had also been employed as his father's part-time assistant for six years. He was steeped in the nature, demands and difficulties of the job, and had lived all his life in the domestic quarters above the Institute. It must have seemed an obvious choice for the committee, if they thought of it as a choice at all.

Throughout his 33 years as superintendent, Colin showed that he was more than capable of the tasks which his father and the committee bequeathed to him. Unlike George, he also had the advantage of some formal training. The announcement of his death in the *British Deaf Times* in 1953 concludes:

> *Mr Stephenson got his commercial training with Messrs Thomas Firth and Sons, after which he went for a course at Manchester University, arranged by the Council of Church Commissioners for the Deaf and Dumb, a body of which he later became a member. When he received his diploma as a fully qualified missioner he was automatically included in the list of first-class interpreters.*

The date of this diploma course is not given, but George Stephenson told the committee of his intended retirement some months before the event, so it is likely that Colin left his employment with Firths in time to obtain the qualification; he commenced his duties only five days after his wedding. The diploma confirmed that he was prepared for the life to come, not just by experience and family tradition, but also now by an element of formal training.

Moreover, Colin had a partner who proved ideal for him and for the Sheffield deaf. Only days before his father's formal retirement, on March 20th 1920 he married the 24-year-old Doris Marie Gould. The Goulds were not from Sheffield; Doris's father Alfred Edward was born in Hoxton and Doris and her mother Florence in Holloway. By the time her younger brother Eric was born in 1905 the family were living in Hackney, but between then and the 1911 Census, Alfred, a gas fitter, moved his family to 172 Cobden Road, Sheffield from which Doris was married nine years later. Ambition brought Alfred to Sheffield; his occupation in 1911 was Gas Company Superintendent.

The couple met at work. The short obituary of George Stephenson in the *British Deaf Times* explained:

> *His youngest son, Mr Colin Stephenson, succeeds him in the work, and in this connection an interesting presentation has been made by*

the employees of Thomas Firth and Sons to Mr Colin Stephenson and to his bride, Miss Doris Gould, both of whom were employed by the firm. Mr Stephenson, who was a senior clerk in the forge department, was presented with a silver cake basket, and Miss Gould was given an oak case of stainless cutlery. The wedding took place at St Paul's Church, and on returning from the honeymoon on March 25th, Mr Stephenson took up his duties at the Institute.

The record shows time and again that Doris was a source of strength and support to Colin and the deaf, not only during his lifetime but continuing after his death when their son Alan was superintendent. And after Alan's resignation she took his place until the Institute closed. The contrast between her 40 years of active service and George's second and third wives, Lena and Mary Hannah, could hardly be greater. She was a warm and welcoming presence; I remember her with affection and in fact more clearly than either Colin or Alan.

★★★

Colin came to office at a difficult time for the country, the Association and deaf people, as shown in the annual report for 1920 and in Colin's first major editorial for Dacty. The committee were worried about the financial position because of 'the great depression' after the war, with the consequent rise in unemployment and the cost of relief. Colin's report as superintendent was shorter than his father's usual contribution, but equally paternalistic in tone:

> *The personal affairs of every deaf and dumb person have been my special care, and I have endeavoured to teach them to be more independent and thrifty. Those efforts have been to some extent very successful, inasmuch as many of the more intellectual members have recently managed for themselves minor affairs of which they would otherwise have claimed my attention, thus giving me greater opportunity to help their less fortunate friends.*

His message in the *Dacty* editorial for January 1921 suggested he was as pious, didactic and determinedly positive as his father:

My dear friends, let me first wish you all a very happy and prosperous New Year. I know that the outlook at present is not very cheering. Many of you, my deaf friends, are now on short time, others are completely without work, owing to slack trade; still with all this we can be happy. There is no reason to go about with a long miserable face; trust in God. He will watch over you and the surest proof that you have faith in Him is a smiling face in times of adversity [...] The different difficulties brought about by the Great War cannot be removed at once, but you, my friends, can all help. If each one will do his or her bit, it will bring the time of peace and comfort much nearer.

He urges his members to work a little harder, to keep a clean and respectable home, and for the women to ensure their menfolk feel valued. Then he sets out his own stall:

It is now nine months since I was appointed as your superintendent, and it is quite evident, by the way you all bring your troubles and worries to me, that I am your true friend as well as missioner, so I feel privileged to say a few straight words.

The words were certainly straight; he chided his 'dear friends' over the whole range of the shortcomings which George had identified, with the single exception that Colin, on this first occasion at least, said nothing about the evils of drink. His first complaint is the poor sales of *Daily* on which the Association loses money regularly – if each member bought two copies and a third for a friend, the situation would be transformed. What his readers felt about this at a time of economic depression and unemployment is not recorded. Secondly, though he agreed that attendance at Sunday services had improved since his appointment, it was still not good enough. Out of about 300 members, an initial attendance of 30 had increased to about 60, but he was looking for a figure nearer 150 by the end of January. They were happy to come to the Institute during the week to play billiards, but:

on Sunday you stay away. It is necessary if you wish to succeed in life, to study the Scriptures. Take all your examples from the good men in the Bible, especially the life of our Lord and Saviour.

Then he turns to the Institute itself, created he says entirely for their benefit and maintained by public and philanthropic support. His readers come only to play billiards and sit and talk, but they:

> take absolutely no interest in the welfare of the association [...] all I ask is that you all remember that everything costs money, and it is up to you as sportsmen to subscribe as much as you can afford. Do your bit and perhaps our hearing friends will be disposed to do more.

All this is strong stuff from a newly appointed superintendent not yet 30 – there was to be no softening of the pious paternalism of the previous regime. It also seems that Colin was well aware of the fragile finances of an institution which depended entirely on modest charitable donations and the support of the professionals and businessmen who constituted his committee. At a time of economic recession and industrial unrest, some of the committee members had their own worries. In 1920, Daniel Doncaster and Sons Ltd took financial shelter within United Steel Companies, though Samuel remained Chairman and the family resumed control in the 1930s.

Apart from straight talking to his deaf readers about their shortcomings, Colin was happy to give his views on the political situation, much as his father had railed against the slaughter on the Western Front. However, bearing in mind the interests of his employers, he is careful to appear neutral on the struggle between capital and labour. In his May editorial he welcomed the news that the railway and other transport workers (but not the miners) had cancelled their intention to strike, and then asked what lay behind such damaging disputes:

> In my own mind it is because people are forgetting God and thinking only of themselves. Here we have two classes of people, owners and miners; both parties have the same idea that one is getting too much money; it is not for me to say who is right, but there is a plain fact that according to the press and their actions, that, rather than give way one to the other, they will plunge the country into trouble and endeavour to starve the people – men, women and little children.

The next two editorials show the contrast between his exhortations to smile and trust in the Lord, and the realities of the situation – an extraordinary mixture of the missioner, the social worker and the mendicant friend of his deaf members. 'The coal strike is causing so many of you to be unemployed and thus causing poverty', yet, he says, it has its compensations. The furnaces cannot be fired up, so the air is much cleaner, and there is much pleasure in rambling through the valleys and moorland of the Peak District. But for Colin it was not enough to be thankful for small mercies. His members were not only enjoying their walks in the good weather and cleaner air from Monday to Saturday, but also on Sunday. This was not good enough; Sunday was not a day to walk but to talk to God, and attendances at services had dwindled again. 'You prefer to walk. I sincerely hope that in future you will attend more regularly.'

And then, after criticising of the politics of industrial unrest, urging his readers to look on the bright side and smile whatever the hardships, chiding them for preferring to walk in the fresh air rather than worship in the Institute, there was a single sentence which reveals the underlying reality:

> *We are very grateful to Messrs Greatorex for their kindness in sending five quantities of tripe for distribution to the poor.*

★★★

This is the context in which Colin and his young bride entered their long period of service, raising their own three children and striving unceasingly to alleviate the hardship and handicap of their members. Poverty was a constant reality in the first few years and rarely less than acute by modern standards. Their work included unceasing efforts to find employment for the men and giving meaning and value to the lives of the women, facilitating communication with the hearing world through their command of sign language, providing a social centre where the deaf could enjoy friendship and leisure, and perhaps most importantly to Colin, offering spiritual guidance. All this they maintained within an Association whose finances were increasingly fragile as the years went by. One victim of financial difficulty was *Dacty* itself, even though it limped on for another few years. For the first five years after Colin's appointment, the accounts show a continuing small loss on the magazine which George Stephenson had founded in 1901 as a penny monthly. For a few years it became a quarterly at a higher price and made a profit, but in 1930 it lurched back into loss and is never mentioned again. With such a low circulation and no worthwhile return to the Association, Colin doubtless saw it as an unnecessary drain on his limited time.

The leadership of the committee changed during Colin's first years. In 1923, Wilson Mappin resigned as President of the Association after 25 years in office, to be replaced by James Dixon, the cutler who had been a committee member since the Institute opened in 1886 and who, with his wife, had entertained the deaf members every Christmas at their home. However, after less than two years he retired from business and moved to the South, to be replaced as President in 1925 by Ronald Matthews (later Sir Ronald), a leading industrialist who remained in post until his death in 1958. The Doncaster family were still heavily involved, with the cousins Charles and James Doncaster on the committee until they both died in 1947, when they were replaced by Charles's son, Basil.

In the same period there were two significant changes in the local deaf community. First, as we saw in Chapter Three, the Sheffield School Board decided in 1895 to discharge their responsibility for the education of deaf children under the 1893 Act by 'temporarily' sending them to residential schools in Doncaster, Leeds and Manchester. It is difficult to imagine the effect of this on family lives already handicapped by profound deafness, whether of parents, children or both. In his report for 1921, Colin said the Institute had 289 adult members plus 70 children being educated 'elsewhere'; by the following year, there were 295 adults plus 90 children, all now attending the newly opened Maud Maxfield School for the Deaf. This specialist school was finally set up by Sheffield Corporation, largely as a result of incessant pressure by Miss Maxfield over the previous 25 years. There is little comment on this development in the reports of the Association, but we can well imagine the consequent improvement in the lives as well as the finances of the families involved.

Secondly, the area served by the Association began to expand. In 1924, the committee formally extended its operations to Rotherham, leading in the first year to an increase of twenty adults for whom Colin was responsible, a number which was to grow as profoundly deaf individuals were identified. Then there was a further extension of responsibilities to deaf residents in parts of the West Riding closest to Sheffield. Initially, these additional burdens were not matched by any additional finance, the committee merely expressing the hope that the continuing low level of public donations and subscriptions might thereby be increased, a hope which was largely unrealised.

1925 was a crucial year for the Stephenson family and the future conduct of the Association. Colin himself was so 'seriously ill' that he was unable to work for most of the year. The medical record remains elusive, but we know from Rev Firth that the constant difficulties in walking from his foreshortened leg resulted in a dislocated hip which became so painful and disabling that his leg had to be amputated at the hip. (Firth, 1985, p100) Thereafter he walked with crutches, until in due course he was fitted with an artificial leg, (which is how I remember him).

This terrible experience had one positive consequence. Doris Stephenson was only 24 when she married and was immediately thrown into the unremitting life and labour of the Institute. In the first few years she played only a minor part in her husband's work; their first child, Marie, was born in 1923. In the following years, however, it became clear that she was hard-working and influential in much of the social work of the Institute, especially with the women, and there is no doubt from all the evidence that she was universally liked and valued, so much so that in the final two years of the Association's active life she became de facto superintendent.

For Doris the long months of Colin's illness were a baptism of fire – from that time onwards she was an integral and indispensable part of the organisation. This was reflected first in the creation of a Sheffield Deaf and Dumb Lodge of the Church Benefit Society (to grant sickness and other benefits to subscribers) of which Doris was Secretary; second by the committee's comment in the 1926 report that subscriptions to the Association had actually increased 'largely due to the efforts of Mrs Stephenson who has so ably carried on the work during the serious illness of her husband'; and third by the front page of the 1927 report which listed the committee members and trustees, the superintendent, and, for the first time, Mrs C Stephenson as 'Hon. Asst Superintendent'. Note the 'Hon.' – there is no sign that Doris was then or ever paid separately for all the work she did; the salary bill for 1927 was £267, exactly the same as in the previous year and actually less than it had been in 1923 and 1924. No doubt this was due to the increasing frailty of the Association's finances, in a year when the first major repairs to the Institute were required and electricity was installed.

The annus horribilis of 1925 finished on a better note, with the birth ten days before Christmas of the couple's second child, Alan, who 27 years later was to succeed his father as the third Stephenson to be superintendent. The third child Christine was born four years later, but even caring for three young children did nothing to discourage Doris in her increasingly valuable contribution to Colin's work. In contrast to George's last two wives, never even mentioned in the surviving reports, the committee said in 1928:

> *This report would not be complete without mention of Mrs Stephenson, whose help and service have been of inestimable value. Every duty she has undertaken has been carried out with efficiency and thoroughness. Her services are much appreciated.*

★★★

Following his recovery, Colin resumed work within Sheffield at his usual frenetic pace, walking less because of his handicap but using the tram or occasionally taxi to do the rounds of his growing flock in their homes; visiting hospitals and workhouses to support the ill; acting as interpreter in court and whenever deaf individuals needed to communicate with local and government agencies. The economic situation remained grave and the main thrust of Colin's work in those difficult years remained the unending search for employment for deaf people. The committee's contribution to the annual report, signed off and no doubt written by the Hon. Secretary, was rarely detailed; the report for 1926 was unusual in emphasising the employment difficulties due to 'trouble in the coal industry'. In other words, the largely abortive General Strike and the continuing strife between miners and coal owners:

> *It will be realised that the Deaf and Dumb are largely helpless in time of trouble and shortness of work. The inability to communicate with hearing people places them at once at a disadvantage, and*

that, with the prejudice against them which still exists amongst employers of labour, would place them in a distressing position if it were not for the efforts of this association.

In fact, in that year alone, his first year with only one leg, Colin made no less than 301 visits to employers, seeking work for his members, resulting in sixteen jobs obtained, ruefully said to be better than the previous few years of short time working and unemployment; this continued into the 1930s with much consequent hardship amongst the deaf community. After the 1929 crash, working-class poverty in Britain was of a severity and scale almost unimaginable today, and deaf people were affected at least as badly as the hearing. The Association supplied what it could, on a piecemeal philanthropic basis, but only to its own registered members; in 1927, the committee report had advised against encouraging:

> *deaf and dumb beggars [...] The efforts of the association are devoted to the needs of the Deaf and Dumb of Sheffield and district and every case has special attention and assistance in the way calculated to be most helpful. In this respect our committee appeals for gifts of boots and clothing of every description which are urgently required.*

In 1928, Colin says of the annual Christmas distribution that:

> *every member was given a stone of flour, two rabbits and a cake. Several parcels of groceries, pairs of new boots, clothing, and bags of coke were also given [...] these gifts were made possible by subscriptions to the Christmas Parcel Fund.*

The accounts show the total cost was £23.15.11d.

★★★

Like George before him, Colin was aware of the need for all those involved in deaf welfare to consult and where possible work together in the common interest. Ernest Abraham had tried to provide a national forum through the Guild of St John of Beverley to which George Stephenson attached great importance, both under Abraham and then in his old age with its revival under Selwyn Oxley. Colin did not share his father's enthusiasm for the Guild; it is never mentioned again in Association documentation and I could not find Colin's name in Oxley's copious papers. Like many others in the field, he probably realised that the Guild was effectively a one-man band and that any successes it had were largely confined to rural areas in the South and West.

Fortunately, for the cause of deaf welfare, there was now a more widely based and conventionally structured organisation which came to play a significant role in the modern history of British deaf people. In 1911, the National Bureau for Promoting the General Welfare of the Deaf had been founded and in part financed by Leo Bonn, a deaf merchant banker. Until then, although the BDDA (now BDA), acting as a pressure group, had been very active in the interests of deaf people since 1890, there was no other formal organisation working on a national basis. The stated objectives of Bonn's foundation were to centralise information and investigation into the problems faced by deaf people and to raise and pursue issues in communication with government and other agencies. Dominated at first by teachers and therefore educational issues, and bedevilled like so much else by the exigencies of the Great War and the economic difficulties which followed, the early years were disappointing to its supporters, but on 1ˢᵗ April 1924 it was completely reconstituted as the National Institute for the Deaf and from then on developed rapidly as a representative national organisation.

In 1926, mindful of the very variable coverage and quality of deaf welfare, the NID called a national conference, aiming to widen its influence and create regional associations. Although it was 1950 before coverage was complete, the first such regions were created for Scotland, the North and the Midlands in 1928, and Rev Firth noted that:

> *Colin Stephenson was a familiar figure at the national and regional meetings and conferences of social workers and chaplains to the deaf, partly because of his disability but also because he played a full part in the proceedings.*

> (FIRTH, 1985, P101)

Colin also realised that central government was now getting involved; the Association's 1929 report showed that the NID had finally brought the plight of deaf people into the political arena. Mr Matthews said he had read with interest Stanley Baldwin's speech at the National Institute for the Deaf. Baldwin had pointed out:

> *and quite rightly too – that the deaf and dumb received very little sympathy compared with the blind, and in his opinion the deaf and dumb in many ways are more shut out from social life than the blind.*

By the time these comments were published Baldwin had been defeated in a General Election after four years as Prime Minister, but two years later returned to government as Lord President of the Council in Ramsay Macdonald's National Government and became PM again in 1935, so his views were significant, and were reflected in a new emphasis within the Ministry of Health. Previously, there had been little focussed or specialised provision for the deaf minority; although the Ministry had Regional Welfare Officers with responsibility for all handicapped persons, it was not until 1963 that there was a civil servant within the Ministry with specific responsibility for the problems of deaf welfare. Nevertheless, whether as a result of the efforts of the NID, the BDDA, or the Guild of St John of Beverley or all three, political attention was specifically drawn to the problems of deaf people; when governments show interest in a previously neglected area, the usual response is to commission a report, which is exactly what happened next.

In the Association's 1930 annual report, Colin remarked on the importance of research being done into the problems of the deaf by a Dr A Eichholz. Born in Manchester in 1869, Eichholz had a stellar academic career as a young man, and became an Inspector of Schools in 1898. Already the President of the East End Social Club for the Deaf, a primarily Jewish society (he was married to a daughter of the Chief Rabbi) he was appointed in 1903 as His Majesty's Inspector for Deaf, Blind and Defective Schools. He was therefore vastly experienced and widely regarded as a pre-eminent authority, and in 1930, he was appointed jointly by the Ministry of Health and the Board of Education to prepare his *Study of the Deaf in England and Wales* (HMSO, London, 1932). Although there had been research into the problems of deafness as long ago as the 1889 Report of the Royal Commission on the Blind Deaf and Dumb, which led to the 1893 Act, the Eichholz Report was the first authoritative survey for 40 years, and Lysons called it 'the most thorough investigation of the condition of the deaf adult, and indeed the only government enquiry exclusively concerned with the deaf'. (Lysons, 1965, Introduction) During Dr Eichholz's research into the existing provision he visited the Sheffield Institute and Colin was relieved to report to his committee Eichholz's view that Sheffield:

> is a well conducted mission and a highly creditable element in the network of the welfare societies of the country.

Legislative changes also impacted on Sheffield, as on all the missions. The Local Government Act 1929 abolished at a stroke the Boards of Guardians, parish unions and the workhouses they had administered since the Poor Law Amendment Act 1834. The old framework for the relief of the indigent, old and sick was replaced by various statutory functions of local and central government. In Sheffield, the workhouses at Fir Vale and Ecclesall became Fir Vale Infirmary (later the City General and now Northern General Hospital) and Nether Edge Hospital respectively. The Boards of Guardians were replaced by municipal Public Assistance Committees. For several years, the Sheffield Boards of Guardians had made an annual donation to the Association of £21, hardly munificent in view of the widespread hardship. As from 1930, this subvention was replaced by one from the Sheffield PAC, initially at the same low level, but with profound long-term consequences; for the first time there was a cash nexus between the Association and the local authority.

The committee were increasingly worried about the Association's finances. The total of individual donations and subscriptions had varied from year to year, occasionally boosted by legacies, but the overall level had hardly increased since before the Great War, whereas expenses continued to grow; salaries rose from £170 in 1912 to £312 in 1934. In 1932, the committee complained bitterly at the level of public support – 'The Association has been working for the welfare of the Deaf for 67 (sic) years and does not receive the support from the public that it deserves.'

In 1933 they returned to the issue – 'the Institute is sorely taxed'. Responsibility had been accepted for deaf people in parts of the West Riding as well as Rotherham, so that numbers were up but income was static. For the first time, the committee also suggested that larger premises were required, with a special room in which religious services could be held and an outside space for sports and open air activities. In 1932, the AGM was held for the first time in the Town Hall, in the presence of the Lord Mayor, who said he regretted the financial position and, perhaps rather tartly, 'he would advise the Association to make more widely known the good work it was doing.' In 1933, he hosted the AGM again and personally appealed to the people of Sheffield for greater support.

The Lord Mayor had identified what was now a fundamental weakness in the governance of the Association. There had been little difficulty raising substantial funds to build the Institute in 1886, under the guidance of wealthy philanthropists and their social and business contacts. Once the Institute was built and costs were low, the committee could always rely on the generosity of individuals amongst the founding committee to fund unexpected expenses. A list of regular repeat donors was established and with considerably fewer deaf members in the early years, the whole operation could be run on a shoestring, but over the decades, the situation had changed. Costs had increased, especially salaries and maintenance of the ageing Institute, and responsibilities had expanded to include neighbouring areas; no new financial resources had been identified, the subscription list had remained static, and the steel industry (from which such a high proportion of the committee and trustees were drawn) had gone through some difficult times. No effort had been made to increase support from the general public, small subventions from local charities had not increased, and neither the Hon. Treasurer nor the superintendent were ever formally tasked with raising funds. In this context greater involvement by the local authority was perhaps the only and logical answer, and with that involvement, sooner or later, some degree of control would be inevitable.

Again in 1935, the annual report was low key if not downright gloomy. The committee bemoaned yet another deficit on its current account and a corresponding deterioration in the balance sheet, and darkly remarked that this situation could not continue. They also emphasised again the need to move the Institute out of the city centre but that any such move seemed financially impossible.

★★★

How such pessimism can change in a year! In 1936, the committee reported that an a offer of £7000 had been accepted for the Charles Street premises, so that after 49 years the Institute lost its home and was able to look for an alternative. It is not clear from the record whether the contract to purchase the new premises had been signed before or after the contract for the sale of Charles Street, but in any event considerable refurbishment and alteration were necessary and for nine months the Sheffield deaf and the Stephenson family were homeless. Assistance was given on a temporary basis with accommodation for various purposes at the Friends Meeting House in Hartshead, and in rooms provided by the Vicar of St Pauls and the Minister of Burngreave Methodist Church.

The temporary lack of a home and a centre was the bad news; the good news was that against a sale price of £7000 for Charles Street, the purchase price and initial costs of the new premises at 57 Psalter Lane only amounted to £2170.10.9d. Most of the alterations and additions, however, took place in 1937; the accounts for that year show a final overall cost of the new premises as £5723.5.8d.

Originally called Sharrow Bank, 57 Psalter Lane, on the corner of Cherry Tree Road, was a substantial eighteenth-century gentleman's residence. From 1820, it had been the home of the Newbould family, originally edge tool manufacturers who became large land owners in Nether Edge and elsewhere in Sheffield. The last residents were the bachelor lawyer John Newbould and his unmarried sister Elizabeth, and after John died in 1880, Elizabeth retired to Leamington Spa. The property then passed through several hands but by the 1920s it was the home of William Tyzack, another steel manufacturer, from whose family the Association made its advantageous purchase. Sharrow Bank was to remain both Institute premises and Stephenson family home until the Association closed its doors in 1960.

The new Institute was formally opened on 11th October 1937 by the Bishop of Sheffield. Colin remarked in his report how pleased he was with the new home, and particularly the inclusion of a separate and newly constructed chapel at the side of the original building, as well as a substantial garden area at the rear for recreation and outside activities. The Bishop visited again in February 1938, for a ceremony which illustrates Colin's dual role as superintendent of all the worldly concerns of the deaf community and missioner to their spiritual needs. The occasion was reported in the *Sheffield Morning Telegraph*:

> *The Bishop of Sheffield will visit the Church of the Sheffield Association for the Deaf and Dumb, in Psalter Lane, on February 13th to license the superintendent and missioner Mr Colin Stephenson as a Diocesan Lay Reader. Mr Stephenson, who acts as a Good Samaritan to over 300 deaf and dumb people, has been a Lay Reader for some years, and when he becomes a Diocesan Lay Reader he will be fitted to conduct services in all parts of the Sheffield Diocese.*

> *The service will be of particular interest. It will be conducted by Mr Stephenson, orally and by finger spelling, and the Bishop's address will be interpreted by Mr Stephenson to the congregation of deaf and dumb people.*

The chapel was important to Colin, as it would have been to George, as well as those of the deaf members who shared their piety. It contained an elaborate font and altar as well as the memorial chair to the Dixon infant mentioned earlier, all created by deaf Sheffield craftsmen, and by the time the Institute closed there were also stone wall plaques commemorating the service of both George and Colin; all these artefacts were transferred to the present Deaf Club in Grange Crescent but are now unused because there is little demand for religious services there.

★★★

The move to 57 Psalter Lane was a substantial change, but more was to follow. On the national level, following the Eichholz Report, the Minister of Health issued Circular 37, which recommended Public Assistance Committees to fund services for the deaf in their areas, specifically the search for employment. In Sheffield, Rev Firth tells us:

> *Colin Stephenson succeeded in making a satisfactory financial agreement with the Council and worked really hard to get his people back into employment.*

(FIRTH, 1985, P101)

The committee report for 1937 gives more detail, though without specific credit to Colin for the agreement which effectively added some years to the Association's independence:

> The committee has been pressed for some time to undertake responsibility for finding employment for the deaf in the districts of the West Riding not covered by any association. After considerable negotiation, an agreement has been negotiated with the Sheffield Corporation, the County Borough of Rotherham, and so much of the administrative area of the County Council as is within the area covered by the scheme of the Sheffield Corporation for dealing with blind persons.

Receiving the same level of support as the blind, however belatedly, might have been viewed ruefully by the deaf community; nevertheless this agreement and the move to 57 Psalter Lane considerably reduced the committee's perennial concerns about the static level of individual donations. The transformation in the Association's finances was immediate. Since 1930, the Sheffield Public Assistance Committee had continued the donation by its predecessor Boards of Guardians of a nominal £21 per annum with no subvention at all from either Rotherham or the West Riding; from 1937, under the terms of the agreement, the Association received a total of £500 per annum, comprising £250 from the Sheffield PAC, £100 from Rotherham and £150 from the West Riding. These figures remained unchanged until 1950 which might seem strange to modern readers, but having achieved such an advantageous settlement the committee and Colin were no doubt relieved that for a few years at least they were left to get on with the job they had always done, and with no major direct involvement by the local authorities. The only exception was that the Rotherham and West Riding local authorities, but not Sheffield, were now given representative places on the committee.

★★★

Now the threat of war began to dominate. Colin's annual report for 1938 refers to National Service, ARP Wardens and the like. He also mentions the Golden Wedding of two of the members – the husband was an 81-year-old retired tailor, but in spite of his age 'he has dug deep and erected his own air raid shelter'. Both committee and Colin commented in the 1939 report on the numerous difficulties caused by the outbreak of hostilities. Air raid warnings were a serious problem as of course the conventional sirens were useless for the profoundly deaf, and efforts were made to set up a cascade system of telephone calls to the Institute and to properties adjoining the homes of deaf families.

Colin himself added to all his other duties with war work, as reported by the noted local historian and Sheffield city librarian Mary Walton, a near neighbour of the Institute. In 1958, in number 28 of her series of 'Paragraphs of Sharrow History' in the parish magazine of St Andrews, the local Anglican Church, she introduced the Institute to her fellow parishioners. She said of Colin:

> He is well remembered in Sharrow. I myself particularly have in mind his presence at the Air Raid Information Bureau in the Central Library all through the difficult days after the air raids of December 1940, where he was constantly at hand to advise the deaf.

As for deaf people themselves, the coming of the war had one advantage; as in the Great War, unemployment ceased to be a problem. By virtue of their disability, no deaf individuals served in the armed forces, though Colin remarked that some of the younger men were disappointed and would have done so if they could. Notwithstanding the subventions from the PACs, Colin did feel the need in his 1939 report to appeal to the public for greater support, a complaint which had always previously been left to the committee. With this appeal he summarised very clearly the objectives of the Institute, perhaps already looking over his shoulder to any direct assumption of some or all of those functions by the Council. By this time, restrictions on paper were reducing the length of the annual reports, so Colin was uncharacteristically brief:

> A CHURCH where the deaf can have services in their own language AN EMPLOYMENT BUREAU
> A HEADQUARTERS where the deaf can bring their troubles to one who realises

A CLUB where they can gather for amusement and social intercourse
AN INTERPRETER for all occasions. In fact we provide, as far as possible, alternatives for hearing and speech for those who are without.

During the Sheffield Blitz of December 1940, a number of bombs dropped in the Nether Edge area and the Institute roof was damaged and windows blown out; fortunately nobody was injured. Numbers registered with the Institute were at an all-time high, so Colin's work was as demanding as ever: 377 adults in Sheffield, 32 in Rotherham and 51 in the West Riding. In 1941, the committee reported that:

the war has of course brought many difficulties for the Deaf and Dumb but Mr and Mrs Stephenson had, as always, done everything possible to help those who are terribly handicapped.

Colin was already thinking about the longer term; in his 1943 report he said that:

post war problems are being carefully considered and much thought given to the effect of the Beveridge and Tomlinson Reports as far as the Deaf and Dumb are concerned.

With his involvement with the Northern region of the NID and the new and closer relationship with the local authorities, Colin now took a less parochial view of his and the Association's work. This is clear from his report for 1944, delivered to the AGM after the conclusion of the war in Europe. This was his 25th such report and he took the opportunity to look back at developments, not primarily in Sheffield but on a national basis. He detailed the central role of the NID in relations between the local societies and central government, and emphasised the importance of the Eichholz Report: 'although this did not accomplish all we could wish, it was a beginning'. He also referred to the 'Placement Grants', namely the subventions from the local authorities in return for his work in obtaining employment and points out that 'recently Employment Exchanges have been instructed to inform the Local Society of any deaf brought to their notice', so that some of the special attention previously accorded to the blind was now being paid to the welfare of deaf people.

He also gave a personal tribute to Doris. After describing how far the Institute had succeeded in making good citizens of so many of the deaf he said:

> *Perhaps I may be forgiven for a feeling of pride that a little of this is due to my personal interest and endeavour. We are like a big family and their anxieties are ours, and their successes fill us with thankfulness. Here I would like to say that without the help and interest of my devoted wife, whatever success has been achieved would have been considerably less. I mention this because this year sees also the twenty-fifth anniversary of our wedding*

This anniversary was marked by a celebration and presentation at the Institute. Doris's importance was now emphasised by describing her on the title page of the 1945 report not only as 'Hon. Asst Superintendent' but also 'Hon. Superintendent of the Mothers Meeting'; note, however, the 'Hon.' remained for all her duties.

★★★

It is, however, apparent from the 1945 report how little had changed in the day-to-day operation of the Sheffield Institute since before the war, notwithstanding Colin's grasp of the wider issues and the enormous social and political changes about to transform the country. With peace came a resumption of all the social and sporting activities and other functions which Colin had succinctly listed in 1939; the committee were again concerned about the low level of donations from individuals and businesses. They also expressed the hope that the local authorities might increase the Placement Grants, perhaps unlikely given the more or less full employment in the immediate post-war period. The appeal to their fellow citizens was repeated in 1946, but neither then nor later with any marked result.

In his address to the AGM in 1947, Sir Ronald Matthews first had sad news of a personal nature. Both Charles and James Doncaster died in that year; grandsons of Daniel Doncaster II, they had been trustees of the Institute and committee members for many years. As Sir Ronald said, 'from the very beginning of our existence the Doncaster family were closely associated with our fortunes and took a close and personal interest in the work.' The connection was not severed: Charles's son Basil was elected to the committee and the new Hon. Secretary was the accountant Jarvis Barber, a member of the Quaker family with whom the Doncasters had been closely associated in the foundation of the Association and then through business and intermarriage.

Then Sir Ronald turned to the possible effects of national policy on organisations like his – 'I cannot at this stage forecast what developments may take place in the care of the Deaf as the result of recent legislation.' He believed the work of voluntary societies and experienced superintendents would be needed 'and should be supported for many years'. Colin certainly knew what might be coming; in his report he said he was pleased the National Assistance Bill then before Parliament recognised the needs of deaf people and he was watching developments very closely. Both he and the committee were conscious that the proposed legislation might add to the Association's burdens with no corresponding increase in revenue. By 1948 the Association was responsible for 529 deaf adults in Sheffield, Rotherham and the West Riding; the salaried staff had doubled by the recruitment of a Mr C Roberts as assistant superintendent, so that salaries rose from £490 in 1946 to £730, and in 1949 a Miss Howard joined the staff and salaries increased again to £926. These developments were national in scope and potential, and Colin reports his attendance at many meetings of the NID, its Northern region, its Deaf Blind Committee and the Church Missioners to the Deaf.

The reason for all this increased local and national activity is clear from the report of the 1948 AGM:

> The committee is in negotiation with the local authorities with a view to agreeing on the most efficient way of complying with the requirements of the National Assistance Act 1948.

The word 'requirements' was misleading. Section 29 of the 1948 Act *empowered* but did not *require* County Boroughs and County Councils to make arrangements for:

*promoting the welfare of persons who are blind, deaf or dumb and
other persons who are substantially and permanently handicapped
by illness, injury and congenital deformity or such other disabilities
as may be prescribed by the Minister.*

It was 1960 before these powers became mandatory for deaf people, but by
that time virtually all the local authorities had made their arrangements.

★★★

How this affected the Sheffield deaf community, and why it was different
from most other areas, is detailed in the next chapter, but became
increasingly clear during the last years of Colin's life. Progress was slow;
in the 1949 report the committee said that negotiations with the Council
were now in abeyance because all parties were waiting for the Minister
of Health to give guidance on what would constitute an acceptable
scheme, and the Minister was in turn awaiting a report from his Advisory
Committee. Meanwhile, the committee was simply carrying on, although:

*owing to the continued rise in prices and very inadequate public
support the association is faced with a large excess of expenditure
over income.*

Colin was more trenchant in his report, asserting that nothing of value
to deaf people had so far resulted from the 1948 Act. He defined the real
problem of his members in the strongest terms:

*In the general social life of the community the totally deaf are the
loneliest people in the world, and one of our main objects is to
alleviate this loneliness as far as possible or as the Superintendent
of the Gloucester Institute said, the deaf are alone in a silent world.*

By 1950, Colin's assistant Mr Roberts had been replaced by Alan
Stephenson, Colin's only son and like his father 'born to the job' and
raised on the premises. Only 23 years of age and recently granted the
National Diploma of the Deaf Welfare Education Board, we cannot doubt
Alan's initial commitment. Given the financial fragility and the legislative

uncertainty, he may have wondered just how his future would develop, but he was soon to learn. There was still no movement in negotiations with the Council or any further guidance from the Minister. The finances if anything were worse. As Sir Ronald put it to the AGM:

> *unless matters are put on a proper footing, the time would shortly come when the association would be without funds at all.*

Perhaps an exaggeration, but understandable in an experienced businessman; the balance sheet now showed the main assets as the written down value of 57 Psalter Lane and gilts with a nominal value of £8749, producing an income of £205. For once Colin was blunt in his assessment. He dug out the information for 1877 and pointed out that in that year there had been just 80 adult members and expenditure of £128 compared with the current year with 528 adults and expenditure of £2045. He could also have said that the level of individual subscriptions had hardly increased throughout the period, certainly not since the Great War, so that without the subventions from the local authorities since 1937 (still at the same level) the President's apocalyptic prediction might have come true already.

1951 was a better year, financially at least. Income had increased markedly, partly by two donations of £97 from Daniel Doncaster and Sons Ltd and £100 from a Thomas Nicholson, but largely because the local authorities had finally increased their contributions: £650 from Sheffield, £150 from Rotherham and £200 from the West Riding, thus doubling the guaranteed income from £500 to £1000. Moreover negotiations had recommenced and:

> *it is hoped and anticipated that the association will be appointed agents on behalf of the corporations of Sheffield and Rotherham and the West Riding County Council [but terms have] not yet been agreed upon.*

That Sir Ronald was being unduly optimistic becomes clear when we look at internal City Council documents in the next chapter, but the next year's annual report only notes that negotiations were 'no further forward'. Although there had been further one-off donations of £248 and a total including regular subscriptions of £506, the financial situation continued to deteriorate. With costs increasing it must have been clear to the committee and to Colin that reliance on private generosity was no longer tenable; the only source of financial salvation would be the local authorities, acting under the powers given to them by Section 29, replacing the generosity of philanthropists with rate income from the population as a whole. It would still be possible for the council and the Association to negotiate a properly funded agency agreement, as happened elsewhere, provided there was goodwill and a sensible non-confrontational approach on both sides. This, it appears, was not to be the case.

Perhaps such an outcome could have been achieved if Colin Stephenson had survived and repeated his successful negotiations of 1936/7, but he died on 28th July 1953. His death certificate shows multiple causes of death: uraemia, polycystic disease of the kidneys and arteriosclerosis. In its report for the year the committee announced the death with sincere regret – 'after a long period of ill health which Mr Stephenson had fought with the greatest courage for the benefit of the deaf.'

Courage had been the hallmark of his life and career. First, there was the accident which left him lame from boyhood, the long and no doubt agonising ill health as a young man and father of a young family, culminating in the amputation of his leg, and the fight back with the aid of sticks, crutches and eventually a false leg. There was the homelessness of the family during the hiatus of the delayed move from Charles Street to Psalter Lane, the steady deterioration in the Association's financial position over much of the 33 years he was superintendent, and finally, the fear that negotiations with the Sheffield Corporation might fail and bring to an end the Association and Institute which he and his father had effectively run single-handedly for more than 80 years. All this demanded moral and physical courage of a high order. Perhaps it was a mercy that he did not survive to see the end game, but left that to his widow Doris and his son, Alan, who was appointed his successor as inevitably as Colin had been appointed to succeed George.

7

ALAN AND DORIS
STEPHENSON 1953-1960

'Official Duty and Private Compassion'

It would be idle to pretend the last years of the Association were happy, for the committee, the Stephensons or their deaf members. There is no trace of the annual reports for the crucial last three years 1958–60; perhaps they were never produced, because by early 1959 (when the 1958 report would be prepared) it was clear that the Association had no future. Alan Stephenson had already resigned, the chairman Sir Ronald Matthews died during the year, and the committee, the trustees, the City Council's Public Health Committee, and the Charity Commissioners were increasingly involved in the mechanics of closure – to say nothing of the Stephensons, whose family home had been above the Charles Street and Psalter Lane Institutes for over 70 years. None of this may have seemed inevitable when Alan Stephenson succeeded his father; the committee and Alan continued the struggle for survival as long as they thought there was any hope of saving the organisation and its work.

Alan's appointment was unquestioned; both Colin's obituary in the *Sheffield Telegraph* (30th October 1953) and his death notice in *British Deaf Times* reported (in exactly the same words) that 'a few years ago his son, Mr Alan Stephenson, became Assistant Superintendent, in readiness to succeed him.' Alan had not always been sure of his vocation. Three years after his appointment he was interviewed for the *Sheffield Star*. According to the reporter, Jacqueline Wilkie:

He tells me he never thought he would follow the family tradition;
he did not think he had the patience. But nevertheless I heard the
association's president, Sir Ronald Matthews, say of him only this
week that he was the 'undisputed friend of the deaf', and it would
be little short of a disaster if the bond between them was broken.

The article is significant for what it omitted; it was written when the City Council had already set up its own department for deaf welfare and withdrawn all support from the Association, crucial developments of which Sir Ronald and Alan would have been only too well aware. Either they said nothing, or asked Ms Wilkie to ignore these uncomfortable facts.

Alan's annual reports as superintendent are instructive in both content and manner. In the early years Colin's own reports as superintendent reflected George's authoritarian, paternalistic and pious style, but soften with his growing maturity and show a greater awareness of the national context of the voluntary societies and the developments which might limit their practical independence. Alan was only 27 when he became superintendent and was only in post for five years. Nevertheless, his reports reflect his Deaf Welfare Education Board qualification; they are thoughtful and endeavour to show that the work of missioners like himself was uniquely valuable, providing a personal service to deaf individuals and families unlikely to be met in any larger organisation, however well intentioned. Neither his father nor his grandfather would have thought such justification was necessary.

At no time did Alan specifically argue for the retention of the Association and the Institute under an Agency Agreement. He may not have thought it politic and negotiations on such matters were the province of his committee. He had neither the experience nor the regional and national influence which had enabled Colin to negotiate a satisfactory arrangement with the local authorities in 1936/7. Now they had acquired powers under Section 29 it became a question of how Sheffield and other councils would exercise such powers.

According to Lysons, by 1950 only seven local authorities had schemes already approved by the Minister; the number grew to 71 by the end of the following year and then rose steadily to 137 in 1960. (Lysons, 1965, Table 8, p91) Now the government decided that the Section 29 powers should become mandatory, and the Minister issued Circular 15/60:

The Council of every County and County Borough shall be under a duty to exercise their powers under Section 29 in relation to persons ordinarily resident in their area who (a) are deaf and dumb or (b) are substantially and permanently handicapped by illness, injury or congenital deformity.

Why were the "deaf and dumb" finally singled out in this way? The reason is clear, as Lysons pointed out – after the passage of the Act in 1948 the Minister had indicated that the provisions of Section 29 were *not* to be treated as mandatory *except for the blind.* (Lysons, 1965, p92)

The schemes devised to comply with Section 29 varied widely. In 1962/3 Lysons surveyed all the relevant authorities (except the four county boroughs and four counties in London and the Home Counties still administered by RADD), a total of 75 county boroughs and 45 counties. The large majority (66 county boroughs and 35 counties) had concluded full Agency Agreements with the voluntary organisations operating in their areas, and a further nine county boroughs and all the other eight counties had created a mixed system with some services supplied by themselves and the remainder by one or more surviving voluntary bodies. (Lysons, 1965, Table 9, p93)

Only six councils had instituted a full deaf welfare service operated directly by their own Public Health Committees: Barnsley, Bournemouth, Gateshead, Rotherham, Sheffield and Tynemouth. It is noticeable that three of these areas where the local authority dispensed entirely with the services of established voluntary societies were in what is now known as South Yorkshire and two in the North East; only Bournemouth was outside the old industrial North with its pronounced Labour domination; looking at the Sheffield example it is clear this was not a coincidence.

★★★

The Association's 1953 report showed no progress towards a negotiated Agency Agreement, perhaps because of Colin's mortal illness during much of the year and Alan's inexperience. Following the 1948 Act, Public Assistance Committees were abolished, and the Council support was now shown in the Association's accounts as 'Welfare Committee Grants'. The Council had accepted liability for the welfare of the blind in 1927, assuming the functions but still co-operating with the Royal Sheffield Institute for the Blind, and for many years there had been a Blind Welfare Sub Committee of the Public Health Committee; in July 1948 the name changed to the Disabled Persons Welfare Sub-Committee. Thereafter it was this body (for brevity now referred to as the DPW Committee) which dealt with the detailed implementation of Section 29 and in due course created the Council's own deaf welfare service, subject to approval by the parent Public Health Committee and the full Council. For this reason its discussions, the reports it received and the recommendations it made enable us to trace the sequence of events culminating in the closure of the Institute – not least because the accounts in the Association's own annual reports are incomplete and to some extent misleading.

The draft minutes and reports of the DPW Committee meetings for the years 1943 to 1957 are held by the Sheffield Archives. (Although described as 'draft' they have every appearance of being the finished article, which is just as well because the minutes and reports for the remaining period to 1960, and for several years after, are incomplete and as explained above we have no Association's annual reports after 1957). As in the debate between the Association and the school board in the 1890s, I make no apologies for the detailed account of the deliberations of both sides during the key years. It shows how they failed to understand each other, and how their contrasting social and political attitudes helped to end the Association's history of service of nearly 100 years.

There are two telling aspects of the DPW Committee minutes. Firstly, there are quite detailed reports on services for the blind, but much less about deaf people and the provision planned and later put in place for them. Secondly, part of the explanation is clear from the monthly count of disabled persons registered with the Council; the total blind count was always between 900 and 1000, compared with a more variable figure between 200 and 300 deaf (in Sheffield alone), a reminder that one reason for the comparative neglect of deaf people had always been their smaller numbers and relative 'invisibility'.

There was an early indication of what was to come. In November 1948, the members were reminded that if they decided to terminate the 1937 Agreement for an annual subvention to the Association they need only give one month's notice, *but* the notice had to expire on 31st March in any particular year. At the same meeting a proposal was received from the West Riding authority for the agreement to be continued; they had no intention of setting up their own deaf welfare service. The request was deferred, but later agreed; at this early date the Minister had not approved any Sheffield scheme. Nevertheless, the DPW Committee were already thinking about their Section 29 options. In July 1949, it was agreed the Chairman and also the Medical Officer of Health should attend the AGM of the Northern Region of the NID, and in November the Chairman was appointed as a member of the Association's 'Placement Committee', a significant move not even mentioned in the Association's annual report. This 'watching brief' became a regular feature of the DWP minutes and the members began to receive regular reports on the Association's work in obtaining employment for deaf adults.

From January 1950, the minutes referred to discussions with Rotherham and West Riding about future provision for their deaf citizens, though without any agreed decision. In December 1950, it was reported that the Association had offered to act as agents under Section 29 for all three authorities in return for a subvention of £3750 per annum, a startling increase on the £500 in force since 1937. This was deferred pending receipt of further guidance from the Minister but as a temporary measure it was increased to £1000. A couple of months later, the DPW Committee Chairman was appointed to the Executive Committee of the Northern Region of the NID; the Council's future intentions were becoming steadily clearer, if not yet to the outside world.

In November 1951, the Council submitted its scheme for a full deaf welfare service to the Minister, a clear signal that there was no intention to enter into an Agency Agreement or share any responsibilities with the Association. In June 1952, it was reported that a scheme submitted by the West Riding County Council had received the Minister's approval, leading to a conference of all the voluntary societies in the area. The Council sent an 'observer' only, as their own scheme had not yet received approval. For several months the minutes have few references to the deaf population, until a report from the Medical Officer of Health to the meeting in January 1953. His officers had now started formal registration of all deaf Sheffield residents who would need welfare services; 95 had been registered by 31st November 1952, but the total had grown to 317 by the end of the year and to 328 in February 1953. The Council now possessed the details of most if not all of the Sheffield members of the

Institute, an even clearer indication of the intention to replicate and as soon as practicable replace all its functions with their own self-contained service.

It is inconceivable that the Association's committee still remained unaware of the growing threat, which is no doubt why they wrote to the DPW Committee in April 1953. Another 'serious deficiency' had appeared in the Association's 1952 accounts, a substantial increase in the grant from the local authorities was long overdue, and an urgent meeting was required. This was agreed, and the seriousness of the situation was recognised by deputing the chairmen of both the DPW Committee and the parent Public Health Committee to attend.

The meeting was held in May and reported to the DPW Committee in September. The Association had decided there was no point in asking for less than they needed; they now proposed that the combined subvention from the three authorities under the 1937 Agreement should be increased by £1500 from 1st April 1954 and another £1500 from 1st April 1955. Whether this bold approach was politic is questionable, and of course Colin Stephenson was in very poor health in the first part of 1953 and actually died between the meeting and the report. As it was, the response was brutal and effectively final:

> *The sub-committee having in mind that the continuance of the agency agreements with the Sheffield Association in Aid of the Adult Deaf and Dumb would involve a substantial increase in contributions, and being of the opinion that so far as Sheffield is concerned they would now be directly responsible for their own cases, request the three local authorities to confer on the subject with a view to a recommendation being made for the termination of those agency arrangements on 31st March 1954.*

Although only a submission from a sub-committee to its parent committee and to the other local authorities, there was little chance of the 'request' or the 'recommendation' being refused. For some reason, however, which is unclear from the record, there was a delay in implementation; the issue was not mentioned again until March 1954, when it was agreed to renew the £700 Sheffield contribution for the following year ending 31st March 1955. Nothing further appears in the minutes until December 1954 when the Medical Officer of Health reported that the Association had renewed its offer to supply a full service for the adult deaf of Sheffield under an Agency Agreement, but now on a per capita basis of £7 per annum for each of the 330 registered deaf citizens, an annual cost of £2310. He estimated the cost of direct provision by the Council would be £2000 per annum, but:

> *Arrangements would probably have to be made with the association in connection with religious and recreational services for the deaf and dumb.*

The report emphasised that time was short, as one month's notice was required if the current agreement was to be terminated on 31st March 1955, a year after the sub-committee had originally recommended. The decision was immediate and unequivocal; it was time to resolve the impasse and the Town Clerk was requested to serve the necessary Notice of Termination. There was no discussion about any arrangement to support religious or recreational activities or any attempt to calculate the likely cost, and no mention of the long history of the Association's service to deaf people or the future of the substantial Institute building in Psalter Lane. The sub-committee never doubted what they would recommend to the Council or that it would be accepted. They had only been waiting for the right moment.

All this had finally become clear to the Association and to Alan Stephenson by the time of the 1954 report, issued and probably prepared after receipt of the Notice from the Council. Before giving the bad news, the Secretary Jarvis Barber announced a positive new departure; an agreement for the Association to act as agents for the Derbyshire County Council, similar to the arrangements being formulated between many local authorities and local voluntary societies in compliance with Section 29, and Derbyshire was to join Rotherham and West Riding in appointing representatives on the committee.

Only then did Barber refer to the loss of the annual support from Sheffield, an essential element in the Association's income since 1937. He mentioned this devastating development but gave no explanation at all. Perhaps in view of the minimal notice given, and the warnings from the Medical Officer of Health about the 'religious and recreational services' which the Association might continue to provide, the Council did agree that a final Welfare Committee Grant of £700 should be paid (in arrears) during the following year; thereafter the financial situation would be dire indeed. Perhaps the Council was losing patience with whatever discussions had taken place, and the minimal time gap between decision and implementation was a deliberate ploy to bring the Association to the negotiating table. If so, it had the opposite effect. Indeed, even the Council seems to have been taken aback by its own speed of action, for it was only at the same DPW Committee meeting in January 1955, which renewed the grant for a final year, that they approved in principle the appointment and salary scales of a supervisor and assistant officers for deaf welfare. There was no organisation, no premises, and as yet no experience of how to fulfil the needs of the deaf community for which the Association had been solely responsible for almost 100 years.

For the Association's committee, the failure of negotiations and the apparently precipitate decision of the Council presented real difficulties. They were still providing a wide range of welfare, social, religious and employment services to over 300 deaf adults in Sheffield, as well as smaller numbers from three neighbouring authorities, and were about to lose much of the largest guaranteed source of their income. At last, and perhaps far too late, the committee realised that the static total of small annual donations from a few score well-to-do individuals, a few companies and a couple of local charities, plus the interest on a steadily declining set of investments, would never pay for the services they had traditionally provided or maintain the substantial Institute and home for the superintendent and his family.

As the Lord Mayor had advised twenty years earlier, they finally understood the need for proactive fund raising within the private sector. The 1954 accounts show how far attitudes had changed. Special donations were now sought and had been received from the Queen Victoria and Johnson Memorial Trust, the Church Burgesses Trust, the Town Trustees (both these last two being old established Sheffield charities) and the Sheffield industrialist and philanthropist Sir Stuart Goodwin. These totalled £750, a little more than the impending loss of the Council's grant. Even if this level of support could be renewed and retained, the Association's main area of influence had always been Sheffield and the profoundly deaf of the city were the main focus of its welfare work. If

Sheffield Council had withdrawn their support and refused to contemplate an Agency Agreement, how was the Association's work and staff to be replaced? The 1955 annual report made this brutally clear. The Council had relented only by extending their grant to March 1956, and they had already appointed James Dean as Supervisor of Deaf Welfare, together with an assistant, and a nascent service was being put in place. At the AGM, Sir Ronald referred to:

> *the fact that during the year the Sheffield City Council had set up their own organisation for welfare work on behalf of the Deaf and Dumb and that at the present time although the association had offered to place the whole of its organisation and facilities at the disposal of the City Council there was no cooperation between the two bodies.*

★★★

The Association was still staffed, equipped and experienced to provide a full deaf welfare service but now had to accept that the local authority was legally empowered to provide the same service and had actually started to do so. Even now the financial situation remained superficially satisfactory; the special donors of the previous year had repeated their generous gifts, and as well as subventions from the other three local authorities, the last payment from Sheffield Council had recently been received.

Alan's 1955 superintendent's report contained two passages emphasising the unique contribution which he felt only a full-time superintendent could provide, recognising (though not admitting openly) that the work of the Association, if it survived at all, would have a much narrower scope in future and would necessarily involve some cooperation with the newly appointed Council officers.

Firstly, he entered into the long running debate between manual and oral teaching methods. Today we can agree with Alan that for any organisation dealing with large numbers of deaf children or adults of widely differing needs and abilities, the combined method comprising both lip-reading and sign language was the right approach, but at that time virtually all profoundly deaf Sheffield children were taught in the exclusively oral Maud Maxfield school. Alan emphasised the importance in court proceedings, hospital admissions, and medical appointments, of having someone able to help with concepts and terminology which might be vital to the individual's health and future. In entering this debate he was anticipating that much of his welfare work might soon be absorbed by the Council, yet making a strong case for the continuing importance of established professionals, not because of any paper qualifications but because they had interpretative skills honed during a lifetime's intimate experience of communication with deaf persons about their problems.

Secondly, he emphasised the importance of the social activities, sport, games, educational and religious meetings, and the more general welfare work he and his mother, father and grandfather had provided on an individual and group basis for three generations. He must have feared that under the City Council, with all its responsibilities for other handicapped groups as well as the wider population, at least some elements of such personal and quasi-familial work would be lost. Interestingly, he used the phrase 'Deaf Club' which is now common parlance. What the usage implies is that there is or needs to be some centre catering specifically for the general social needs of the deaf community, given their unique difficulties in communicating or socialising with the hearing population. This need would still exist however integrated individuals might become in education, employment or the wider social context. This thought was echoed by Mary Walton in her historical piece on the Psalter Lane Institute in the *Sharrovian*, already quoted in Chapter Six. She accepted that in the modern era, many functions were better provided by the local authority or central government:

> but there are individual and detailed needs which the Church and the voluntary society can in their turn claim to be better qualified to satisfy and it is to be hoped that in the future an arrangement can be made in which both official duty and private compassion will be allowed to play their appropriate parts.

★★★

The 1956 annual report still showed the Association in survival mode. Notwithstanding the Council's growing involvement, the number of deaf persons registered with the Association was greater than ever at 549, including 411 from Sheffield, 67 from the West Riding, 40 from Rotherham and 31 from Derbyshire. Special donations of £1150, including £500 from the Church Burgesses alone, continued to disguise the financial shortfall, although expenditure again exceeded income, and the future was looking less and less certain. It is extraordinary that in neither the 1956 nor the 1957 reports is there a single reference to the Council's developing an essentially competing deaf welfare service. Both reports have to be compared with the DPW Committee minutes to get the full picture. The March 1956 minutes record a further request from the Association for a grant of £500, but the sub-committee, 'after considering the Association's financial resources', decided that 'the application be refused'. In July 1957, the Medical Officer of Health reminded the sub-committee of its previous decision and reported a further application from the Association; the sub-committee saw no reason to change its views.

Yet a casual reader of the 1957 report might suppose that all was well. Even the finances, though still in deficit, were improving with a similar total of special donations plus £770 from the Sheffield University Students Rag Committee who had been persuaded to make the Association the chief recipient of their profits for the year. Surely a committee dominated by successful businessmen must have realised that one-off donations, however generous, would never replace a properly constituted regular income, large and reliable enough to ensure solvency and an independent future existence?

★★★

Whatever the committee may have thought, it soon became clear that Alan Stephenson had no illusions, neither about his personal position nor the prospects for privately funded charitable care for the Sheffield deaf. In 1951, he had married Beryl Saberton from Southend-on-Sea. It is not known when Alan and Beryl decided there was no future for them in deaf welfare work in Sheffield; perhaps Beryl disliked making her home in the Institute with her mother-in-law Doris and her sister-in-law Christine, who had returned to the Institute with three young children following the breakdown of her marriage. Perhaps, as the third Stephenson to act as missioner to several hundred profoundly deaf individuals, living on the job and inevitably sacrificing at least some of the privacy and pleasure of family life, Alan himself had finally decided there was no future for him in the Institute. He resigned as superintendent and he and Beryl left Sheffield in the summer of 1958 and moved to Looe in Cornwall where they opened a shop and their only son Timothy was born the following year.

The only surviving internal document from this final period of the Association is the December 1958 edition of the *Sharrow Magazine* which Alan had started for the deaf community as a much shorter and more cheaply produced successor to his grandfather's *Dacty*. There had been just three previous issues over a two-year period and they contained little of historical value or interest. The editorship was taken on by Alan's assistant Clive Davis and his first editorial commenced:

> *It was with regret that we bade farewell to our superintendent Mr Alan Stephenson and his wife Beryl last September. It is always sad to say goodbye to a good friend; but we wish them every success in their venture in Cornwall. All will read 'Niagara's' comments with full agreement.*

'Niagara' is a pseudonym but his or her account of the Stephensons' departure is worth summarising. Clearly Alan was well respected and his departure much regretted. Niagara reports on the many deaf members from Sheffield and elsewhere who attended a leaving party on 13th September 1958 at which Alan and Beryl were given an 'electric boiler', perhaps more practical than sentimental in value – 'Although we were doing our best to put on a smile on that evening it was no use pretending our happiness was not rather forced.' He goes on to say how proud they have been of Alan's connection with the Institute:

> *He has won himself a reputation for leadership in matters of welfare and recreation. To those of us who have been in closer touch with him and have known him best he has been more than wonderful [...] Although the evening by no means marked the end of our esteem and affection it was sad to remember that Mr Stephenson's presence amongst us was no longer a reality but a kindly and treasured memory.*

The question for the Association was simple: how to replace Alan? The Stephenson family had effectively run the Association on behalf of the committee for over 80 years, and through three generations since 1886 the family had known no other home; their lives and those of their deaf friends were inextricably intertwined. In the long run the strength and longevity of the connection might have become a weakness; perhaps it already had. Nevertheless, it was not surprising that the new superintendent was Doris Stephenson. Approaching retirement age, she had devoted almost 40 years to serving the deaf community. By now the committee must have accepted there was no future for the Institute, that the Council were determined to assume all the functions the Association had undertaken since 1862, and that Doris was the obvious caretaker manager until the doors were closed.

At a time when many local authorities were considering the provision of deaf welfare, including possible cooperation with local voluntary societies, it is surprising that the Sheffield situation was not even mentioned in the leading national journal which for over half a century had served, documented and where necessary argued powerfully for the interests of the deaf community. (The title of the monthly *British Deaf Times* was replaced at the end of 1954 when it amalgamated with two other journals to form the bi-monthly *British Deaf News*.) However, it may be that the editors were given no indication the problems existed. Each issue featured short reports from local societies; and the same few societies reappeared regularly. Sheffield was one of the few. Between 1955 and 1960, there were sixteen reports from the Institute. Each one contained a bright and breezy account of social events; annual parties, seaside trips, sporting achievements and the like. In the last edition of 1955, it was reported that a branch of the BDDA had opened in Sheffield, so they would certainly have been aware of the local situation. At the end of 1956, there was the first Sheffield use of the phrase 'Deaf Club', already indicating that the Association's functions might be reduced to the purely social rather than the full gamut of welfare work. The same issue mentioned that Alan Stephenson was the auditor of the Yorkshire Association of Welfare Officers, suggesting that he at least was not isolated from the wider context of his role. The Sheffield report in the first issue for 1959 congratulates 'our old superintendent Mr Alan Stephenson and his wife Beryl' on the birth of a son, and expresses the hope that they will visit the Institute soon. Even the issue in the autumn of 1960, when the Association finally closed, contains no more than a cheerful report of the last party, and the event was only given full significance by the *Sheffield Telegraph*. In these chatty and largely inconsequential reports in *British Deaf News*, there is no suggestion that the closure of the Institute was of any significance.

***

There is no surviving internal record of the last two years, but it is clear from the local press that the closure in 1960 was accompanied by some bitterness. It may have been inevitable, given the financial uncertainty, the resignation of the last professionally qualified superintendent and the decision of the City Council to create an entirely self-contained deaf welfare service, but it was not amicable. The defiant justification in the *Sheffield Telegraph* by Alderman W E Yorke, Chairman of the Public Health Committee and a Labour stalwart since the 1920s, reflects the frosty tone of the abortive negotiations of the previous years. He was replying to a leading article headed 'Unreasonable Decision' with subheadings 'Unwise' and 'Unjust'; in those days the *Sheffield Telegraph* was a determinedly Conservative organ, reliable in its opposition to much of the Labour-dominated Council's policies.

Alderman Yorke first set out his own credentials as a selfless volunteer for public service and an elected representative; he emphasised that the Council had in the past and would continue to make substantial grants to the voluntary sector. He paid tribute to the Association for its past services but he was certain that the Council could now provide a better service for deaf people. He refers to a letter dated 12th December 1955 from the Association in which they:

> agree in principle that the Corporation owing to its greater resources, should ultimately be able to provide a fuller service than a voluntary body would do.

This letter was dated eight months after the Council had given notice of terminating the existing agreement, which suggests that the committee had already accepted the Association's future was finite. Indeed it is apparent from Alderman Yorke's account that by this time the Council was fully staffed with qualified officers to care for the 3000 citizens suffering from varying physical and mental handicaps. This included training and placement services for the handicapped to the extent, he claimed, that there were more deaf and dumb persons in employment than at any time in the past. On the issue of social activities the Council had already budgeted £50,000 for a centre for disabled and handicapped persons on a city centre site. This comprehensive and now fully active scheme, he said, had been commended by the Minister of Health on a recent visit to Sheffield.

He then detailed the history of relations between the Council and the Association from the date of the first agreement in 1937. He confirmed that the Association had requested the Council to increase its contribution to £7 per head of the registered deaf and dumb, about £2500 p.a. The Council had asked itself two questions: could they provide a service at less cost by employing their own staff, and could such a directly provided service be more efficient and comprehensive? The answers had been clear for some time; the scheme devised by the Council had been drawn up several years previously and approved by the Minister in the early part of 1952. The Association had been informed of these conclusions in August 1953 and 'it could therefore have caused them no surprise when they were given notice to terminate the Agreement from 31st March 1955'. He accepted that the Council had initial staffing difficulties, and had invited the Association to discuss the effects of the new arrangements; yet no discussion took place until October 1955, 'after we had overcome certain obstacles in the appointment of certain technically trained staff, and our scheme was in full operation'. Eventually, a meeting did take place at which, Yorke said, the Association was still trying to persuade the Council to appoint them on an agency basis, but it was too late: staff now appointed would have to be dismissed, costs would be increased, and 'there would be a consequent lowering of the standard of service at which we are now aiming'.

The phrase 'now aiming' implied that the Council's service, whilst now irreversible, was far from complete or satisfactory, which no doubt explains why the Association was able to limp on under Alan and then Doris for several more years. It also explains why Alan, as a young married man hoping to start a family, could see no future in the post he had inherited from his father and grandfather. There is no doubt how the Council saw the future. Alderman Yorke's last paragraph was both congratulatory about the past but dismissive about the future:

> *I am sure we should all salute the local association for its services in the past, but we should now realise that there will be very little left for them to do as far as Sheffield is concerned, and I note from their balance sheet that their assets are in the region of £12,000, which is mainly derived from Sheffield sources, and this, of course, could be available for the Sheffield deaf and dumb in any supplementary service the association may care to provide for many years to come.*

Neither Alderman Yorke nor the Association in its annual reports made any mention of future provision for the deaf citizens of Rotherham and the nearer parts of the West Riding and Derbyshire for whom the Institute had provided services with contributions from their local authorities. Perhaps this was another reason why the doors were not finally closed until 1960, although given the distances involved it is unlikely that many members from the outlying areas came to 57 Psalter Lane on a regular basis. The three authorities would need some time to make alternative arrangements, but the new premises for the Sheffield deaf and other handicapped groups, which Alderman Yorke said were planned at a cost of £50,000, were not opened in nearby Grange Crescent for over twenty years, and until then 57 Psalter Lane continued to be used as the Council's 'Handicapped Persons Centre'.

★★★

So 'closed its doors' is a metaphor. Nevertheless, the deaf community were undoubtedly conscious of the great change. Under the heading 'Association Just Misses Century', the *Sheffield Telegraph* of 26th September 1960 reported on a farewell party the previous Saturday at Psalter Lane to mark the 'taking over' of the Association by the Public Health Committee. For 98 years they had 'succoured and found employment' for the Sheffield deaf, and Doris was quoted as saying that:

> *It's a pity that we have to lose our 400 members especially just short of 100 years of service to them.*

The report detailed the long connection of the Stephensons with the Association, and relates how the deaf men and women, 'using their own hand tapping language (sic)' came up to Doris to commiserate with her. A photograph encapsulated both the family connection and the future of deaf welfare. It shows three of George Stephenson's great grandchildren (Christine's children John, Vicki and Sally Anne, whose home was now at the Institute) and with them their grandmother Doris and, smiling benignly, James Dean, the Council's Deaf Welfare Officer. Henceforth, he and his successors would be directly responsible for the services which the Association and the Stephensons had provided ever since Thomas Widd was sent from Leeds to Sheffield in 1862 and first met Daniel Doncaster II and John Brown.

★★★

In order to formalise the take-over, legal decisions had to be taken by the City Council and the Charity Commission. On 22nd August 1960, the Public Health Committee passed two resolutions. The first was headed 'Sheffield Association in Aid of the Adult Deaf and Dumb – Acquisition of Property':

> That subject to the receipt of any necessary consents, the sum of £8500, together with a sum to be agreed in respect of costs, be paid to the Sheffield Association for the Adult Deaf and Dumb for the acquisition of their freehold interest in the land and buildings at 57 Psalter Lane for use as a handicapped persons centre and that the Corporate Common Seal be affixed to any necessary documents.

The second resolution was presumably a quid pro quo demanded by the Asociation's negotiators, especially with regard to religious observance, and was headed 'Undertaking re. provision of Welfare etc. Services':

> That approval be given to the terms of an undertaking to be given to the Sheffield Association in aid of the Adult Deaf and Dumb which provides that the welfare and religious services for the deaf and dumb at present provided by the Association at 57 Psalter Lane will be provided by the Corporation on a comparable scale, subject to their being sufficient demand for such services and that the Town Clerk be authorised to sign the necessary undertaking.

So much for the property and the functions of the Association, but what of the contents of the Institute and its chapel, some of which had been crafted by deaf members of the community over many years? Presumably this took longer to negotiate, together with the removal of the Stephenson family's own possessions to their new homes, but a further resolution was passed on 24th October 1960:

> That subject to the receipt of any necessary consents, the sum of £585 be paid to the Sheffield Association for the Aid of the Adult Deaf and Dumb for certain fixtures and fittings in accordance with the details now reported, at the Deaf and Dumb Institute 57 Psalter Lane, which premises the Corporation has acquired from the Association.

The Association was a registered charity (and remained so until 2013, see Chapter Eight) and its regulation under the Charities Act 1960 was henceforth governed by a scheme approved by the Charity Commissioners on 23rd October 1961. The remaining funds, (the unused capital plus the net proceeds of the sale of the property and the fixtures and fittings at 57 Psalter Lane) were invested in the name of the Official Custodian for Charities and administered by a body of three nominative and six co-optative trustees, who had to be resident or engaged in business in or near Sheffield. The first co-optative trustees largely comprised those who had served on the committee for the last few years. The first chairman was the accountant Jarvis Barber, who for the last couple of years had been both Hon. Secretary and Hon. Treasurer and the last descendant of Daniel Doncaster II to play any part in the Association, Basil Doncaster having died in 1959. The others were John Matthews, a retired bank manager, Percival Phillips, a retired steel company director, the solicitor Brian Pye-Smith, John Osborn, a director of the family steel company and Conservative MP, and Reverend Reginald Robson. (Robson was vicar of St Andrews, the parish church, and had become closely associated with the Institute; he had organised a substantial collection to add to the special donations when it was still hoped to keep the Association afloat.)

After proper administrative expenses, the next item provided that the trustees:

> *may pay to Doris Marie Stephenson who was the superintendent*
> *of the buildings known as 57 Psalter Lane Sheffield and formerly*
> *belonging to the charity as from the date of her retirement from that*
> *post a pension at the rate of not more than £2.10s a week out of the*
> *income of the charity.*

Despite the 'may' and 'not more than' it is believed the pension was paid in full until Doris's death in 1971. It was not overly generous; accommodation within the Institute had been integral to the Stephenson family since 1886, including 40 years of Doris's family life, and her younger daughter Christine and three young children were also displaced.

Otherwise the trustees were empowered to use their income to make grants to 'deaf and dumb persons over sixteen' living in and around Sheffield, especially:

> *for the purposes of the religious, educational and recreative welfare*
> *of such persons and the donation of money in aid of the funds of*
> *any institutions or organisations established or to be established and*
> *having for their object any of the purposes aforesaid […] [but] the*
> *funds or income of the charity shall not be applied in relief of rates,*
> *taxes or other public funds.*

Finally, there is a schedule to show the total funds now available and invested by the Official Custodian: £6,379. 18s.6d in 4 ½ % Conversion Stock 1964 and £9,764.10s.1d in 4% Consolidated Stock, a total of just over £16,000.

So, 99 years after the inaugural meeting set up by James Foulston and his committee from Leeds, together with Thomas Widd and Daniel Doncaster II and chaired by John Brown as Mayor – almost certainly attended by George Stephenson's profoundly deaf parents amongst many others of their friends and well-wishers – the Association was left with modest capital and trustees empowered to pay a small pension to the last of the family to serve the deaf community, and otherwise make grants to supplement the work of the Council.

★★★

What are we to make of this dispiriting end? In part it was an example of a historical process originating in the Victorian era and culminating in the immediate post-war period; replacing or supplementing private philanthropy by comprehensive national or local provision funded out of general taxation or local rates. In the period after 1960, many of the missions to the deaf were to close, absorbed by local authorities under the provisions of the 1948 Act or acting on their behalf and with their financial support under Agency Agreements. On the other hand, the very first of the missions to close its doors was Sheffield. Why?

In the first place, almost from the opening of the Charles Street Institute in 1886, the Association was slow to adapt to changing circumstances. It is symptomatic that the format, length and contents of the annual reports were almost unchanged from 1887 to 1957. The membership of the committee and the Hon. Secretaries and Treasurers were similarly slow to change, including for many decades members of the founding Doncaster family and their Doncaster and Barber descendants, together with friends or colleagues in the professions and the steel industry. From 1937, representatives of two of the local authorities were included by virtue of their financial support, but at no time after the retirement of Daniel Doncaster III and Robert Renton Eadon was there any deaf committee member, nor does any deaf member of the Institute contribute to the annual report.

The committee and their superintendents (and their wives, though no woman was ever elected to the committee) shared a strong sense of social duty in the best traditions of Victorian philanthropy, combined in the case of the Doncasters and the Stephensons with profound deafness in their own families. In the early years there was no difficulty in attracting substantial capital donations and annual subscriptions to fulfil the objectives they had set themselves. Nevertheless, it seems that after this first period the organisation failed to move forward as the original founders died and were replaced by their younger relatives or business and professional associates.

One constant, from well before the Great War, was the committee's complaint that the citizens of Sheffield did not appreciate the value of the Association's work, or offer sufficient financial support. Looking at the lists of subscriptions printed in the annual reports, two features are constant: that the same 100 or so names appear for years at a time, and most of the amounts they volunteer are in the region of £1 or £2. The total varies but until the last desperate years in the mid-1950s, there was no marked increase after the Edwardian period. The committee were aware of the increasing risks of reliance on such a static source of income, but made no effort at all until it was far too late to widen the base of support or encourage donors to increase their gifts in line with inflation.

Perhaps there was another weakness which in the long run perpetuated the impression of an increasingly sclerotic organisation – the simple fact that the same family effectively ran the Institute for all its active life after the first nine years under Joseph Farrar. It was not that George, Colin, Alan and Doris Stephenson failed to give their all to their work of care and support; indeed for most of the time it was literally a 24-hour job, 365 days a year, living as they all did within the Institute. The problem was rather that the committee, meeting when required and quite properly giving their superintendents full responsibility for daily management and themselves fully absorbed in their own business and professional careers, were content with the status quo and seemingly never even considered whether anyone else should be appointed when a vacancy occurred.

There is no doubt that George was a forbidding and authoritarian figure in his work for deaf people, in his family life, and (when he chose to take part) in the wider world of deaf welfare. The fact that he took up the work at the age of 26 and remained in post until retiring at 75, and moreover established his youngest son as his assistant, left the committee with little chance of considering an alternative appointment in 1920. Certainly, there is no evidence they ever did. Exactly the same could be said in 1953; Colin had taken over at the age of 27, worked unceasingly on both local and national levels for 33 years, and ensured that his son obtained the National Diploma qualification. Alan commenced his career as his father's assistant, and like Colin became superintendent at the age of 27. By 1958, it was long past the time when the committee could look for any outside recruit, and they must have been grateful that there was still an experienced family member to take over, despite her gender, age and lack of formal qualification.

In the post-war context of radical social and political change, an organisation in which both the governing committee and the professional carers had seemed almost unchanged for nearly a century could easily be seen as outmoded and inadequate. Add to this the chronic financial difficulties of the Sheffield Association, and the development of a more publicly accountable and solidly financed model was inevitable. As the voluntary movement matured, in the field of deaf welfare as in many other areas of social life, governments and politicians began to accept that the state should play a larger and finally, more dominant role.

The increasing influence of the National Institute for the Deaf and its regional organisation, the Eichholz Report, the support the voluntary societies received from the Public Assistance Committees after 1930, and the whole paraphernalia of the Welfare State embodied for deaf welfare in Section 29 of the National Assistance Act 1948, ensured that the voluntary movement declined over the years, even if many missions were able to continue their work under Agency Agreements in areas where the local authority was unwilling or unable to create their own inclusive departments.

Yet none of this tells us why Sheffield was the *very first* such voluntary society to fold its tent and steal away. Two factors were of primary significance, both exemplified in Alderman Yorke's letter in the local press. Here perhaps more than elsewhere in the country there was a real contrast in values and assumptions between the voluntary and the municipal. On the one hand, Sheffield was then, as it has been throughout the modern era, a citadel of municipal socialism, with an unbroken Labour majority on the City Council from the 1920s to the 1980s and, with two short-term exceptions, continuing to the present day. As an integral part of the post-war Labour government's creation of an inclusive Welfare State on Beveridge principles, the Council was empowered and then required to create comprehensive systems to care for all handicapped persons and set about the task as soon as appropriate advice was received from the Minister of Health.

The organisation the Council replaced could be seen as poorly financed and unchanging, founded and still governed by an unelected and self-perpetuating group of precisely those wealthy and middle-class businessmen and professionals the city councillors were most likely to distrust – private steel owners, their professional advisers, a Conservative MP and an Anglican vicar. So it is not surprising the Public Health Committee decided it was right to replace the Association with a specialist department financed by the rate-paying citizens of Sheffield and staffed by officers appointed by their elected representatives. There is no reason to doubt that both sides had the interests of deaf people at heart; it is simply that a cultural clash rooted in social and political history led to completely contrasting ways of serving those interests.

***

That leaves only the most uncomfortable of questions, briefly mentioned in the Introduction and in summarising George Stephenson's work in Chapter Four. Were the roles and functions of the missioner/ superintendents of the voluntary societies wholly beneficial, or were there inherent disadvantages which would become more obvious as society evolved; was the model entirely fit for purpose, and if so for how long? Questions like these were implicit in the provisions of the National Assistance Act and in the bitter stand-off between the Association and the Council in the final five years, but they were only raised openly by some of those most closely concerned in the following years.

In his thesis, Lysons not only detailed the history of the voluntary movement; he also analysed the contemporary situation. He described, and to some extent queried, the staffing, qualifications, training and status of the missioners, and although never published in book form, his findings were well known to professionals in the field. Indeed, the most insightful contemporary critique I have found was the work of an unexpected hand. We have met Rev George Cuthbert Firth (1919–1997) as the author of *Chosen Vessels*. A fourth generation Anglican clergyman, Firth compiled his survey during retirement from a lifetime's service as a missioner, with a wealth of largely laudatory biography and personal or second-hand anecdotes about his fellow missioners, including the Stephensons and over 100 more.

It is therefore all the more intriguing to read his clear-sighted and often caustic summary of the missioner role in his review of Lysons' thesis in the Winter 1965 issue of *British Deaf News*. At the time of this review Firth was still an active missioner, and it was written twenty years before his much gentler *Chosen Vessels.*. His doubts about the role were apparent in his description of the typical missioner's lifestyle, quoted by Lysons and reproduced in Chapter Three. Although written as a review, Firth's 1965 essay is more of a commentary on the main issues, in some ways more powerful because it is not obscured in the painstakingly thorough accumulation of factual material in Lysons' own text.

Firth bemoans the lack of historical material available before Lysons commenced his research, welcomes all the factual findings unreservedly, and describes the results as:

> *Perfectly frank and perfectly fair [...] Mr Lysons draws a picture of muddle, parochialism, sectarian interest, lack of imagination, stubborn traditionalism, and a particular folly to which I shall refer below.*

He starts by reverting to the old quarrel between the oralist schools and the signing institutes:

> *The deep wound in the body politic, as regards the deaf, is the antagonism between schools for the deaf and the missions. Whereas in the early days of manualism, the school not only gave birth to the mission, but its teachers went beyond the school gates to become the first missioners; with the coming of oralism all this was reversed and the two became independent and antagonistic.*

Firth, pointing the moral more succinctly than Lysons, blames both sides for this antagonism. It is the responsibility of both the adult welfare societies and the schools to ensure a smooth transition from one to the other; the children should be taught by whatever system is best suited to their individual needs and aptitudes; as they move back into the adult world of the societies, the schools must prepare them thoroughly for this sometimes difficult transition.

Secondly, many missioners regard their total dedication to their work and the lives of their deaf members as an advantage, but from his own experience and observation of others in the same role, Firth sees the dangers:

> *Many (missioners) have few interests outside the deaf, live among them, marry them, have friends among them, eat, drink and sleep deafness from morning to night… Lysons feels there is a danger that the welfare worker will tend to impose his own religious, political and philosophical opinions on people who know no other point of view than his.*

Naturally, this leads to the question of recruitment of deaf welfare workers:

> *Lysons says frankly that deaf welfare would do much better if the workers were better educated. He says it is a pity that there is not a wider field of recruitment than the accident of birth (of deaf parents) or of personal affliction (deafness in a child, or in the man himself) which lead so many, quite understandably, to volunteer for entry into deaf welfare work.*

What is the likely result of antagonism between the schools and the missioners, entirely engrossed in and sometimes overwhelmed by their many duties, and recruited so often from deaf families? Here we revert to the question of a deaf subculture – whether it exists and if so its significance. Firth was not convinced there is such a creature, but it was a powerful enough idea to have clear and damaging effects:

> *Again Lysons says there is clear evidence that a deaf 'subculture' is fostered by the missions, whether deliberately or subconsciously. This tendency, which is so sharply resented by the schools, has been greatly exaggerated, but it exists nonetheless. To a certain extent the deaf themselves, manual or oral, demand a retreat from the exigencies of the hearing world. Like tends to attract like, and deaf societies of one kind or another are bound to persist.*

A missioner himself, as devoted to his charges as any of his colleagues, Firth nevertheless came to believe that in the end, integration in hearing society is the ultimate objective, insofar as it is possible and achievable and is actually what deaf individuals want for themselves. He echoes Lysons' plea that if only missioners and others would just stand back and do some basic research, most especially into what deaf people need and want, everybody would be much happier.

Finally, Firth reaches conclusions which he says are implied rather than openly stated in Lysons' thesis; here he is at his most acerbic, in a manner which Lysons might have felt excessive in an academic treatise. He says the word 'missioner' is not accidental; it refers not only to the evangelical motives of the early workers, but is uncomfortably close to 'missionary' – a pioneer in a hostile world:

(The missioner) had to do everything for himself. He sought out the deaf, studied and cared for their problems, organised their employment and their domestic social life. He spoke for and fought for the society which employed him; organised that as well, and touted for its funds. He helped to recruit, train and establish the status of his colleagues. He encountered and overcame the prejudice or indifference, and sometimes the hostility, of powerful social forces, to obtain the co-operation and assistance he needed for the welfare of the deaf.

Martin Smith described in stark terms the role which he embodied and then made to 'vanish' over his 26 years in Leeds: 'The missioner's role was in essence to manipulate the emotionally charged ground between benefactors and receivers. The missioners determined need and dependency but maintained control over their charges and their own jobs.' (Smith, 2011, p97) How and why did this uniquely isolated and demanding role develop? Firth is very clear:

It happened in the deaf world because the missioners have allowed it to happen. Societies have raised enough money for their superintendent's modest salary and expenses, and have considered that this constituted the full discharge of their obligations to the deaf; and have been only too glad, thanks to the missioner's oversensitive sense of duty, to escape any further responsibility.

Firth had no doubt that this era was coming to an end. The societies and their missioners only had a future if they accepted the need to work with those with the financial resources and professional skills to support deaf people in accordance with all their needs, and they must accept this lesser role without sacrificing their personal lives in a constant striving to be all things to all deaf persons.

Every member of a Society Committee should be led to give his whole personal time, attention and talents to the deaf people in the care of his Society; and the trained worker should deliberately school himself to work as a member of a team, and insist that others so regard him. His greatest service to his beloved deaf will now be to talk, and fight, and organise himself out of a job, or at least into the background [...] The plain fact is we are just not up to it on our own; we haven't enough education, influence, time or numbers to carry the job any further. It is time the pioneer boys began to take a back seat.

This powerful and effective critique was testament to Firth's courage and clarity of thought, as well as to Lysons' groundbreaking research of which it was nominally a review. Both of them anticipated and were reflected in the experiences of the following 25 years described in telling detail by Martin Smith, which are touched on by way of contrast to the Sheffield story in Chapter Eight.

★★★

I located Lysons' thesis early in my research, and it was extremely useful in the first narrative draft, as was Firth's *Chosen Vessels*. In fact, none of this account would have been possible without them. The review in *British Deaf News*, however, only came to my attention quite late, and immediately seemed relevant to any final summary of the demise of the Sheffield Association and the careers of the Stephensons.

I should emphasise that although Firth probably knew and may have met both Colin and Alan Stephenson, neither he nor Lysons had any direct knowledge of the Sheffield situation. The Institute had already closed a couple of years before Lysons completed his thesis and five years before Firth's article. Yet in both cases, all they said could easily have been based on the Sheffield experience, a very paradigm of the voluntary society and the role of its missioners. In fact, Sheffield was in one respect unique; as Firth said it was the only voluntary society dominated for almost all its existence by the professional leadership of three members of the same family. (He could have said four, to include Doris.)

What may not have been unique but was certainly unusual was the degree to which the committee was led for nearly all its history by a close knit self-perpetuating group from a narrow social band, initially comprising the Doncasters, the Barbers, and their business colleagues and friends, and rarely extended much further. The committee's role has to be assessed; they may have left the administrative detail and the welfare work to their superintendents, but it was for them to decide policy. If Lysons and Firth had been asked to advise them in the vital last few years, they might have urged a more active engagement with the work of the Association for which they had accepted responsibility. If the Association was to have a future at all it would have to be in partnership with and as agents of the Council; this was something the committee never recognised or accepted. They showed no appreciation of the inevitable, persisted in an ad hoc search for charitable donations, and maintained this doomed strategy even after the Council had created its own department, appointed its own staff and cancelled its financial support for the Association. They failed to understand that the social and political context had changed so much that the model their predecessors had created in the late nineteenth century needed substantial modification. They had to swallow their collective pride and find a role in which deaf people could still benefit from the long experience of their successive superintendents. There is no evidence that they did so.

And what of the superintendents themselves? George Stephenson was almost a caricature of Firth's typical missioner, with all his virtues and faults. The son of profoundly deaf parents, a pious and dominant personality, engaged with the deaf night and day for almost 50 years and for the last 34 of those years living with his wives and children in the Institute. Within that enclosed setting he regarded his 'deaf and dumb friends' as an extended family for which he was totally responsible, catering for all their needs and problems, sermonising and educating them, insisting on abstinence and high moral standards, directing their leisure activities, acting as their interpreter and intermediary with the outside world. As he said himself, a self appointed foster father.

Colin Stephenson shared his father's devotion to the deaf members of the Institute, his pious certainties about their intrinsic worth and the moral standards to which they should aspire, and like George, he saw them more like an extended family than clients for whom he provided professional services. He thought of himself as their teacher and guide, a spiritual and temporal father figure. Yet there were differences between father and son; Colin began to play a substantial part in national organisations for the deaf and had a greater understanding of the social and political context of his work and the financial limitations of the voluntary movement. His managerial and negotiating capacities led to the amicable settlement he made with Sheffield Corporation, Rotherham and the West Riding in the late 1930s, winning at least a temporary relief from financial weakness whilst ceding no significant interference with his work. He was moving with the times in ways his father would scarcely have recognised, but within the Institute the paternalistic ethos was unchanged – 'their anxieties are ours'.

Given the privations of the 1939–45 war and the creation of the Welfare State, it is difficult to know how far Colin adjusted his thinking to allow for the profound organisational changes implied by Section 29 of the National Assistance Act 1948. What we can say is that he maintained the total authority within the daily life of the Institute which Firth and Lysons believed could not be sustained. Yet, had he survived another few years he might have reached a satisfactory resolution of the stand-off with the Sheffield Corporation. Impossible to say, better simply to quote an experienced social worker with deaf people, herself the child of a deaf family who were members of the Institute during Colin's lifetime and before, who in discussion with me said of the Stephensons: 'Whatever you say about them, who else *was* there in their time to help the deaf in the way they did?'

In the end it was Alan Stephenson who faced the rapidly changing political situation and the threat to his career and the future of the Association which the family had served since the 1870s. Like both his father and grandfather he came to the work through the accident of birth and a deaf heritage; like them he was only 27 when he became superintendent, and had lived his entire family life within the Institute. His later career in deaf welfare (after a few years in Cornwall) showed that he was capable of working successfully within a local authority and its financial resources. What he could not survive in Sheffield was the determination of the Council to create its own organisation and the equal determination of his committee to remain financially and organisationally independent. He inherited a role which was no longer tenable. For the Stephensons, and the Sheffield Association, after nearly a century of service, their work was done.

8

THE LAST HALF CENTURY 1960-2015

*'There was No Evidence to Support the Argument for the
Superiority of the Voluntary over the Statutory Services
which is Becoming Increasingly Fashionable'*

In October and November 1960 *The Silent World* reprinted a paper given
by P S Taylor to the AGM of the Western Region of the NID. Taylor was
one of the authors of the Younghusband Report on the future of social
work training, and was invited to the meeting because the wide-ranging
recommendations of the report included sections on deaf welfare and his
audience needed clarification.

Taylor summarised the history of the voluntary movement, the early
involvement of local authorities in the 1930s and the powers they were
given by the National Assistance Act 1948. The reactions of the authorities
had been variable, which was unsatisfactory:

> *The first thing to be done, we thought, was to persuade the
> authorities to take a greater interest in work for the deaf and to
> increase the number of people in the local authority service who
> know something of their needs.*

How was this to be achieved? The report envisaged that social workers
would be mainly responsible for deaf welfare and recommended that
one or more in each authority should learn to communicate with deaf
people; it was also hoped that the authorities would provide deaf clubs
and social activities, but perhaps with a nod to the evangelical history of

much of the voluntary movement they should not assume responsibilities for spiritual care, merely ensure it continued to be available. Taylor said his colleagues did not want to appear too prescriptive about administrative arrangements, as far as they were concerned co-operation between the local authorities and the remaining voluntary associations would be perfectly acceptable. It would be undesirable to have a split service, but 'with goodwill on both sides' there was a lot to be said for a service which combined the statutory and the voluntary. For instance, the Deaf Welfare Officer to be appointed by the authority might well be the superintendent of the local voluntary society. Spiritual care might not be appropriate for Council employees but could remain the work of chaplains appointed by each diocese. Nonetheless, the expectation was clear. The greater part of deaf welfare should be provided by the local authorities, so perhaps his kind remarks on the historic contributions of the voluntary sector and the chances of future co-operation were designed to quieten the fears of those of his listeners whose careers had been based in the missions.

An earlier article in *The Silent World* had suggested the Younghusband proposals implied a steady decline in specialist Deaf Welfare Officers on grounds of economy, which Taylor emphatically denied. In fact, he expected each authority would need to employ at least one officer fully qualified by the Deaf Welfare Examination Board, but he accepted that the local authorities had the resources to provide a full deaf welfare service which the uncertain finances of voluntary societies could not guarantee.

Taylor made every effort to convince his listeners that there could be a continuing and important, if lesser role, for the voluntary sector. Nevertheless, at the end of the day the Younghusband Report centred on training for the nascent social worker profession, with a nationally recognised Certificate in Social Work and a National Council for Social Work Training. It was hoped that the NID and others involved in deaf welfare would be represented on the Council, and that all social workers would be required to obtain the certificate and could then further their training, experience and status by specialisation in deaf welfare under the DWEB.

So Younghusband proposed that deaf welfare would cease to be the preserve of charitable societies with their voluntary committees and missioner/superintendents, and instead of being parcelled out between Public Health, Education and Children's Departments services for deaf adults would be included within the growing remit of social work.

Whereas Public Health Committees regarded deaf people as discrete individuals with a particular handicap, Social Services would see them as one client group amongst many. Following the recommendations of the 1968 Seebohm Report all this would be overseen under the Local Authority Social Services Act 1970, supplemented in the case of deaf and other handicapped groups by the Chronically Sick and Disabled Persons Act 1970.

★★★

Within the new framework of social worker teams employed by local authorities, what place could be found for the surviving voluntary societies? We have seen the answer in Sheffield, but could a partnership of the charitable and the municipal work elsewhere? It is ironic that one of the few published accounts of successful cooperation comes from Leeds, the cradle of the voluntary movement in Yorkshire including the foundation of the Sheffield Association in 1862. Martin Smith's whole career in deaf welfare from the 1950s to his retirement in 1992 provides the answer – yes, it could. There were many difficulties along the way, political and personal, and many major issues to be resolved. At the same time Smith was acutely aware that he had to move decisively away from the traditional role epitomised by the Stephensons. The essence of his story is clear from his title – *The Vanishing Missioner.*

Martin Smith had no family or other connection with deaf adults or schools, or with Leeds, before he commenced training with the Leeds Incorporated Institution for Blind and Deaf People which became his life's work. He spent the first four years as a trainee, obtaining a qualification from the Deaf Welfare Examination Board followed by five years working at the deaf institutes in Cheshire and Oldham. From these experiences he learned much about what he saw as right and wrong in the way missions had operated, and particularly that deaf people had found it only too easy to rely on their superintendents to be available 24/7 to deal with all their problems, whether crucial or trivial. Already, he was beginning to question the traditional role for which he was being trained:

> *I had lived and worked in a busy community whose members had been taught how to behave. They had within the Institute a*

well ordered routine designed to provide them with something of a life. Hearing people who were immensely powerful controlled them. These people were the missioners, the welfare officers or the superintendents; each name was interchangeable. The missioners because of the role as a carer of souls. The welfare officer because of the growing aspect of local authority influence and funding. The superintendent because of the traditional role, which Victorian society required for people who live in institutions with or without walls. The role wrapped them together.

(SMITH, 2011, P22)

Smith returned to Leeds in 1966 as superintendent of the institute's Deaf Department with nearly 700 deaf members; like George, Colin and Alan Stephenson he was not yet 30 years of age. Six years after the Sheffield Institute closed, he was faced with two huge issues which the Stephensons had hardly met and never had to surmount; working on an occasionally fractious and divisive basis with the Social Services Department of Leeds City Council, and simultaneously redefining the role he had inherited from generations of missioners in a way which made sense in the second half of the twentieth century. The struggles this involved over the next 26 years are too detailed for this account and any reader who wants to understand how he succeeded must read *The Vanishing Missioner*, but certain salient aspects of the story are relevant to what happened in Sheffield both before and after 1960.

The role of Principal which Smith developed for himself remained relevant in a rapidly changing social climate and fostered an independence of choice and decision by deaf people which were rare within the traditional institutes. It was not all plain sailing; Social Services became increasingly involved in the whole range of deaf welfare, a process to which Smith strongly objected. He would have preferred to provide social service functions within the Leeds Institute on an agency basis with 'his' own social worker team. This was not to be, so that Smith's role as Principal was inevitably reduced, but he continued to redefine his relationship with the deaf community through empowerment, refusing to make decisions which they could and 'should' make for themselves and cajoling them to form and to staff their own committees for social and everyday administrative purposes. Smith is not convinced by the concept of a deaf subculture, but emphasised in discussion with me that for deaf people domination by old style superintendents has been largely replaced by a culture of choice and independence – this was the real benefit of making the missioner vanish.

In the 1970s, the Leeds Institute had to purchase new premises and the move clarified Smith's approach to services for deaf people which he summarised for his committee in his 1975 annual report:

> *Now we could look at our building and say, there are three levels of service:-*
>
> *1 Providing technical assistance for those who wish to remain independent, and could be helped in their independence by physical aids*
>
> *2 Providing statutory assistance to handicapped people*
>
> *3 Providing the hearing impaired with the facilities to develop their own social and recreational life, freed from the strain and embarrassment of communication with hearing people. This area to be for those who recognise and accept their disability.*

This categorisation of social needs seems very different from the discrete subculture envisioned by Harlan Lane and Paddy Ladd. I cannot evaluate such contrasting perspectives, but Smith certainly identified two of the essential elements which distinguish profoundly deaf people from the rest of society; their central problem is one of communication, and where this is acute enough to seem insurmountable they may choose to remain apart, to opt for segregation rather than integration, to regard themselves as Deaf rather than simply deaf.

★★★

I have drawn particular attention to this aspect of Smith's thought because it links with another source. What Smith learned from practical experience of working with deaf people seems remarkably similar to the insights in Sally Sainsbury's *Deaf Worlds* (1986), and specifically her subtitle *A Study of Integration, Segregation and Disability.* An academic specialist in disability studies, Sainsbury based her research on detailed interviews with over 170 deaf people of both sexes and varying ages, including those living at home, in institutions, hostels, hospitals and psychiatric units. The result is a detailed description of the central issues facing deaf people 25 years after the Sheffield Institute closed.

Sainsbury surveyed many aspects of deaf lives in the 1980s but had much to say about the formal network of services. The central problem for the profoundly deaf was and always had been communication and interpretation. Apart from deaf parents, siblings or close friends from the deaf schools, other family friends and neighbours were of less use in resolving the problems of the speechless. The same was true of carers in institutions, unless they had an adequate level of signing skills. The result was that deaf people often preferred to socialise within the deaf clubs; they were integrated into their own subculture but segregated from hearing society. For this reason it was vital for the formal network to be adequately staffed by qualified BSL signers and to have 'on tap' skilled interpreters for dealings with medical, legal and other external authorities. Whether these essential communicators were available through the voluntary movement or social service departments was less important. In 1985, Sainsbury could still say that 'many' local authorities continued to provide deaf services through the voluntary sector and the deaf clubs which were 'largely the creation of the voluntary specialist societies'. On the other hand, she did not share the nostalgia of some for the good old days of the missioners:

> *But there was no evidence to support the argument for the superiority of the voluntary over the statutory services which is becoming increasingly fashionable. The type of facility rather than the method of financing is the most important factor in creating an ambience within which deaf people feel at ease in their relationships with the hearing community.*
>
> (SAINSBURY, 1986, p224)

Because Section 29 of the National Assistance Act was not detailed or prescriptive, the local authorities tended in the early years to replicate what they had provided for blind people since the 1920s; home visits and employment opportunities, two but only two of the traditional functions of the voluntary societies. But during the 1960s and 1970s, a much wider range of social services became important and for deaf welfare this placed great emphasis on the need for skilled interpreters. In turn this had an unfortunate effect, the marginalisation or segregation of deaf people and their specific needs:

> *The needs which the deaf shared with other groups for family support and so on would be emphasised, while the interpreting role of the deaf specialist would be utilised only when substantial problems of communication arose. But in practice considerable ambivalence soon emerged about the role of specialists, and their relationships with area teams and with non-specialists generally. In recent years it has become clear that the effect of the emphasis on genericism and the focus on work with families, and particularly with children, has been to isolate the deaf specialist.*
>
> (SAINSBURY, 1986, PP. 225–6)

Sainsbury's interviewees attached great value to deaf specialists with full communication and interpreting skills. One group she interviewed was particularly distraught when the only competent signer on their local authority staff left and was not replaced; often where nobody was available to interpret, deaf individuals preferred to keep their problems to themselves. If profoundly deaf people were to avoid isolation and achieve some degree of integration, communication with their social workers and the provision of interpreting services were equally necessary. In the missions led by superintendents with full signing skills, both functions were fulfilled by a single dominant figure with all the dangers inherent in that role, but if deaf people are to benefit from a team of professional social workers it is vital that a sufficient number have the appropriate skills.

Sainsbury concluded that the chance of successful integration depended on the individual's degree of deafness and intellectual and psychological capacity to achieve usable communication with the hearing world without undue reliance on the support of signers and interpreters. The more profound the deafness, particularly in the absence of readily available interpreters, the less the chance of integration into hearing society and the more important the social comfort of the deaf community, whether or not this amounted to segregation from the 'outside' world.

The conclusions which Sainsbury reached from her painstaking research are clear:

> *It became apparent that the existence of the deaf community added another dimension to the question of what constituted integration, and what was meant by segregation. For while deaf people usually engage in normal activity, they do not do so with the hearing. Most appeared to be effectively insulated from the hearing society by the deaf community.*
>
> (SAINSBURY, 1986, P296)

She also returned to the importance of specialist social work provision and the danger of it being marginalised in the well-meaning effort to integrate deaf welfare services within the normal framework of general provision:

> *The importance of the deaf community in sustaining deaf people in their attempt to achieve a way of life which closely resembled that of the hearing raises the question of the role of specialist provision. In the recent past there has been a tendency to denigrate specialist provision in the interests of normalisation and integration. Yet it is the logic of this study that there is a need to reinforce and extend specialist provision.*
>
> (SAINSBURY, 1986, P296)

The profoundly deaf rely heavily on their integration into the deaf community and to that extent are socially segregated from hearing or 'normal' society. Yet they have as much need of contact with that society as anyone, and only the specialist social worker is able to provide the necessary means of communication:

> *And because they mediate between the deaf and hearing worlds across the full range of activities, including for instance employment, their role is much wider than that normally associated with social work.*
>
> (SAINSBURY, 1986, P298)

★★★

Taylor's 1960 paper to the NID clearly indicated how the Younghusband authors envisaged the development of social work for deaf people. Martin Smith's memoir shows how it was possible for the voluntary sector to continue its traditional work in tandem with the local authorities and at the same time transform the role of the traditional missioners so that such co-operation remained workable, and by the 1980s the new framework was sufficiently established for Sainsbury to examine its effectiveness through the eyes of deaf service users. For an authoritative view on how deaf welfare services progressed over the next years, we move forward to the 1990s and the ominously titled *A Service on the Edge* (1997).

This sober and sobering document was the report of an 'Inspection of Services for Deaf and Hard of Hearing People' by the Social Services Inspectorate of the Department of Health. It was based on a rigorous inspection of provision in eight local authorities, chosen to be representative and including urban and rural areas, North and South, and two London boroughs. Neither Sheffield nor Leeds were included, and in only one of the authorities was there still an active voluntary association cooperating with the social services department. The inspectors acknowledged that much good work was done at various times and in various places, but 'the quality and extent of the services across the authorities was disappointing with only one presenting a generally satisfactory picture'.

The legislative framework had recently changed again and fresh thinking and a revised approach were needed:

> *In the past services for people who are deaf or hard of hearing have been seen as a specialist area because of the particular communication needs which arise. Mainstream managers and specialist staff have not always understood the issue or felt able to influence practice. However the Disability Discrimination Act 1995, (now subsumed in the Equality Act 2010) now requires all parts of social services to take reasonable steps to make their services available to deaf and hard of hearing people. Additionally the role of specialist teams is evolving, increasingly moving away from approaches which encourage dependency rather than independent living.*
>
> A SERVICE ON THE EDGE, 1997 (INTRODUCTION)

So what was presently wrong? Why was the service 'on the edge'? It started at the beginning; procedures for assessment were poorly developed or non-existent and deaf people themselves were often unaware of the existence or importance of assessment. The specialist services which were provided were bedevilled by overwork, a lack of focus and little effective management; there was rarely any provision for the vital gap between school and adulthood; and the provision of equipment for help with communication or safety was patchy. On the crucial area of communication and the skills required, general social workers were not fully aware of the needs of deaf people, and of the specialists only 18% had Stage 3 qualification in BSL which is considered the minimum for effective support. The provision of interpretation services was inadequate in seven of the eight authorities; it was often provided by specialist workers with inadequate skills who were already under great pressure, there was a shortage of fully qualified independent BSL/English interpreters, and in hospital environments there was frequently no interpretation available at all. Access even to the specialist social workers was often problematic because few reception staff had any signing abilities, which led to frustration on both sides with reliance on written notes, simple gestures or (unbelievably) answerphones; access to other areas of social service departments was even more hit and miss. Information about available services for the deaf was poor or incomplete and inaccessible to anyone without a good command of written English. Above all, at the top of the departments there was limited strategic thinking and too much reliance on traditional practice; there was little or no effective consultation with the deaf community as the actual or potential users of the services provided.

Local authority social workers and their managers must have been disheartened by these stringent conclusions, but at least the inspectors made recommendations on how matters could improve. At the outset it was vital that assessment of the needs of deaf people should take account of the cultural and the disability models of deafness, highlight the risks of dependency, allow for the long term future of young deaf adults, and include consideration of ethnic minorities and those with complex needs. A cursory scheme of 'one size fits all' would never meet the need. Social workers with deaf people need to be aware of the risks of dependency, respond to assessed needs and consider counselling and support on an individual basis where problems were multiple or acute. Similarly, the provision of environmental equipment should be based on assessed needs and not just on a restricted list of those items which the local authority happens to have in stock. Hard pressed social work departments might well consider cooperation with voluntary societies or other community organisations or deaf-led groups, where appropriate even ceding to them decisions about the levels and types of provision most needed. Above all there needed to be an adequate capacity for both communication and interpretation, and a clear understanding of the difference between the two.

This is only a bare summary of some of the detailed suggestions which the inspectors made, sufficient to show just how far they believed the authorities were falling short of their responsibilities under Section 29 of the 1948 Act and the further requirements of the Disability Discrimination Act 1995. The criticisms date from 1997, and others can judge what effect they have had since then; the intention here is only to set a context within which to gauge any changes in the position of deaf people in Sheffield since the Association and its Institute ceased to play any part in 1960.

It is also important to acknowledge that both before and since the publication of *A Service on the Edge* there have been several technical and other developments which have helped some deaf people to achieve a greater degree of independence within the hearing world and to feel proud of their community. From its early development in the 1950s, and more general acceptance in the last two decades, the cochlear implant, colloquially the 'bionic ear', has been fitted to over 10,000 deaf people in Britain and some 400,000 worldwide, and has been of great benefit to most of the recipients. However, the implant requires expensive surgery, and can take up to a year to become effective, and only in the last decade has it become routine in the NHS to screen babies for hearing loss. During recent years the controversial and also expensive small scale development of auditory-verbal therapy (AVT) has in combination with cochlear implants enabled a small number of profoundly deaf children to achieve 'normal' educational development and integration into mainstream schools. However, it has to be said that both the implants and AVT remain controversial in the deaf community, many of whom believe that British Sign Language (BSL) fosters and sustains a proud community and subculture which would be poorer if the 'best' and most able deaf children are absorbed into 'normal' hearing society. Again we can see the contrast and potential conflict between the cultural and disability models of deafness, and the debate between oral and manual instruction of deaf children. Chief among the proponents of BSL has always been the British Deaf Association (formerly the BDDA) and their collective view is well expressed on their website:

> *We believe that Deaf people have the right to full participation in our society, signing BSL and using both written and spoken English. We therefore believe in bilingualism – something like 80% of the world is bilingual. We want Deaf people to be part of this majority [...] We believe that Deaf children do best when they learn BSL and English. Some deaf children will never have enough hearing to make use of their hearing aids or cochlear implants to the same extent as the rest of the population. They are deaf. For those children BSL is essential as a first language because it is a visual language. Once they have learned the basics they can learn a second language which would be English.*

> (WWW.BDA.ORG.UK)

The rapid development of the internet and mobile phones are less controversial in their specific and far-reaching benefits for deaf people. The capacity to locate information, resources and assistance online would have been unthinkable for deaf people only 20 years ago, and for hearing people it is difficult to imagine the release granted by the ability to communicate by email and texting to friends, family, carers and all the authorities and institutions which govern modern life. To the extent this enables the individual deaf person to participate more fully in social life; it inevitably dilutes the exclusivity of the deaf subculture, but there is no question such technologies release the profoundly deaf from at least some of the isolation which has been their historical lot. More than once in meeting deaf people and others I have been told that the young take much less part in the social life of the deaf clubs; the use of computers and mobile phones is often given as a main reason, and it already seems clear that the smartphone is among the most significant technical changes in the life of deaf people today.

The other really important advance in the last few years has been the recognition by HM Government in 2003 that BSL is a true language. Sign language has a long history and BSL has always been a rallying point for the BDA, the British Deaf History Society and all proponents of the importance and value of the deaf subculture. As we have seen, its use was deeply distrusted in education from the 1880 Milan conference until at least the second half of the last century and the opposition of signing and oralism has highlighted contrasting views of deaf life and welfare. It is not for me to engage in that controversy, but what follows from government recognition is the chance to analyse the 2011 Census returns and gauge the extent of profound deafness and the use of BSL in modern Britain.

We looked in Chapter One at the various estimates of the deaf population, and 'estimates' is still the right word; deaf registration with the local authorities is not compulsory and practice varies widely. One practical measure of the profoundly deaf population could be the numbers who habitually use BSL which is where the 2011 Census might be useful; the answers to any question vary with the precise wording of the question itself, and therein lies the problem.

For England and Wales, the question was simply 'What is your main language?', for which the first tick box alternative was English, the next and only other box was 'Other, write in, including British Sign Language'. For BSL the figure was 15,487 out of almost 54 million, approximately 0.03% of the population, which many in the field were convinced was far too low a figure; the BDA for instance pointed out that the Department of Health's GP Patient Survey for 2012 contained a question 'Are you deaf and use sign language?' to which the answer (admittedly only from a sample) suggested there were over 100,000 signers in England alone. Unlike the Census question, of course, this total included those who regarded English as their main language, some of whom would be hearing members of families with at least one deaf individual. More importantly, it was argued that the question of what is one's main language is dependent on the circumstances of its use; earlier estimates of the use of BSL varied from 30,000 to 70,000.

For Scotland the Census question was quite different: 'Do you use a language other than English at home?' for which there were three tick boxes to choose from: 'No, just English', 'Yes, British Sign Language' and 'Yes, other, please write in'. There were no less than 12,533 in a Scottish population of about 5.1 million who ticked the second box, approximately

0.24% or eight times the proportion for England and Wales! There is one obvious explanation of the difference; the Scottish figure includes the use of BSL as a second language; it is rare for all members of a family to be profoundly deaf and it may only require one person to be deaf for the rest of the family to consider English as their main language, to learn and use BSL to communicate with the deaf individual(s).

So I decided (and was advised) to ignore the Census evidence when estimating how many Sheffield citizens today are profoundly or at least sufficiently severely deaf to rely on BSL and be eligible for whatever welfare support is available. Instead, I reverted to Appendix G of *A Service on the Edge* in which the authors gave a rough guide to local authorities of how to calculate the numbers in their own areas. The figures quoted were derived from *The Informability Manual* by Wendy Gregory (HMSO, 1996) and give a total of 250,000 with profound hearing loss, a proportion of 0.5 or 1 in 200 of the population, and 62,000 who use BSL, a proportion of 0.1% or one in 1000. These extracts relate only to those two categories, and not the very much larger figures of those with some form of hearing disability or who use a hearing aid. Nonetheless, the report's final words on the estimates suggest that reliance on formal registration is suspect and that the problems are far wider than many authorities had realised:

> Figures from the 1995 registers of Deaf and Hard of Hearing People (Department of Health, 1995) and the findings of this report confirm that local figures seriously underestimate incidence. It may be therefore that services have not been developed because the scale has not been recognised.

Based on these simple 1997 guidelines, the number of profoundly deaf people in a city of over half a million like Sheffield would be 2500, and there would be perhaps 500 who use BSL whether as their only or second familial language. But in fact nobody to my knowledge has ever suggested a figure as high as 2500. Nevertheless, the 500 who have a use for BSL must be regarded as a minimum estimate and happens to be the figure suggested to me from within the social services department, and is not so different from the membership of the Institute before closure. Compared with the blind, the uncertainty about numbers shows again how severe or profound deafness can not only isolate deaf people from the social life of the hearing but makes it doubly difficult to measure the nature and extent of their needs.

★★★

What follows is not a detailed history of care for the adult deaf in Sheffield since 1960, merely a sense of how it has developed, derived from various sources including deaf people and others concerned with their welfare, either named below, included in the Acknowledgements or anonymous by their choice, and set within the context of the foregoing sketch of the national position.

Until 1960 the needs of the Sheffield deaf were assessed and supplied by the Association and the Stephensons. The family's contributions ended with the death of Colin, the resignation of Alan and the retirement of Doris; the remaining history of the Association as a registered charity is quickly told. The *Sheffield Telegraph* of December 8th 1960 carried a report of the Association's AGM headed 'Deaf and Dumb need support – Institute sale in final stages'. The Chair was local solicitor Brian Pye-Smith and the Secretary was Jarvis Barber, by then the only remaining descendant of the founding families. It was agreed that the remaining capital should be used to fund 'pressing needs' which the Council were unable or unwilling to meet, and the perennial appeal for donations was repeated. At last, however, a note of realism crept in. According to the report the committee was 'unanimous in disapproving the purchase of other property for Institute purposes'.

The remaining capital amounted to just over £16,000 and continued to be administered in accordance with the scheme approved by the Charity Commissioners in 1961. In due course, however, there were two significant changes. Like the BDDA and RADD the trustees bowed to modern sensibility and dropped the word 'Dumb' from the title. Secondly, perhaps because the administration of a small fund was too much for a group of otherwise busy independent trustees, the responsibility was entrusted to Voluntary Action Sheffield, an independent charity with close connections to the Council, created to support voluntary and community organisations in the city. Some years later the work was handed to South Yorkshire Community Foundation. Set up in 1986 at a time of economic and social difficulties in the county, SYCF raises considerable sums to support community projects and organisations. In recent years the Association's income varied between £4000 and £5000, the majority of which was disbursed in grants of not more than £300 each. Eventually, the Association's status as an independent charity was seen to be anomalous and on 9th April 2013 its registration was cancelled. After consultation with the Charity Commissioners the remaining capital was transferred to SYCF and remains as a discrete fund and is still administered under the terms set out in 1961.

★★★

Colin Stephenson summarised the functions of the Institute under five headings: a church, an employment bureau, a headquarters (where problems could be brought and listened to and perhaps solved), a club, and an interpreter service. To what extent has the Council replaced those functions whether directly, by subsidy or outsourcing of services? And what about deaf people: do they feel as well served as under the Stephensons at the Institute? On this last question I have no BSL so I have not been able to discuss sometimes sensitive or uncertain issues directly with deaf persons; my contacts have been limited to three visits to the two Deaf Clubs. On each occasion I was greatly helped by my interpreter, a hearing person with phenomenal signing skills, and I give her special thanks in my Acknowledgments. I have not attempted to survey the opinions of deaf adults as a whole; the views I report represent just a few of those willing to answer my queries and none are identified by name.

The Council had purchased 57 Psalter Lane, but deaf people still needed somewhere to go, and the building continued in use for over 20 years, renamed the Handicapped Persons Centre, a resource and meeting place for various groups, with the evenings being reserved for use by the deaf community. Alderman Yorke had identified a capital sum to provide a purpose-built centre for deaf people in the city centre and after a delay of two decades modern premises were opened in 1985 at 105 Grange Crescent, not in but a little nearer the centre than Psalter Lane. Again these capacious premises were not reserved for deaf people alone but were and remain shared with other handicapped people. The facilities include a bar, snooker table and a carefully separate area for religious services in which the altar, font and other artefacts of the Psalter Lane chapel were imported including the chair identified at the end of Chapter Two. There are also plaques commemorating the service of George and Colin Stephenson, which, however, proved too heavy to be attached to the walls of a modern building! 57 Psalter Lane remained empty for several years, fell into disrepair and was eventually demolished and sold for development as a small housing estate in the 1990s.

Grange Crescent is home to the deaf-led Sheffield Deaf Sports and Social Club with a constitution approved by the Charity Commission, thus fulfilling one part of the undertakings given by the Council in 1960. Unfortunately, that is not the only social provision for the Sheffield deaf and this is one of the most curious features of the modern story – Sheffield is believed to be unique in having not one but two Deaf Clubs. The origins of this duplication remain shrouded in mystery to outsiders. Apparently, due to personal difficulties or antagonism between a few key figures in the deaf community, a break-away group was created in about 1984 and assigned rented premises by the Council in the city centre, under the title Sheffield Central Deaf Club (SCDC). This second 'rival' social club had to move out of Council premises and is now housed in an upper room of the Methodist centre at the Victoria Hall, and the split remains as complete and apparently irreconcilable as ever. In any event, the Council finally did fulfil its commitment to provide and pay for premises, and uniquely on not one but two sites. How does the deaf community feel about this split? I have no idea; it was made very clear that feelings are still so strong that to even mention the subject would be enough to end the discussion – that tells its own story.

The creation of SCDC was not the most important change affecting the Sheffield deaf in the 1980s. Since 1921, almost all deaf children had been educated at the Maud Maxfield School; there was a break after the original premises in East Bank Road were destroyed by enemy action in the war until the school relocated in 1954 to purpose-built premises in Ringinglow Road on the leafy western edge of the city. However, integration was the new watchword and 'mainstreaming' the educational corollary, and (as with blind children) parallel provision was developed in several primary and secondary schools in the city. In those schools the deaf children are taught by both oral and where appropriate, manual systems including BSL. After more than a century of sometimes bitter dispute, this must be regarded as progress. I had read elsewhere of draconian punishment for children who used sign language, which I took with a pinch of salt until I was told by a deaf member at SDSSC that she had been caned at Maud Maxfield for conversing with another child in what both of them regarded as their common language. Despite its exclusive concentration on oral teaching methods, for which Maud Maxfield had a national reputation, the deaf community had great affection for the school and many were sad when it closed in 1984. For sixty years it had provided not just education for the children but a link which helped to maintain group solidarity, with almost all deaf people making their first social contacts at the school and then moving together to the common resources provided by the Institute.

By that time, and particularly after the 1970 Act, the responsibility for deaf welfare had transferred from the Public Health Department to Social Services. Potentially this had two profound effects, really two sides of the same coin. First, there were concerns amongst organisations for deaf people that the provision of services by general social workers would eventually obviate the need for deaf specialists. This was the fear which Taylor tried to allay in his 1960 paper to the NID; it was apparent from *A Service on the Edge* that the danger remained in 1997. Second, less obvious but in the long run even more significant, was a change in emphasis from the disability to the cultural model of deafness, with deaf people seen not just as individuals with a particular handicap but as a discrete social group with their own language and community life. And as general social workers came to see deaf people as a community seeking an independent lifestyle and integration into mainstream social life, there would inevitably be less emphasis on the continuity of care and supervision which the missioners had provided in the institutes. The deaf were now thought to be able to resolve their personal problems and make their own decisions, and social workers would only be involved where they had statutory duties. Today, for instance, I was told that social workers were rarely seen at Grange Crescent. The Stephensons regarded it as part of their duty to visit deaf individuals and their families on a regular basis, whether in hospital or their own homes. This was particularly valuable to the frail and elderly, irrespective of any immediate or urgent need, and this quasi familial relationship has disappeared completely. The changing ethos was best described in a personal communication from one of the specialist social workers, now retired, writing to me in April 2014: 'They were trying to make deaf people more able to conduct their own business and not rely on social services. The idea was empowerment but I suspect it was because they didn't have the resources to carry on as the missioners did.'

This 'vanishing' of the missioner role is not because Social Services or individual social workers had ceased to care, it was and is policy to encourage deaf people to take greater control of their own lives. Martin Smith was determined to downplay the authority of the role for which he was trained. He told me he had a notice on his office wall in Leeds: 'Don't come to me if you can do it yourself.' In the early days from the 1970s and into the 1990s, Sheffield Social Services certainly had the staff and the resources to meet their *statutory* responsibilities. What became known as the Sensory Impairment Team, serving deaf, blind and deaf-blind, had a staff of 12 under its senior officer, and on the deaf side several of the social workers had the traditional family background of parents who had been members of the Institute themselves and had continued to be active in SDSSC. There was a worker specifically concerned with the welfare of the small but difficult group of the doubly handicapped deaf-blind. The Sheffield deaf also had a unique facility in Deaf Advice Service Sheffield (DASS), the only specialist advice service for deaf citizens in the whole country. DASS was somewhere the deaf could feel comfortable in taking problems they felt unable to discuss with non-specialist social workers. In 1879, the Association and the Sheffield School Board had created the first free day school for the deaf in England; DASS showed the city had not lost its capacity to pioneer services for the deaf community

★★★

In assuming total responsibility for deaf welfare, the Council had never intended and was not required to provide everything the Association and the Stephensons had offered; spiritual welfare, social and sporting activities, and the search for employment were never regarded as part of Social Services' remit. Otherwise, in the early years at least, both the resources and the organisation were more than adequate to the needs of deaf people and would not have deserved the criticisms directed at many authorities in *A Service on the Edge*. Even today, to search the Council's voluminous and informative website, you might think it all still matched the promises of Alderman Yorke and the fully staffed and well-intentioned Social Services Department of the 1980s and 1990s. Unhappily, it has to be said that if the will is still there, the resources are not, a bleak situation which is almost certain to continue and worsen over the next few years.

An internal report in 2005, hopefully entitled *A Fresh Start,* was commissioned by the Council to examine and suggest a remedy for the wasteful and antagonistic duplication of the two social centres, SDSSC and SCDC. Careful questionnaires were sent to a large number of users of deaf welfare services and relevant member organisations and investigations undertaken in other towns for comparative purposes. The results were disappointing; only a quarter of the questionnaires were returned, and there still seemed to be no appetite to resolve the long-standing feud within the deaf community. The report recommended setting up a single centre which would be more than just a social club and encompass for instance the work of DASS and hopefully draw together the two separate groups. Also, the Council should utilise the funds from the disposal of the premises in Surrey Place then occupied by SCDC towards the project, and the undertaking to the deaf given in 1960 should be updated. It was also hoped that the deaf youth club would be revived and encourage a larger participation by the younger generation. Whatever the reasons, and financial stringency must have played a major part, none of this has yet come about.

With the best will in the world, a much reduced number of specialist social workers could not replicate all the services which were on offer in previous years. The Sensory Impairment Team no longer exists as such, and from its total of twelve workers in the 1980s the senior council officer responsible for deaf, blind and deaf-blind welfare has a total staff of four, two for the deaf and two for the blind; the worker with the deaf-blind has been lost. The youth club has not been revived because there is no longer a social worker responsible for the children who could organise and run it. In early 2014, as another consequence of reduced funding, the unique contribution of DASS has been 'lost' by being absorbed into the CAB. The focus of social work generally has moved to problems of old age, dementia and the interface between the NHS and Social Services, so with the shortage of specialist staff and resources it is inevitable that access by deaf people to welfare provision is increasingly similar to the hearing population and less specifically related to their separate and identifiable needs.

Premises have been provided for deaf community purposes, still at two different sites, though how long the double expense can be justified must be doubted. What is provided by SDSSC and SCDC has to be run by the deaf members and their committees, and that is right and accepted by them. Having visited both centres, there seems to be a marked preponderance of the older generation. Without any formal organisation for young people, especially for the crucial period between education and adulthood, that can only become more pronounced. When deaf members were asked about the absence of the younger generation, shoulders were shrugged; I was told they rarely appeared, and then only on Saturdays. They were thought to prefer pub life and in any event they were as absorbed by smartphone resources and communication as other young people. Social life at the Deaf Clubs, particularly SDSSC at Grange Crescent, remains important to the older generation, but several members said it was not the same as in 'the old days' of the Stephensons. It is no longer 'one big family'; social life is more independent from outside influence or the domination of the missioners but perhaps also more isolated from the wider community.

★★★

It was never expected that the Council would offer the spiritual care which was so important for the voluntary societies and the piety of missioners like the Stephensons. However, the Council did undertake in 1960 to ensure such care remained available as long as there was a demand. The undertaking was fulfilled by the provision of the separate area at Grange Crescent and the transfer there of the accoutrements of worship from the chapel at Psalter Lane; it has now been closed because there was such little demand. The closure does not seem to have caused much anguish amongst the deaf members; the Stephensons would have been appalled. There is a diocesan chaplain to the deaf community, though no specific fund to maintain the service. In 2014, I talked to the then incumbent who was also responsible for four parishes and so had limited time to devote to her duties as chaplain. She knows BSL and visits the deaf clubs in Sheffield and Doncaster from time to time, but has had neither time nor resources for Rotherham and Barnsley, which are also in the diocese. She is hoping to be more proactive in her retirement and perhaps this is one area where this admittedly minority interest might expand again. In any event it remains the responsibility of the Anglican and other churches, not the Council.

A major part of George and Colin Stephenson's work was visiting employers to obtain jobs for their deaf members, convincing employers of their competence, and interceding whenever the relationships proved difficult; readers will remember the extraordinary number of visits which George in particular recorded every year. With the creation of 'placement grants' in the 1930s, this was how Sheffield and most local authorities first became involved; never doing the work themselves, but recognising the necessity and paying the voluntary societies to do it for them. However, under Section 29 the authorities no longer considered this was part of their duties; employment was an area where the deaf could and should be encouraged to stand on their own feet. When I asked a group of the Sheffield deaf how work was obtained, the answer was simple – you go to the Job Centre. (Interestingly, Martin Smith, for all his efforts to foster deaf independence, told me that the search for employment was one aspect of missioner work which had been really valuable and which he still hopes can be restored within the voluntary institution in Leeds.)

So if the Council no longer attempts to replicate, directly or otherwise, the recreational, religious or employment functions originally provided by the missioners or superintendents except by providing premises and finance for the self-led Deaf Clubs, how best to describe the work actually done by the few remaining specialist social workers? There has to be an assessment procedure when deaf individuals need assistance with specific social problems; the Council also supply mechanical devices to facilitate telephone communication, fire and emergency alarms, TV and radio reception and the like, but what else? There is a document on the City Council website: 'Services for people with impaired vision/hearing', and a senior Council officer gave me the following summary:

> *Social care support for d/Deaf people encompasses a very wide range of services from help with complicated correspondence to the more vulnerable in the deaf community (often with additional disabilities) perhaps with a formal package of home support. Drop-in services on Tuesday mornings and Thursday afternoons*

have been a long-standing service to deaf people. This worked well with DASS who were open to callers on Mondays, Wednesdays and Fridays (but of course DASS no longer exists as a separate organisation). The role of social care staff has moved away from the idea of the 'missioner', who represented the needs of Deaf people, to ensuring that Deaf people have proper access to all Council services and that the necessary 'reasonable adjustments' (as required by the Equality Act) are made. This usually involves the provision of a qualified BSL/English interpreter and some basic awareness training to help others understand the specific needs of the Deaf person.

It is this last sentence which takes us back to Sainsbury and the most central issue of all; the necessity of clear communication and interpretation. In their silent world, how are the profoundly deaf to be heard and their needs assessed and met? How does an authority like Sheffield manage to provide such a basic need, beset as they are by staff shortages and the seemingly endless reduction in resources imposed by central government? Fulfilling other local government responsibilities has often been met by outsourcing, privatisation, charging fees to the end user of services, or any combination of such devices, all designed to provide what is needed at less or no cost and to exert less pressure on shrinking budgets. Increasingly that is the way the beleaguered service has gone with the deaf community. It is estimated to take up to ten years to achieve full fluency in BSL to a level at which interpretation is reliable in complex situations like hospitalisation, courts of law or tribunals dealing with mental health, employment or benefits. If it was ever realistic to expect a modern Social Services department to employ such linguistic paragons, that time is fast receding. These days, when a qualified interpreter is required, the Council usually has to utilise one of the professional interpreting services; sometimes nobody is available, however urgent the need. The cost is significant and can only become more so, and though there is no actual rationing there is inevitably a rigorous test of need in each individual case.

There is a further alternative in Sheffield, and although it is in the early stages of development and is a form of privatisation, it is very impressive. I was recommended to meet and interview the young directors of Communication Independent Limited, a small company founded in 2011 to provide precisely the individual service their title suggests. As always during my research, I have found the greatest understanding of the problems of deaf people amongst those with personal or family experience, and CIL is no exception. One director is the child of deaf parents and was particularly incensed by the lack of understanding of her father's plight during hospitalisation, and was herself for several years a member of the Council's sensory impairment team; the other is herself profoundly deaf. At this early stage they have enough to do with referrals direct from the Council; the two directors make the assessments and supervise the ongoing work with deaf individuals by one of their eight part-time support workers. What they are effectively trying to provide is the dedicated and specialised support for deaf people which is increasingly challenging for the Council's general social workers with all the myriad and changing demands on their services. That support is grounded in the central issue of communication which for the profoundly deaf is unique, and uniquely difficult. With the right support, they believe that by treating each deaf person as an individual, they can facilitate a multi-disciplinary approach covering all the services available from the various departments of the Council and enable deaf individuals to feel they are independent citizens. This is in direct contrast to the missioner model where one man assumed the responsibility of serving all the needs of each deaf person through his contacts with the outside world, but it is also more specialised and focussed than general social work, in effect a replication of the sensory impairment team which the Council can no longer sustain.

Meeting the CIL Directors left a more positive feeling about the future of deaf welfare, but the combination of enthusiasm and experience in one small dedicated organisation will never be enough. It still seems to me, as it does to the older deaf people who remember the Institute, that something was lost through the inability of the Association and the Council to work together in the interests of the deaf community. The missioner or superintendent role as practised by the Stephensons was clearly outmoded by the 1950s, as Lysons, Rev Firth and Martin Smith recognised, but it had real value for deaf people of that era. It gave a personal, focussed emotional dimension to care which is inevitably difficult for beleaguered Council staff, a dimension which an organisation like CIL might begin to restore.

★★★

Many of the themes I identified in the Introduction remain relevant – the conflict between the oral and manual approaches to deaf education, the importance of sign language, the contrasting cultural and disability models of deafness and Deafhood, and the inevitable differences in emphasis between the voluntary, statutory and outsourced or privatised approaches to social care. Sainsbury's research centred on communication and the contrast between integration and segregation as likely outcomes; *A Service on the Edge* revealed how far care had fallen short of the ideal some 50 years after the National Assistance Act empowered the local authorities to provide the deaf welfare formerly the work of charities and the Church.

Evaluation of the national position has to be left to the academics, the administrators and the polemicists. In Sheffield, the profoundly deaf are a relatively small group and are (both literally and metaphorically) without a strong voice. From what I have read and been told in an effort to summarise what has happened in the last 50 years, neither integration nor segregation seems appropriate. My impression is that Sheffield's profoundly deaf population may have become more independent as individuals but less cohesive as a social group, certainly less so than at any time between the opening of the Charles Street Institute in 1886 and its closure at Psalter Lane in 1960. Perhaps the high point of their community life lasted from the opening of the Maud Maxfield school in 1921 and the closure of the Institute in 1960. In those years nearly all deaf children were educated at the same school and then maintained social contact and friendship through the Institute. This vital link was fractured firstly by the transformation of Psalter Lane from Institute to Handicapped Persons Centre and secondly, by the closure of the Maud Maxfield school in the belief that educational 'mainstreaming' would lead to greater integration.

It seems that developments since then have simply magnified the difficulty in maintaining a sense of community. About the same time that Maud Maxfield closed, some of the adults, for reasons which remain unclear, added to the fracture by establishing a rival community centre. The younger element might have stayed closer to each other with the benefit of a youth club, but this has closed and not yet revived. The adults had the unique resource of DASS as an alternative to Social Services, but now this too no longer operates as a separate organisation. The rundown of the Sensory Impairment Team and the declining numbers of specialist social workers further reduces the commonalty of interest and resource. To dispense with the traditional missioner and replace him with a dedicated team of professionals is one thing, but when that team is drastically reduced, not by policy decision but simply by financial constraint, the sense of belonging to a valued group declines.

Outsourcing support and communication as well as interpretation services may restore some of the professionalism and specialised care, but not necessarily the sense of community. Deaf people are not alone in the modern fragmentation of community life. As in the hearing population, some will be able to harness the new technologies to access their needs and communicate with others without close and continuing social support. But where this is difficult or impossible, the profoundly deaf are uniquely disadvantaged. "Alone in a Silent World"? This phrase from an old style missioner described lives which the voluntary societies and the specialist schools were created to transform. It remains to be seen how far the developments of the past half century have changed those lives for the better.

Appendix One

Thomas Widd, Ernest Abraham, Arthur Doncaster and Kate Oxley

Thomas Widd

Given his humble origins and profound deafness, Widd's major role in the foundation of the Sheffield Association would justify an honoured place in the history of care for the deaf. Yet when he left Sheffield in 1863 he was still only 24 and his subsequent career was even more remarkable. After his marriage to the deaf Margaret in early 1864, the young couple moved briefly to Whitehaven in Cumbria where their first son was born but died two days later, and then to Clerkenwell in east London; in both places he worked in the printing trade. Through this occupation he met Charles Dickens, said to have been the godfather to his second son Charles Arthur Widd; Dickens also contributed to the cost of the Widds' next move, emigration to Canada. They settled in Montreal, where Widd realised that although there were several Catholic schools for the deaf there was no provision for the Protestant minority. Within a short time he had founded and become Principal of the Protestant Institute for Deaf Mutes with Margaret as matron. As in Sheffield, he started by contacting and befriending the deaf, then created newspaper publicity and looked for financial support. This came from a wealthy Montreal businessman, Joseph Mackay, who paid for the construction of the institute. Very recently, as part of a project by Concordia University of Montreal, Widd was accorded due recognition, as reported on September 6th 2013 in the *Montreal Gazette*, a local English language newspaper. Apparently, the origins of what is now the Mackay Institute for the Deaf had been almost completely forgotten, until research was undertaken by a teacher of the deaf whose own parents had been pupils there and knew something of the story. As a result, a commemorative mural was installed in the institute and Widd is now accepted as the true founder. Deaf historians may agree with the wry comment in the report, that the previous neglect of Widd's role was 'an example of how deaf people have been written out of their own history'.

Even then, Widd's contribution to deaf institutions was not done. The harsh Canadian climate was bad for his health, and in 1883 he moved his family to the warmth of Los Angeles. There he soon became recognised as a leader and teacher of the deaf, and in 1889 was a prime mover in the foundation of the Los Angeles Association of the Deaf of Southern California, of which he was the first 'Secretary, Treasurer and Missionary'. The initial meeting was held in the Guild Room of St Paul's Episcopal Church which then became the centre of a range of activities very similar to those provided for the deaf by the Stephensons and their committees in Sheffield. In 1896, like Colin Stephenson in Sheffield some 40 years later, Widd was appointed by the Episcopal Bishop of Los Angeles as a Diocesan Lay Reader. Following this distinction, he made contact with his old colleagues in England and a detailed account of his work in Los Angeles was printed in Abraham's *British Deaf Monthly* in 1897 (Vol. 7, no 73, pp. 13–14). This must have resulted in George Stephenson sending Widd the Annual Report of the Sheffield Association for 1896, because Widd mentions this in his detailed account of his Sheffield experiences in December 1897 in *British Deaf Monthly* (Vol. 7, no 74, pp. 34–35). This article provides much of the detail used by George Stephenson in 1911, and Boyce and Hayes in 2007, in their accounts of the events of autumn 1862.

Thomas Widd died in December 1906. By any standards it had been an extraordinary life. Deaf from childhood, he became a writer of considerable skill and force, evidenced by the letters he wrote to the Sheffield press in 1862 and the excerpts of later work in the appendices to Boyce and Hayes' book. At different times a printer, gardener, teacher and missioner to the deaf, but above all a leader in the foundation of voluntary associations for the care of the deaf in three countries on two continents.

Ernest Abraham

Although not deaf himself, Ernest Abraham's later career is as impressive as Widd's. When in 1901 his uncertain health forced him to a second resignation from the Guild of St John of Beverley, as editor of *British Deaf Monthly* and as missioner to the deaf of Bolton, he was still only 33. He was invited to be Chaplain to the Adult Deaf and Dumb Mission in Melbourne, Victoria, by Frederick John Rose, a profoundly deaf Englishman who had emigrated some years earlier and was one of the founders of the Victoria Mission. In 1901, the mission was run entirely by volunteers and had no substantial premises. According to research by John Flynn in 2001, Abraham was the first full-time missioner to the deaf in the whole of Australia, and the energy and chutzpah he had displayed in England was to bear fruit in this new home. According to a laudatory article celebrating his first 25 years in Australia in the *Argos* newspaper of Melbourne on 9th October 1926, headed 'Deaf Mutes' Cause – Mr Ernest Abraham's Life Work', he had 'raised the status of the deaf and dumb people of this State to as near normal as conditions will permit'. As soon as he arrived in Melbourne he had embarked on 'an extensive publicity campaign' which resulted in the erection of an institute building for the association as early as 1904. Within a few more years he had secured free compulsory education for all deaf children and persuaded the State government and private philanthropists to create a church dedicated to the deaf, and other buildings for social and educational use by the deaf community. Perhaps most remarkably, again with the aid of a grant from the Premier of Victoria supplemented by his own fundraising activities, in 1909 and still only eight years after first setting foot in Australia, he established:

> a home for aged, infirm, mentally defective and blind deaf mutes[…]
> Mrs Abraham becoming the first matron. The success of this home
> is practically wholly due to her services. She entered on the difficult
> and nerve wracking task of controlling and training this terribly
> afflicted section of humanity with a dauntless spirit.

The details of Abraham's fundraising and property deals, described in the *Argos* and elsewhere, are testament to the business acumen which

Rev Gilby had reluctantly acknowledged in England, and the crucial caring work of his wife reminds us of Mrs Widd's work as matron of the Protestant Institute in Montreal (as well as Doris Stephenson's support of Colin in Sheffield for more than 30 years). Given their unpromising beginnings – a deaf youth in rural East Yorkshire and an orphan in South London – Widd and Abraham should surely be counted amongst the giants of Victorian philanthropy.

Arthur Doncaster

Arthur was born in 1856, the youngest of Daniel Doncaster II's ten children and probably the most severely affected of the three who were congenitally deaf. The relative deafness of the three siblings is difficult to judge from Census returns alone; it is not mentioned for Daniel III until 1901 and only once for Phebe; both of them are described in the notes given to me by a family member with the old-fashioned phrase 'stone deaf'. In Arthur's case it is much clearer: he is classified as deaf and dumb from birth in each of the Census returns from 1861 to 1911.

Arthur's disability was sufficiently severe for him to need private tuition. He never went to school, and was tutored at home by Joseph Farrar, the deaf graduate of the Doncaster school who was part-time superintendent of the Sheffield Association from 1862 to 1871. Arthur was still at home in the 1871 Census, aged fifteen, but by 1881 was living as a lodger at 77 Vincent Square, London, described as a 'naturalist employing one man'. (Many of the Doncasters were enthusiasts for natural history; Arthur was the first of three who became professionals in the field.)

Sometime after moving to London, Arthur met another naturalist, William Watkins. In 1879 they went into partnership. The business was on the Strand and entitled Watkins and Doncaster, 'Naturalists' Equipment and Framed Specimens'. The partnership did not last and by 1881 Arthur was sole proprietor. By 1891, he had bought the house at 26 Earlsfield Road, Wandsworth which remained his home until his death. He never married but from the time he bought Earlsfield Road he was accompanied and supported by his deaf sister Phebe (1847–1924). A noted Quaker, an elder of the Friends Meeting House in Wandsworth, a peace worker and prison visitor, and editor of a tribute to two Quaker martyrs who had perished in Madagascar in 1884, Phebe must have been as indomitable and strong-minded as her deaf siblings.

Arthur received specimens from all over the world which he would take to the British Museum for identification and classification; he established a reputation as a world expert on tropical butterflies. He learned French and German, in order to communicate better with his customers, and if they called in person he would converse with them by means of a slate and chalk which he carried round his neck. He was a keen mountaineer, and visited the Alps every year from the 1890s until the outbreak of war in 1914. (Rev Gilby's autobiography recounts how he was an all-expenses-paid guest of Doncaster on one such trip in 1901, where he made several climbs which terrified him but were meat and drink to his indomitable host.) He also made his own contribution to those less fortunate than himself; for several years he was a committee member at the Tower House Home for Adult Deaf and Dumb Men at Erith in Kent, where he was a colleague of Selwyn Oxley.

He died in 1931, aged 75, after a long and successful life during which he demonstrated that the affliction of total deafness need not be a barrier to a business and professional career or personal fulfilment – especially if, like all the Doncasters of his generation, he was amply cushioned by financial independence. The business he created did not die with him; Watkins and Doncaster flourishes to this day, since 2013 from a base in Herefordshire, 'specialising in the supply and manufacture of equipment for the study of the Natural Sciences'.

Kate Oxley née Whitehead

It would be unfair to remember Kate Oxley only as a devoted helpmate and occasionally acerbic biographer of her husband. As individual if not as eccentric as him, she was born in Goole on the Humber estuary in 1896, the daughter of a dock labourer. She lost her hearing as a result of scarlet fever at the age of 8 and was a pupil at YIDD from 10 to 16. Although profoundly deaf for the rest of her life, she never let the handicap stand in her way; she published several historical novels as well as a very successful series of cat books for children. In the early 1920s, now living in Hull, she became friends with Walter McCandlish and through him was introduced to Selwyn Oxley.

The couple corresponded for some time, and Kate helped Selwyn by typing some of his endless reports and correspondence, all in his almost indecipherable spidery handwriting. After a couple of years she moved to London, where she was befriended by Rev Raper, and by degrees became Selwyn's secretary and general amanuensis. As she ruefully remarked later, she may not have realised at the time what a life's work she was giving herself, but whatever her misgivings then or later, the couple married in 1929 and her future was fixed.

The Guild of St John and work for the deaf were not all Selwyn and Kate had in common. They shared a love of pedigree cats, or perhaps more accurately an obsession. They had a large number, including those they enrolled as members of the Guild. It was Kate who established what seems to have been the first cat museum in Britain, perhaps in the world, in the home which they shared with the offices and library of the Guild. I cannot be alone in finding it difficult to imagine what the unsuspecting visitor would make of this extraordinary household. Again, we are indebted to Rev Firth who said of the museum that it encompassed:

> *cat clocks, cat automata, cat pictures and embroideries, cat cartoons, cat clothes, cat masks, cat toys, cat-decorated articles, and cat crockery and china.*
>
> (FIRTH, 1985, P.114)

By the time of the final move to Cheltenham in 1939, complete with Guild library and cat museum, Kate calculated that in addition to the mass of loose documents, slides and photos, the library contained 5000 volumes, and the cat museum some 20,000 items. We know what happened to the library, but the cat museum and all its contents seem to have vanished into thin air. Perhaps only cat lovers and feline historians can assess the magnitude of the loss.

Appendix Two

'Sheffield's Backward School Board'

Letter from George Stephenson to British Deaf Monthly June 1899

Dear Sir,

Reading your remarks in the April BDM re. the backward policy of the Sheffield School Board with regard to the day school, I confess to a feeling of shame for my native town.

The case looks dark as it now stands, but I sincerely hope, for the credit of the Old Cutlery Metropolis, that wiser counsels will prevail, and that we shall eventually have what we certainly ought to have had before now, viz. a properly equipped school for the education of deaf children.

To think that the very first provincial town to open a day school for deaf children, after the Act of 1870, should now cowardly wish to shirk their responsibility and cry out, 'This little bantling of ours has become unmanageable, and so we have decided to put it out to nurse,' is enough to raise the shade of the Right Hon A. J. Mundella, who so ably represented the town in Parliament for 26 years, and who, when Vice President of the Council, took a lively interest in the promotion of this very day school.

Well do I remember at a prize distribution shortly before the opening of this school, the right hon gentleman proudly boasting that London had its centres for *the education of the deaf,* and amid the ringing cheers of nearly 2000 people (I almost fancy I hear them now), announced that Sheffield would shortly be in the 'proud position of having the first Board School for deaf children outside London', *and that it should be free.*

Well, sir, the school was opened in January 1879, and continued its work quietly to the satisfaction of both the Board and the parents of the children, but, after being certified under the new Act of 1893, a fly dropped into the pot of ointment in the shape of HM Inspector for Deaf Schools, and after considerable friction (owing to the 'Department' refusing to accept the school premises as suitable for the purpose) the 'Board' awoke to the wonderful consciousness that institutions were best for the deaf and dumb and, having done so, sent over a deputation to several institutions to ask if it were not so. Of course they received answers in the affirmative, were hospitably treated, shown over the beautiful palaces, etc., and returning home were strengthened in their opinion, gave their report, and straight away the 15 gentlemen comprising the Board determined to dissolve the Deaf Day School, and send the children away from their homes and friends to receive their education among strangers. And in order to stand well with the ratepayers, they also put up a scarecrow in the shape of £2375 per annum, which they affirm it would cost to educate the children in Sheffield at a day school.

To say the very least, the action of the Board in this matter is of a most retrogressive character, and most undignified, and not at all in accordance with the policy which they adopt in connection with the ordinary elementary schools

I venture to hope that, if they do not see the error of their ways before the next triennial election, some of their places may get filled by others who know *something* about the needs of the deaf.

Geo. Stephenson

Appendix Three

'Is Dr Thompson Serious?'

Letter from George Stephenson to British Deaf Monthly March 1899

Sir,

I have just received a typewritten circular headed 'Training College for Teachers of the Deaf, Castle Bar Hill Ealing', and signed 'E. Symes Thompson, MD, FRCP'.

This circular begins, 'It is with feelings of misgiving that we hear of an association being formed for the spiritual care of the adult deaf.'

Well, sir, this is a revelation! I believe there are over 50 associations for the 'spiritual care' of the adult deaf in the United Kingdom and that also many of these were in existence and doing noble work, many, many years before this College of Teachers (?) of the Deaf was conceived in the mind of the founder. If the writer of this circular did not know of the existence of these associations, he is quite out of court, and not qualified to offer any opinion on the rival systems of instruction of the deaf.

But suppose we take him seriously, which I confess is somewhat difficult. He says that 'with the possible exception of consanguineous marriages, the most fruitful source of congenitally deaf children are the societies for the adult deaf', and goes on to say that 'these adult societies, bringing both sexes of other deaf persons together is the fruitful source of congenitally deaf children'.

In reply to this sweeping statement I submit the following figures, which I prepared simply for my own satisfaction some few years ago, and for the accuracy of which I am prepared to solemnly vouch, as each case I have had under my personal care; the parents many years, and the children from their very birth. They apply to the city of Sheffield. Total number of deaf people: adults 168, children of school age 45, infants 4. Couples both husband and wife deaf 34; 7 of these couples have had no children, 27 couples have had in all 79 children: 3 deaf and 76 hearing. I may add here that since the above, which dates 1890, there have been 16 births, all the children having their hearing. Mixed couples (only husband or wife deaf) 7; 2 of these couples have had no children, 5 couples have had in all 11 children: 6 deaf, 5 hearing. These figures speak for themselves.

The writer goes on to suggest that 'if all were taught on the pure oral system' and were 'looked after by the clergymen of their own parish (the italics are mine) there would not be any reason for bringing them in contact with other deaf persons' and 'that the deaf on leaving school – while well cared for spiritually and morally, by their own clergyman – should be absorbed into the hearing population', etcetera, etcetera. Our learned philanthropist(?) seems to dwell strongly on 'their own clergyman' as if there were no such people as non-conformists. I have a profound respect for our clergy – most of those I know have been very kind to me in my work among the deaf – but I venture to affirm that few, if any of them, know personally any of the deaf who live in their parishes. Our institution is within 150 yards of the church gates, and I confidently affirm that the vicar of the parish knows absolutely nothing about the deaf, nor do I believe that he has ever evinced any interest in their condition either 'spiritually or morally'. I remember in my younger days being called upon to interpret in a police court, the prisoner being a deaf young man who had been carrying on a system of petty thefts during the time he was being prepared for and after his confirmation. So much for the spiritual and moral care of the clergyman.

As to the suggestion that the deaf person goes to church and a relation or friend 'give him by silent word of mouth the sermon or lecture', I should like to ask what good would the deaf person get by this means, supposing it could be done satisfactorily – which I dispute? The writer knows very well that the beauty, the very life of speech, is in the sound, accent, etc.; that without that, speech would be dead, limp, insipid. Would the writer himself like to be condemned to listen all his life to speech without inflection, accents and eloquent passages?

That the accent tone and eloquent sound is to the hearing, so gesticulation by signs is to the deaf, and appeals to the hearts and minds with equal power.

Why do crowds follow eloquent speakers? Not alone for the words they say, but for the tone in which they are said, etc.

To condemn the deaf to the affliction of visible speech without any gesticulation would be an infliction worthy of the Spanish Inquisition. That this should be suggested by an FRCP at the close of the 19th century is almost inconceivable, yet I have it here before me in actual type-writing. Well, sir, I have no desire to take up your valuable space but the last paragraph of this precious document is the coping stone upon the prodigious display of ignorance by the writer. It says, 'The late Dr Armitage paid great interest in the condition of the blind, and he made it clear that blind men should never be called to the same meeting as adult blind women.' Of course, all sensible people will agree with that, for it is evident that for blind people to marry – if poor – is to increase their penury and run the risk of children being brought into the world to swell the ranks of pauperism. But for this Dr Thompson to bring this as an argument for preventing the deaf from marrying, is giving the whole case away, and showing an amount of ignorance of the comparative contrast of blind and deaf people that would be amazing were it not that I have seen the same in more than one place, and it is high time that these Masters of Art and Medicine are brought to a knowledge of their crass ignorance on this important question.

I am, yours truly,

GEO STEPHENSON.

APPENDIX FOUR

"A PLEA FOR THE GUILD OF ST JOHN"

Address by George Stephenson to the first Conference of the Guild of St John of Beverley, delivered at Beverley May 9ᵗʰ 1896 and printed in "British Deaf Mute" of June 1896.

When our Hon Sec wrote asking if I would contribute a paper to the Conference, it occurred to my mind that a plea for the "Guild" would form an appropriate preface to the volume of interesting and instructive papers which will be read before us.

We have been reminded more than once by the Editor of the British Deaf Mute that "For many years past the Deaf of France have kept green the memory of their noble benefactor and teacher, the Abbe de le'Epee". "The German Deaf also honour Samuel Heinicke" and "the Deaf of America are never tired of honouring the name of Thomas Gallaudet".

It has often been asserted that this "Nation of Shopkeepers" are slow in giving honour to the worthy. This may be so, but it is also certain that when we are awakened to our duty we are not lacking in gratitude to the memory of those who have left us the fruits of their good works.

The question has been asked, "How is it that you have not discovered the good deeds of St John of Beverley until over a thousand years after his death?"

I might make answer that we as a Deaf community have not received the full benefits of his good work till the present time.

That is no fault of St John; he followed the example of his blessed Master and Divine Lord by giving speech to the Dumb; he also provided for his health and temporal necessities. And if St John's successors failed

209

to follow his good example and continue the good work he began, we have all the more cause to honour the memory of one who in an age of ignorance and superstition dared to be singular in an act of mercy.

I believe in forming this Guild for the purpose of fostering a feeling of veneration in the hearts of the Deaf, for the memory of the "first teacher of the Deaf" will be a distinct gain and a great help to those who are ministering to their spiritual needs.

In this Guild the Deaf members have a definite object placed before them, and I believe this will be the means of bringing them more and more into Christian unity and fellowship with each other and sympathy with their teachers and ministers.

The Guild has no sect. It is wide enough to embrace all the Deaf who desire to live in peace and unity with their fellows. It's motto is "the love of Christ constraineth us". It's leader the Lord Jesus to whom we all owe allegiance. To the Deaf it in effect says "Come with us and we will do you good". We will listen sympathetically to your complaints, we will advise and help you, and if necessary we will petition the ruling authorities on your behalf. We will congregate with you at the Throne of Mercy and petition the King of Kings in the name of our Great Leader.

All should hail with satisfaction the formation of the Guild. Unfortunately this is not so, for the majority of Missions have as yet declined to become associates with us in this great movement. Possibly this is largely owing to the distance at which some of them are away from Beverley. I notice that those societies in the South of England have not yet joined us – perhaps it is too much to expect that the members of those societies will journey all the way to Beverley for the purpose of Conference and Divine Service, but they could join with us in fellowship, and though not be with us in the body, they could be with us in spirit.

All or nearly all have been asked to join us, I believe. Some have passed the request over in silence, others have declined, and various are the reasons that have been given. The majority say "There is no need for such a Guild" for the existing societies do all that is necessary for the temporal and spiritual improvement of the Deaf. One friend suggests that it "savours of Papacy and saint worship". Well, Sir, all I need say with reference to his suggestion, is that *I* have no leaning towards Papacy. Yet I should joyfully accept that which is good, even if it came from the hands of the Pope himself.

Turning to the oft-repeated assertion that there is "no need" for such an organisation, as the Missions now existing do all that is necessary for the temporal and spiritual needs of the Deaf. It seems to me, Sir, that there is considerable misapprehension with regard to the constitution of the Guild. It is not intended that the Guild should be a separate and independent organisation. But (and here I believe I am echoing the feelings of all our fellow workers) that this Guild shall be one grand organisation composed of *all* the various Missions and institutions throughout the United Kingdom.

Here we have one enormous platform, one aim, one object, where no differences of sect or creed shall be permitted to enter and stir up strife and mar our progress in the Divine life and in the intellectual improvement of the Deaf; where the highest Ritualist and the humblest Primitive Methodist may meet on common ground. Where the very humblest of the Deaf may be sure of meeting with kindly feeling from all who are engaged in the common cause.

We are all aware that missions to the Deaf are of but recent growth – I believe that I am within the truth in saying – that the very oldest cannot date back more than half a century. And yet in this short time such progress has been made, and much been done, and I would add by the Deaf themselves, to improve the morals and the intellects of their fellows.

There are now nearly 80 Missions in the United Kingdom, with over 100,000 members, and most of those – to their honour be it spoken – were originated by earnest Deaf Christians. With one of these Missions I have now been associated for 25 years, and perhaps I may be permitted to say that it has had a fair amount of success. I believe there are over 80 of our members here today.

Well, Sir, we are grateful for this, but I, along with some of my Deaf members and friends, have long felt that something might be done to remove the spirit of …What may I call it? I do not like to call it by the ugly name of jealousy which is too often applied; but there is a something which is constantly arising to the surface, like the "scum" of boiling liquid, but which, unlike that "scum", does not remain on the surface long enough to be removed; but has the most unpleasant faculty of appearing at most inopportune times and disturbing the peace and unity which ought to prevail in all departments of Christian labour, and in consequence prevents that perfect trust in each other which is indispensable to successful Christian effort.

Perhaps it is unfortunate that amongst the existing Missions there is not one universal creed. This cannot be under existing conditions. Yet it is a puzzle to me why the Church of England should look with suspicion on the Nonconformist missionary, or that the Nonconformist should look with envy upon the clergyman.

I candidly confess that I believe our want of unity is largely owing to this spirit. I feel that I am treading on delicate ground, but honesty compels me to be plain in stating what has both impressed and grieved me.

Working quietly in my own little community I have had but few opportunities of mixing with other associations, but being a diligent reader of both our periodicals, I am fully confirmed in the opinion I have expressed.

Although a Nonconformist (Wesleyan), yet I have a feeling of reverence for the beautiful service of the Church of England. But knowing that a very large proportion of our Deaf spring from Nonconformist parents, who desire their children to follow in their footsteps, I have no right to coerce those Deaf into any particular Church; and as we cannot divide them into the several sects to which their families may belong, I would earnestly advocate the teaching of the Gospel of our Lord Jesus Christ setting before them the example of a pure and holy life without adhering to the form of any particular sect.

Whilst the sectarian spirit exists amongst the Churches and Missions for the Deaf, it is impossible to bring about that "unity of spirit and righteousness of life" without which no man can be at peace with God.

As I have already remarked in this Guild we can *all* meet on common ground. The Noble St John of Beverley, Archbishop of York, of the Early Anglican Christian Church, at a time when there was only one Christian form of worship, left behind him an example of Christian charity which we may all follow with profit to ourselves and a blessing to others, and I would say to each individual worker for the Deaf – in the language of our Divine Lord and Master – "Go and do thou likewise".

APPENDIX FIVE

'I HAVE BEEN TO LONDON'

Dacty June 1921

I have been to London and spent 4 busy and happy days in the great city… Naturally you will be curious to learn the occasion of my visit to the Metropolis.

Well firstly I must remind you that the Guild of St John of Beverley is still alive, and under the fostering care of its enthusiastic organising Hon. Secretary Mr Selwyn Oxley, very much alive indeed. There was a time when the Sheffield Deaf and Dumb constituted the first branch of the Guild; some of you older members will, I have no doubt, be able to recall the memorable anniversaries we have spent at Beverley and the Sacred Services in which we have taken part in the beautiful Minster; to me they seem as they recede into the lengthening past as golden memories which advancing years cannot tarnish, which rather grow brighter and brighter.

How my memory seems to recall the time when the nation was celebrating Queen Victoria's Diamond Jubilee, and thus it came about that the members of the Guild caused a life-sized statue to be placed in one of the empty niches in the Minster as our contribution to the celebrations. Then later how we further enriched the decorations by fixing a beautiful window, illustrating Christ restoring hearing and speech to the deaf man (Ephphatha), the whole being executed by the most noted firm in London; the cost of the window which is not a large one was £120, towards which sum the esteemed Vicar of Beverley, Rev Canon Nolloth contributed £20 and the Sheffield branch about £10. All this to you and I is now simply a memory, I will not write anything to reproach you for falling away from your zeal but I am sorry and perhaps some of the younger members who know nothing of all this will after they have read this letter do something to revive the Sheffield interest in the Guild. At present through the indefatigable labours of Mr Selwyn Oxley there are 7000 members of the Guild including Bishops, Archbishops, Earls, Dukes and large numbers of Clergy. In the early days of the Guild none of the London Deaf and Dumb Associations took any interest in it, but now through Mr Oxley's efforts, the London Association with all its branches are attached and what is more they have just erected a church in North London to be called the St John of Beverley Church for the Deaf, and one object of my visit to London was to be present at the dedication of the church by the Lord Bishop of Stepney. This dedication took place on Saturday 7th May, 1120th anniversary of the death of St John whose remains lie under the nave of Beverley Minster. (*Described in Volume 8 of the Victoria History of Middlesex as 'the St John of Beverley Institute for the Deaf and Dumb', this church/institute was built on land made available by the Church Commissioners in 1913, and was first opened in 1920 with additions and the dedication made in 1921; it burned down in 1960 and a smaller centre rebuilt on part of the site.*)

The Dedication and Service was most solemn. The church was filled with a mixed congregation of mostly Deaf and Dumb, the Vicar of the church the deaf Rev Vernon Jones and three other clergymen to the deaf assisting the Bishop. I am so glad to say that my health was good and after the dedication I spent over an hour in intercourse with the Clergy and people and was most kindly received by the London Deaf, some of whom made enquiries about friends they know among the Sheffield members.

It was a happy time and my kind host and hostess Rev W H Oxley and Mrs Oxley, the parents of Mr Selwyn, were most careful for my comfort in every way. I ought to mention here that the Rev W H Oxley who is the Warden of the Guild has all the time, along with his good wife, supported their only son Selwyn in his self-denying work on behalf of the Deaf, and they also contributed largely to the cost of the new church.

I do not think you will be surprised to learn that G H Brooks spent the week in London using his camera to take photographs for Mr Oxley in furtherance of his literary work in connection with the Deaf; he was busy with his camera at the Dedication Service, so probably you will get to see some of the photographs in Sheffield.

On Saturday May 8th my kind friends took me to St Saviour's Church for the Deaf in Oxford Street. We also went shopping and entered the largest shop in London; it was all very interesting but tiring. Then in the afternoon my host the Rev W H Oxley kindly escorted me by means of the Underground Railway and Motor Bus into the city, where we paid a surprise visit to Mr Arthur Doncaster at his place of business in the Strand. It was a real pleasure to both of us to meet just the same as of yore. Kind, amiable and full of information, we spent a happy 45 minutes taking tea in one of Lyons' restaurants and when I left him I felt it was not by far the least enjoyable incident of my visit to London. Mr Oxley, who had not met Mr Doncaster, was charmed with him and glad that he had taken me. Before returning to Victoria Road we went along the Strand and then on the Thames Embankment and viewed the various large buildings and Government Offices, returning again by the Underground. I felt that I had spent a happy and profitable day.

Sunday May 9th was a really memorable day for me, for Rev A Raper, the oldest clergyman to the Deaf in London, Vicar of St Barnabas Church South London, had invited me to preach the Anniversary Sermon of St John's day. I confess that I had accepted his invitation in some tremulation (*sic*) for I have never preached with my hands since November 1918. Again my kind host piloted me, a very long way, to the church; the journey occupied nearly one and a half hours; in the latter part we went beneath the Thames. St Barnabas Church for the Deaf and Dumb is a very small church and seems as if it has been driven like a wedge into a gap in a row of dwelling houses; inside it is very narrow, at the back part behind the reading stand and the pulpit is the altar and Communion rail, behind this portion is a small reading and recreation room. I learnt that though small it is a busy church and Mr Raper is a most faithful and diligent worker for the deaf.

I read the lesson from St Mark vii beginning at the 31st verse and also preached the sermon from the 118th Psalm last three verses. Looking back to that service I feel amazed for it seemed as if I forgot my disablement and for 45 minutes I used my hands almost with my old freedom and thus was enabled once more to witness to the Deaf, and that in London too.

On Monday morning I felt very peaceful and content and so I decided to return home and on intimating this, my kind friend, through the phone got knowledge of the right train and after luncheon sent me away on my return, full of gratitude for their loving care and to my Father in heaven for His great mercy. I arrived at Crow Park at 6.40 none the worse but better for my visit to the great city.

Appendix Six

Obituaries of Selwyn Oxley

British Deaf Times February 1951

The late Mr Selwyn Oxley M.A., USA

It is with profound regret that the British Deaf Times records the death of Mr Selwyn Oxley at his home, Southlands, 59 Queens Road, Cheltenham, Glos.

By the passing of Mr Oxley the deaf world has lost one of its greatest champions, for throughout his life he laboured for the betterment of the deaf and dumb, the deaf, and the hard of hearing, and all his work on their behalf was done in a voluntary capacity.

For over 30 years he had contributed articles and reports of Deaf affairs under the titles of 'S.A.N.O.' and 'the Gleaner' as well as his own name to the British Deaf Times.

Honoured by the French Government as an Officer Instructor Pub. Francaise, and by Gallaudet College USA by the conferment of the Hon. MA degree in recognition of his great work for the Deaf it is more than a passing regret that his work in conjunction with that of his wife went without reward from his own country and Government.

Readers will join us in expressing deep sympathy to Mrs Kate Oxley in her great bereavement.

217

Cheltenham Echo 31ˢᵗ January 1951

Great Work for Deaf and Dumb Death of Mr S A N Oxley

A lifetime of work in the interests of the deaf and dumb has been closed by the death of Mr Selwyn Amor Nathaniel Oxley of Southlands, 59 Queens Road, Cheltenham, on Monday.

Hon. organising secretary and librarian of the Guild of St John of Beverley for the Deaf and Hard of Hearing, Mr Oxley came with Mrs Oxley to Cheltenham from Ealing shortly before the war. He brought with him a remarkable and extensive library of books, papers and cuttings accumulated in the course of a great number of years' service to the cause. It makes what is possibly the most extensive mine of information on the general subject of deafness in the world.

His work as an honorary lecturer and worker among the deaf and dumb took him to all parts of the United Kingdom.
He had a great love of horses and until recently he and Mrs Oxley were frequently to be seen driving about Cheltenham in an open landau.

Mr Oxley claimed the distinction of being the only man in Europe to hold the Honorary MA of Gallaudet Deaf College USA and was the proud possessor of a diploma recording the fact signed by the late Franklin D Roosevelt. With his father Rev W H Oxley, he was responsible for starting the first mission for deaf people in Gloucestershire.

Mrs Oxley, who is totally deaf, is perhaps better known to a large number, particularly teachers and children, as Miss Kate Whitehead, author of the Stubby and Kelly Ann cat books. A feature of Southlands is an extraordinary collection of china cats of all types and sizes.

Notes on Sources

This is not an academic study, more a work of family loyalty and personal curiosity, so I have used no footnotes nor specified precisely the source of every fact and date. I have identified in the Acknowledgements all those individuals who have helped me with information and suggestions. I have therefore listed below the main documentary sources I have consulted. There is no published history of the Sheffield Association, or of the Guild of St John of Beverley; there is no biography of any of the Stephensons, and no detailed survey of the development of voluntary societies for the adult deaf, except Lysons' unpublished thesis.

Annual Reports of the Sheffield Association

Although I have mentioned at various points the limitations of this source, the reports have been invaluable in establishing the course of the Association's history for the years where they are available. Therein lies the problem. The Sheffield City Library holds bound volumes of the reports for the years from 1912 to 1957 (except 1917 when it was not published) but not for the crucial last three years – it may be any such reports were informal and never printed or published. For the earlier years, the City Library holds one extremely fragile copy from 1888, and there are copies for 1907 and 1910 held in the RNID Library. Rev George Firth (see below) also had access to the 1907 report and summarised some of the contents. Each of the reports was produced following the AGM, usually in the spring of the following year, so that the date on each one actually relates to the 12-month period to the previous 31st December. To avoid confusion, wherever I have quoted or summarised any particular report, I have given the year to which it actually relates.

Chosen Vessels – Rev George C Firth (printed and bound typescript, Exeter, 1985)

This unique work consists largely of potted biographies of many of Firth's fellow missioners from the late nineteenth to the middle of the twentieth centuries. Much of the material is based on personal knowledge, either of Firth himself or reported to him by his subjects, though it is impossible to tell from the text itself just how first, second or even third hand the accounts may be. It appears that 'Chosen Vessels' was self-published; the original typescript with line drawings or sketches of some of the subjects was copied and bound by a printer in Exeter where Firth retired, and in my copy the last 50 of the 140 pages are bound upside down! Nonetheless it has proved valuable, containing as it does substantial pieces on George and Colin Stephenson as well as other relevant figures.

Jubilee Souvenir 1861–1911 – Sheffield Association in Aid of the Adult Deaf and Dumb

Written by George Stephenson, and notwithstanding the fact it was published a year early (the Association was founded at the end of 1862, not 1861), this account priced one shilling is the nearest we have to a contemporary history, and has been invaluable. It is now very rare, and I am very grateful to Julie Clarke (see Acknowledgements) for giving me her copy which was a precious family possession, simply because she thought it would be more appropriate with the Stephenson family rather than her own.

Some Aspects of the Historical Development and Present Organisation of Voluntary Welfare Societies for Adult Deaf Persons in England 1840–1963 – C K Lysons (MA Thesis for the University of Liverpool, 1965, unpublished and held by the RNID Library)

Kenneth Lysons was a Senior Lecturer in Human Relations at St Helens Technical College, Lancashire. His detailed and thorough account of the voluntary movement of which the Sheffield Association and the Stephensons were part provided me with a great deal of the background information I needed. It is difficult to know how it could now be bettered, other than by more micro studies of individual societies and their history like my own. Like Lee's 'Beginners' Introduction' it is a unique contribution to an under-researched area, without which no study like mine could be researched or written. It also contains a trenchant analysis of the missioner role which I have chosen to summarise largely through Rev Firth's review quoted at length in Chapter Seven.

The Blind, the Deaf and the Halt; Physical Disability, the Poor Law and Charity 1830–1890 with particular reference to the County of Yorkshire – Amanda N Bergen (PhD thesis for the University of Leeds, 2004, unpublished)

Particularly useful on the Yorkshire Institute for the Deaf and Dumb (YIDD) and the interface between statutory and charitable approaches to disability in the second half of the nineteenth century.

A Gift from Great Driffield – Anthony J Boyce and Mary P Hayes (British Deaf History Society, 2007)

It would have been difficult to tell the story of the first six months of the Sheffield Association without this biography of Thomas Widd by the deaf historian Tony Boyce and Widd's collateral descendant Mary Hayes. Widd was an extraordinary example of triumph over adversity, and his later career is summarised briefly in Appendix One, again based largely on Boyce and Hayes, supplemented by information about his periods in Montreal and Los Angeles gleaned from the Internet.

The Leeds Beacon – Anthony J Boyce (British Deaf History Society, 1996)
A biography of Edward Kirk, head of YIDD, 1883–1924.

The History of the Yorkshire Residential School for the Deaf 1829–1979 – Anthony J Boyce (originally published by Doncaster Council 1990, republished by British Deaf History Society)

Deaf Lives – edited by Peter Jackson and Raymond Lee (British Deaf History Society, 2001)

A series of short biographical accounts of over 40 prominent deaf people, including Thomas Widd (contributed by Mary Hayes) and Kate Oxley (née Whitehead).

A Beginners Introduction to Deaf History – edited by Raymond Lee (British Deaf History Society, 2004)

Very much a pioneer work, and in part 'created to form the basis for Deaf History courses and examinations as part of the growth in Deaf Studies and British Sign Language courses'. Unusually for a work intended as a source book for students and others, it has neither a list of contents nor an index, but it does bring together a wealth of information on the history of the deaf through the ages; it is particularly detailed on the development and importance of sign language and specifically BSL.

The Vanishing Missioner – Martin Smith (British Deaf History Society, 2011)

Meeting Martin Smith in his home only reinforced my impression that this is a uniquely valuable account – part autobiography, part account of 25 years of work as a missioner to deaf people, and part history of welfare provision in Leeds where Smith spent all except the first few years of his career. Above all the story Smith tells amounts to a critique of the missioner role itself as it began to 'vanish' in the second half of the last century. Anyone who wishes to examine the recent history of deaf welfare would do well to start here.

On the Physical, Moral and Social Condition of the Deaf and Dumb – W R Wilde FRCS (John Churchill, Soho, 1854)

This pamphlet was produced in limited numbers for selected readers and formed an Appendix to William Wilde's *Diseases of the Ear.*

Britain's Deaf Heritage – Peter Jackson (The Pentland Press, 1990)

An early survey, prior to the foundation of the British Deaf History Society in 1993.

The Sheffield School Board 1870–1903 – J H Bingham (J W Northend Ltd, Sheffield, 1949)

Alderman Bingham was a stalwart of the Labour party and the City Council and for many years Chairman of the Education Committee.

A History of Education of the Deaf in England – M G McLoughlin (Self-published, 1987)

The only account I have found which attempted to cover the whole of its chosen subject matter.

74 Years Among the Deaf and Dumb – Rev F W G Gilby (Unpublished typescript autobiography, about 1947, held by the RNID Library)

Described by Rev Firth as one of 'several giants among the pioneers of Deaf Welfare', Gilby (1865–1949) was the son of deaf parents and his career included work in Britain and abroad as a parish priest, teacher, missioner and journalist; see for instance his comments on Ernest Abraham in Chapter Five and his adventure in the Alps with Arthur Doncaster in Appendix One. His autobiography is full of insights into the minutiae of deaf welfare throughout his long and varied career.

A Man with a Mission – Kate Oxley (Hill and Ainsworth Ltd, Stoke-on-Trent, 1953)

The biography of Selwyn Oxley, written by his widow and published at the expense of his estate two years after his death.

When the Mind Hears – Harlan Lane (Random House, New York, 1984)

Deafness and the Deaf in the United States – Harry Best (Macmillan, New York, 1943)

Understanding Deaf Culture – Paddy Ladd (Multilingual Matters Ltd, 2003)

Deaf Worlds – Sally Sainsbury (Hutchinson and Co Publishers Ltd, 1986)

An academic study of 'integration, segregation and disability' which was particularly useful in clarifying the position of deaf people since 1960; see Chapter Eight.

A Service on the Edge – Department of Health (1997)
Report of an 'Inspection of Services for Deaf and Hard of Hearing People'
by the Social Services Inspectorate of the Department of Health.

An Industrial Evolution – Ian Dillamore (Completely Novel, 2014)

The subtitle is self-explanatory: 'The Role of the Banks in Industry,
exemplified by 230 years of history of Daniel Doncaster and Sons'. See
Acknowledgements.

Local Sources

I have lived in the Sheffield suburb of Nether Edge for almost 50 years
and the area has a number of links with this story. Sir John Brown
lived at Shirle Hill before he built Endcliffe Hall, John Cole's main
residence was at Prior Bank, Fanny Emma Stephenson was in service
at Brincliffe Towers, Thomas Widd was married and Sarah Stephenson
died in the Ecclesall Bierlow Workhouse, which became Nether Edge
Hospital and is now a housing estate, and George Stephenson and
his third wife Mary Hannah were interred in the General Cemetery
which adjoins the area. Most importantly, the original home of the
Newboulds and later of one of the Tyzacks at Sharrow Bank became
the home of the Institute and the Stephensons for the last 23 years
of the Association's active life. It is difficult to disentangle personal
knowledge built up over many years from the work of local historians
but for more detail the reader is recommended to the local history
section of the Nether Edge Neighbourhood Group (NENG) and
particularly the following publications:

*The Story of the Workhouse and the Hospital at Nether Edge – Joan Flett (ALD
Print and Design, 1985)*

They Lived in Sharrow and Nether Edge – Various contributors including
Joan Flett on Sir John Brown and John Cole (NENG, 1988)

Cherry Tree Hill and the Newbould Legacy – Joan Flett (NENG, 1999)

Newspapers and Journals

Sheffield City Libraries (Local Studies Library) and the British Newspaper Archive

Sheffield Independent
Sheffield Daily Telegraph
Sheffield Telegraph
Young Sheffield
The Sheffield Young Man's Magazine

RNID Library (now Action on Hearing Loss)

The British Deaf Mute
British Deaf Monthly
British Deaf Times
British Deaf News
Silent World
Ephphatha
Dacty
Sharrow News

Other than Lysons' thesis, Kate Oxley's *A Man with a Mission* and the journals itemised above, the main delight of the library is the cache of books, papers, ledgers, photographs and slides comprised in the Selwyn Oxley library, formerly the library of the Guild of St John of Beverley. The origins of some of the material are uncertain, and likewise the proportion lost either by enemy action in 1940 or gifted elsewhere by Oxley during the last years of his life. Nevertheless, as Firth observed, there remains a great deal of historical interest and detail, donated after Oxley's death at his request and subsequently funded by his widow.

Sheffield City Libraries – Local Studies and Archives

Other than the newspapers and journals listed above, local street and commercial directories used to identify addresses and places of residence, the bound volumes of the Association's Annual Reports and the Jubilee

Souvenir, there are only a few items of relevance in Local Studies. Catalogue entries relating to George Stephenson are limited to items reported in the newspapers and journals, and the same is true of 'deaf' or 'deaf and dumb' except for the Charity Commissioners reports and a short memoir by Daniel Doncaster II. There is also a small set of documents on the history of Daniel Doncaster and Sons Ltd with information on the family.

The Sheffield Archives also have relatively little of direct relevance, but it has been very useful to read through the minutes of the Sheffield School Board for the period from 1893 to 1900, to clarify the dispute with the Association and the parents of deaf children; and likewise the minutes and reports of the Disabled Persons Welfare Sub-Committee from 1943 to 1957, especially the crucial years when the City Council decided to create its own deaf welfare service.

Internet

There is much information available at the click of a mouse and I have not been afraid to use it, bearing in mind that accuracy is sometimes difficult to verify. The following are some organisations whose websites I have visited and found interesting or useful during my research:

Action on Hearing Loss (formerly the RNID)
The British Deaf Association
The British Deaf History Society
Sheffield City Council
The Charity Commission
The United Kingdom Council on Deafness (an umbrella organisation)
The Royal Association for Deaf People (formerly RADD)
The Deaf Advice Team – CAB (formerly Deaf Advice Service Sheffield)
The Deafhood Foundation
Deaf Info (primarily mental health and deafness, funded by Department of Health)
Gallaudet University (USA)
RNID Library, deaf history blog, full of detailed information on deaf people, tales, histories and relevant information extracted from the

Library's resources: available at blogs.ucl.ac.uk/library-rnid/category/
deaf-history

The Limping Chicken (deaf news and blogs from the UK)